THE BATTLE FOR
QUEBEC
1759

Battles & Campaigns

A series of illustrated battlefield accounts covering the classical period through to the end of the twentieth century, drawing on the latest research and integrating the experience of combat with intelligence, logistics and strategy.

Series Editor
Hew Strachan, Chichele Professor of the History of War
at the University of Oxford

Published
Ross Anderson, *The Battle of Tanga 1914*
'An excellent book' *Peter Hart*, author of Jutland 1916

Ross Anderson, *The Forgotten Front: The East African Campaign 1914–1918*
'Excellent... fills a yawning gap in the historical record' *Gary Sheffield, Times Literary Supplement*

William Buckingham, *Arnhem 1944*
'Startling... reveals the real reason why the daring attack failed' *The Daily Express*

Brian Farrell, *The Defence and Fall of Singapore 1940-1942*
'An original and provocative new history of the battle that marked the end of the British Empire'
Professor Hew Strachan

David M. Glantz, *Before Stalingrad*
'Another fine addition to Hew Strachan's excellent *Battles and Campaigns* series' *BBC History Magazine*

Michael K. Jones, *Bosworth 1485*
'Insightful and rich study of the battle... no longer need Richard play the villain' *Times Literary Supplement*

Martin Kitchen, *The German Offensives of 1918*
'Comprehensive and authoritative... first class' *Professor Holger H. Herwig, War in History*

M.K. Lawson, *The Battle of Hastings 1066*
A *BBC History Magazine* Book of the Year 2003

Marc Milner, *Battle of the Atlantic*
'The most comprehensive short survey of the U-boat battles' *Sir John Keegan*

A.J. Smithers, *The Tangier Campaign*
'The fullest account of the British Army's first major expedition abroad'
Professor Hew Strachan

Tim Travers, *Gallipoli 1915*
'A book of the highest importance... masterly' *John Lee, The Journal of Military History*

Matthew C. Ward, *The Battle for Quebec 1759: Britain's Conquest of Canada*

Commissioned
Stephen Conway, *The Battle of Bunker Hill 1775*
Martin Kitchen, *El Alamein 1942–1943*
John Andreas Olsen, *Operation Desert Storm*
Michael Penman, *Bannockburn 1314*

THE BATTLE FOR
QUEBEC
1759

MATTHEW C. WARD

TEMPUS

First published 2005

Tempus Publishing Limited
The Mill, Brimscombe Port,
Stroud, Gloucestershire, GL5 2QG
www.tempus-publishing.com

British Library Cataloguing in Publication Data.
A catalogue record for this book is available from the British Library.

ISBN 0 7524 1997 8

Typesetting and origination by Tempus Publishing Limited
Printed in Great Britain

Contents

About the Author

Matthew Ward is lecturer in history at the University of Dundee. He is one of the world's leading experts on the Seven Years' War. His other books include *Breaking the Backcountry: The Seven Years' War in Virginia and Pennsylvania, 1754-1765*. He lives in Dundee.

Introduction

On the morning of 13 September 1759, the armies of Britain and France clashed on the Plains of Abraham outside the city of Quebec in French Canada. The battle was an overwhelming victory for the British forces, but during the conflict the commander of the British forces, General James Wolfe, received a mortal wound. Dying before the battle was even finished, he guaranteed himself a place in the hearts of the British nation as a man who had given his very life for his country. At almost the same time that Wolfe received his fatal wound, the commander of the French forces, General Louis-Joseph, Marquis de Montcalm-Gozon de Saint-Véran, also received a fatal wound. Dying in agony the next day, his death seemed to epitomise the end of the French regime in Canada.

The deaths of Wolfe and Montcalm, full of pathos and drama, loom over the British campaign to conquer Canada. For many authors and historians the conquest of Canada is the story of Wolfe, and its defence is the tale of Montcalm. The conflicts between both generals and their subordinates, which influenced their conduct of the war, have become the story of the campaign, as epitomised by Francis Parkman's monumental *Montcalm and Wolfe*, a sweeping work that unfortunately is almost as much fiction as fact.[1] Attention to the actions of the commanders during the campaign has further intensified because ever since their deaths there has been a fierce debate over the relative merits of their command. Historians have debated whether Wolfe was really no more than a good regimental officer, promoted beyond his capacity, whether Montcalm's disdain for his Canadian troops was responsible for his ultimate defeat, or whether the machinations of the governor of Canada, Pierre de Rigaud de Vaudreuil, served to undo his efforts to defend the country.

Such questions, which focus purely on the actions and decisions of the armies' commanders, portray the British campaign to conquer Quebec through a very narrow perspective. If the campaign is about Montcalm and Wolfe then their deaths must mark the end of the campaign, and the battle of the Plains of Abraham becomes the climactic conclusion of the struggle. Such a view is surely wrong. British control of Quebec was far from secure until the arrival of the British relief fleet in May 1760. Indeed, it could be argued that the arrival of the British fleet in May 1760, though lacking all the drama of the battle of the Plains of Abraham, was in many ways as important as the battle itself. Even with the arrival of the British fleet, the conquest of Canada would take another determined summer's campaigning. The British conquest of Canada was not just one climactic battle, but a protracted campaign which lasted for eighteen months.

A focus on the commanders also fails to acknowledge adequately the roles of the thousands of men who fought in the British and French forces. The fate of Canada was determined not just by the actions of a handful of officers but by the actions of thousands of soldiers and sailors. These soldiers did not form one homogeneous social group. Both armies contained soldiers from widely different backgrounds: from the Canadian militia, skilled in woodcraft, to the highly disciplined regular *troupes de terre*; from the American ranger companies to the fearsome Scottish Highlanders of Fraser's Regiment. In addition to the thousands of soldiers and sailors, hundreds of Native Americans fought alongside the French and hundreds of British civilians accompanied the British army, as sutlers (sellers of supplies and provisions), labourers, nurses and washerwomen. Collected from around the globe, the two armies which met in Canada were vibrant military communities with different traditions and skills. Their role in the campaign, though more subtle than the decisions of their commanders, was equally, if not more, important.

A focus on the commanders also ignores the experiences of civilians during the war. For civilians this war was markedly different from previous wars. The campaign in Canada was in many ways a total war. The French mobilised the Canadian civilian population to resist the British onslaught. Thousands of Canadian farmers – the *habitants* of the St Lawrence Valley – participated in the militia and exposed British troops to constant attacks from French skirmishing parties. Women and children hauled supplies and provided military intelligence. In retaliation, the British waged total war on the civilian population of Canada, destroying villages, crops, and livestock, rounding up women and children and forcing them from their homes. In so doing, the British pushed the eighteenth-century concepts of limited war and the 'rules of war' to their very limits, if not beyond.

There were other forces that also determined the fate of Canada. Some of them could be called long-term 'structural' developments in Europe, far beyond the immediate scope of the campaign. The expansion of British financial institutions, which enabled the government to wage such an expensive campaign, the securing of British naval superiority and the development of new naval and military tactics all aided the British victory. Pure luck also played an important role. Before the 1759 expedition Canadians seemed to have been protected by 'divine providence'. All previous expeditions against the city and colony had failed miserably. During the Quebec campaign, while the British had their share of misfortune, when luck and chance most mattered, particularly on the night of 12-13 September, fortune favoured the British.

This book examines the British campaign for Canada from its origins in the cabinet offices of London and Versailles to the final capitulation of the colony in September 1760. It views the campaign in its entirety and does not concentrate solely on the events of 13 September 1759. The focus is not purely on the actions and decisions of commanders but also examines the experiences of ordinary soldiers and civilians in the British and French armies during the war, and the war's broader impact on the civilian population of Canada. It demonstrates how the campaign deteriorated from the civilised war, fought very much in a European fashion, to the irregular 'war of the worst shape' berated by Brigadier-General George Townshend.[2] For both soldiers and civilians, this 'irregular' war was as important a part of the Campaign for Canada as the more 'regular' combat on the Plains of Abraham.

While the campaign on the St Lawrence is often viewed as the first 'regular' military campaign in North America, fought according to European military traditions, the campaign which consequently emerged was very different from a regular campaign in Europe. While there was one major 'regular' battle fought on the Plains of Abraham in September 1759, and another on the edge of the Plains near St Foy in April 1760, and a large-scale skirmish near the Falls of Montmorency at the end of July 1759, all of which could be regarded as part of regular campaigning, the rest of the conflict was as different from war in Europe as any other operations in North America. Even in these 'regular' battles, combat was adjusted to meet peculiarly American circumstances. Consequently, the experiences of British troops who fought on the St Lawrence in 1759 and 1760 were as alien from the experiences of those who fought on the North German Plain as were those of troops fighting in the Appalachian Mountains or in the tropical forests of Martinique.

It is in the totality of the Canadian war effort that the campaign is perhaps most striking and diverges most from European campaigns. Nearly all adult Canadian males fought at some time during the campaign, a level of mobilisation which would not have been seen in Europe until the twentieth century. Women, children and clergymen all served the French war effort in some capacity, and as such became targets for British reprisals. This marked the Quebec campaign as a very different type of war from that fought in Europe. By examining the totality of the campaign, and looking at the experiences of ordinary soldiers and civilians as well as of officers and commanders, and by expanding the focus beyond the battle of the Plains of Abraham, the 1759 Campaign for Quebec and Canada emerges as a rather different experience of warfare, where the traditions and practices of the British army, in particular, were stretched to their limits.

I

Two Empires

On 23 May 1759, the beacons along the St Lawrence River were lit to announce the arrival of a British fleet in the St Lawrence River.[1] The news caused the French settlers, or *habitants*, who lived along the lower reaches of the river to panic. In haste they hid their women and children, cattle and food stores, in stashes in the forest and prepared for the arrival of the enemy. In Quebec City itself, the target of the expedition, the wealthy citizens evacuated the town for safer locations in Montreal or further up the St Lawrence. Their safety now depended upon the French regulars and colonial troops and militia who were quickly assembling to oppose the British. On board their ships, the British troops watched the countryside slip slowly past and wondered at the beauty of the lower St Lawrence. While eager to land and resolve the campaign, they were apprehensive about the fate which awaited them when they finally landed in the heart of the French empire in North America.

The success or failure of this expedition would depend on a wide variety of different influences. Some of these were very immediate, such as the decisions of opposing commanders and the different strategies and tactics employed. Others were much more long-term, such as the ability of the British and French to equip and supply their forces and undertake prolonged warfare at such a distance from Europe, and also the relative importance both countries placed on North America. The outcome of the campaign would also depend to a great degree on luck, which seemed previously to have favoured the French.

The immediate events which would determine the outcome of this campaign had been set into motion some years previously and were determined by ministers of the British and French crowns. In London, two men in particular influenced affairs in North America. They were Thomas Pelham-Holles, 1st Duke of Newcastle, who had been influential in British politics for over two decades, and William Pitt, who held the important post of Secretary of State for the Southern Department, with responsibility for affairs in all the British colonies and relations with France, Spain and the Mediterranean states. In France, the most influential minister was Nicolas-René Berryer, minister of the Marine and Colonies. He was advised by Charles-Louis-Auguste Fouquet, Maréchal et Duc de Belle-Isle, the minister of war, and Étienne-François, Duc de Choiseul, the minister of foreign affairs. These men would play a major role in shaping the course of the campaign.[2]

These ministers in London and Versailles had not planned on a global war for empire. Indeed, if there were 'imperialists' in the early eighteenth century, they were to be found in large numbers not in London or Versailles, but rather in the North American provincial capitals of Williamsburg, New York, Philadelphia and even Quebec. In the late 1740s, land-speculators from the British colony of Virginia and fur-traders from Pennsylvania had begun to move into the Ohio Valley. This was territory in the interior of North America which both the British and French claimed, although neither occupied. The French had responded by constructing a series of small posts and forts in the region. To Britain's colonists in Virginia and Pennsylvania, this action was seen as nothing less than a French invasion of the Ohio. The governor of Virginia responded by sending a small force commanded by George Washington to oppose the French. When Washington was forced to surrender to the French, Virginia appealed to Britain for aid.[3]

Britain countered by sending Major-General Edward Braddock to North America with two regiments of regular troops, in effect starting a war. When these troops were not just defeated but completely routed at the battle of the Monongahela in July 1755, this provided the French with an unparalleled opportunity. By committing regular troops, the British had in effect declared war on France in North America. The Duke of Newcastle still hoped that the war could remain limited to North America, for 'in North America, the Disputes are; And there They shall remain for us; And there the War may be kept'.[4] Newcastle's hopes proved unfounded. The French were well aware that if the struggle was limited solely to North America the British colonies so outnumbered the French colonies that their weight of numbers would eventually tell. Braddock's defeat, however, gave the French a very rare opportunity. It meant the French had military dominance, if only temporarily, in North America. In Europe, French forces had an overwhelming superiority over the British. In addition, the French had managed to break apart Britain's alliance with Austria and Russia and left Britain with Prussia as her only continental ally. If a war could be fought quickly in Europe, before the British could turn the tables in North America, the French might be able to force some major concessions from Great Britain. The French took the war to Europe by attacking the British-held island of Minorca in the Mediterranean in May 1756. Suddenly, the hostilities had become a world war. In Canada, French regular troops were to hold colonial forces at bay while parties of Indians commanded by French officers were to harass the colonial frontier. In Europe, the French army was to invade and plunder George II's electorate of Hanover.[5]

In its early stages, the progress of the war was disastrous for the British. In 1756, the French captured the important British post of Oswego on Lake Erie, depriving the British of any access to the Great Lakes and threatening the western frontier of New York. In the meantime, Native American warriors descended on the colonial frontier from New York to North Carolina, wreaking havoc. Throughout 1756 British military officers wrangled with the provincial assemblies in each of the British colonies, as they complained about the cost of assisting the war effort, about raising provincial troops to fight, and about the devastation on their frontiers.[6]

In 1757, the British mounted their biggest offensive so far in North America. On 20 June, the commander-in-chief of British forces in North America, John Campbell, Earl of Loudoun, left New York harbour with the largest seaborne expeditionary force ever assembled in North America. Its objective was the French fortress of Louisbourg. Located at the northern tip of Île-Royale or Cape Breton Island, near the entrance to the Gulf of St Lawrence, the fortress protected a large harbour from which ships could protect or intercept convoys of supplies heading into the St Lawrence. Control of the fortress made it difficult for an enemy to send ships or supplies to Canada. Consequently, its capture was vital to allow an attack on Quebec; otherwise the British fleet lay dangerously exposed to French attack. Delayed by bad weather and poor planning, Loudoun did not reach Louisbourg until early August. There he discovered that three French naval squadrons, which included eighteen ships of the line and five frigates, had slipped past the

British fleet in the western Atlantic and made it into Louisbourg. With his naval escort outnumbered by the French, and so late in the season, there was little chance of success. Loudoun returned to New York having achieved nothing.[7]

Loudoun's concentration of his forces against Louisbourg had allowed the French commander, General Louis-Joseph, Marquis de Montcalm-Gozon de Saint-Véran, to concentrate his forces on Lake Champlain and to launch a devastating attack southwards into New York. A French force advanced south from Lake Champlain and besieged the British post at Fort William Henry. The commander of the fort, Lieutenant-Colonel George Monro, wrote desperately to General Daniel Webb, only a few miles away at Fort George, begging for assistance. Webb dithered and was reluctant to expose his force to the French. With no prospect of relief, Fort William Henry's garrison was forced to surrender. An even worse fate was in store. As the garrison marched out of the fort, the Native American warriors accompanying the French descended on the column of British troops, butchering many of them. The fall of the fort created panic along the frontier. Even residents of New York City, 250 miles to the south, fretted about the danger of a French invasion. The massacre of the garrison created resentment and distrust of the French, and especially of their Native American allies.[8]

The French capture of Fort William Henry had other results less beneficial for the French, which would directly influence the campaign of 1759. With French forces so victorious, and the British in such disarray, the civilian governor of Canada, Pierre de Rigaud de Vaudreuil, believed that Montcalm should have advanced further south to take Fort George, or Fort Lydius, as the French called it. The New York frontier lay exposed and from there the French could have laid waste to much of the colony. It seemed a great opportunity for the French to win a decisive victory. However, Montcalm knew that much

of his army was composed of Canadian troops and militia
who were anxious to return to their homes for the harvest.
If the harvest was not gathered, the loss of supplies would
have been a disaster for the colony worse than the loss of a
battle. Furthermore, Montcalm's disgust at the behaviour of his
Native American allies resulted in most of them abandoning
his army and returning home. Montcalm would never again
trust them. Vaudreuil for his part would not trust Montcalm.
Soon he and his supporters began a whispering campaign
against Montcalm. The bitter disputes between Montcalm and
Vaudreuil would seriously handicap French efforts to defend
Quebec in 1759.[9]

After Fort William Henry, the tide of war, both in North
America and around the world, changed in favour of the
British with amazing speed. The British planned three separate
campaigns for the summer of 1758: one from the backcountry
of Pennsylvania on Fort Duquesne; one against the French
fort of Ticonderoga at the southern end of Lake Champlain;
the third a renewed attempt to seize Louisbourg. The British
operation against Louisbourg in the summer of 1758 was the
most important British campaign of the war so far. Louisbourg
was perhaps the most heavily fortified town in North America,
more heavily fortified in many ways than Quebec itself. The
fortress had stone walls several feet thick and was built in
the fashion of European military engineer Marshall Vauban,
with bastions, half bastions, a ditch, glacis (sloping banks) and
cannon mounted where they could sweep all the defences.
Inside were 6,000 troops, regulars and Canadians, militia and
seamen.[10]

The expedition was ready to sail much earlier than
Loudoun's in the previous year. Eight ships of the line had
wintered in Halifax and were ready to sail as soon as the ice
cleared. However, the fate of Louisbourg had in fact been
sealed the previous autumn, when many of the French ships

returning from North America had been captured or sunk by the Royal Navy. In the spring, a British victory in the Mediterranean prevented any ships from leaving the south of France for Louisbourg, while the British squadrons operating in the western approaches intercepted many supply ships. Louisbourg was much more exposed in 1758 than in 1757. The British force arrived on 3 June, but heavy surf prevented a landing until 8 June. Even then, the waves capsized many boats and many men drowned. Ironically, the surf may have provided a degree of protection from the fire of the French troops entrenched along the shore, for the boats bobbing violently in the swell proved difficult targets to hit. Once ashore, the army conducted the siege fully in the European tradition, following Vauban's *On the Attack and Defense of Fortified Places* to the letter. The British rained shells on the town, destroying buildings and ships. The French held out desperately for seven weeks, to ensure that it was too late for the army to continue the campaign with an attack against Quebec. Finally, on 26 July, the French commander, Augustin de Drucourt, asked for terms.[11]

The Louisbourg campaign revealed how British naval and land forces could work together effectively. It also highlighted the potential of several officers, in particular James Wolfe. Wolfe demonstrated his organisational skills by overseeing many of the preparations for the expedition in Halifax, before the arrival of the expedition's commander, Sir Jeffery Amherst. More importantly, he displayed great military acumen in leading the landings and then building the batteries to besiege the city. Wolfe's ability, energy and skill quickly brought him to the attention of the ministry in London. The lessons learned at Louisbourg would directly influence the planning of the campaign against Quebec in 1759.[12]

After Louisbourg, both the British and French had to decide their future commitment in North America and draw appropriate lessons. The fundamental issue to be decided by the ministries in both Whitehall and Versailles was the extent to which it was worth attacking, or defending, Canada. At first sight Canada seemed relatively unappealing. By the middle of the eighteenth century the British and French had both built global trading empires. Commerce was the engine that had driven both countries into conflict in the Americas, Africa and Asia. Both countries had established colonies in the West Indies producing sugar, in West Africa exploiting the slave trade, and in Asia trading in tea, spices and cloth. In comparison, the North American colonies seemed much less significant. For the British, Virginia produced tobacco and the Carolinas rice and indigo (cotton would not be grown in any great quantities in North America until the early nineteenth century). New England and the colonies of New York and Pennsylvania, however, produced little that could not also be found in the British Isles.

For the French, Canada's sole commercial lure was the fur trade. However, following the collapse of the beaver trade in the 1690s, the trade had not been particularly profitable, and had been supported as much to maintain Native American alliances as to generate profits. The population of between 60,000 and 70,000 was insufficient to provide any significant market for French goods, and was scattered along almost 300 miles of the St Lawrence River. By the 1750s the economy was beginning to diversify and in good years Canada's *habit-ants* produced a surplus of grain which could be traded to the West Indies. In years of poor harvest, however, the colony remained dependent upon imports from France. The colony did include access to the Great Lakes and the lands beyond the Appalachian Mountains, but these were too remote in the mid-eighteenth century to be of any great commercial importance. For the French ministry in Versailles there were few compelling reasons to commit substantial resources to the defence of Canada. At first sight, British ministers should also have dismissed any serious thought of conquest in Canada, and concentrated instead on more lucrative conquests in the West Indies, Africa and India.[13]

The importance of Canada was not economic; rather, it was strategic. The reduction of Canada would provide the British colonies which sprawled along the eastern seaboard with a security previously undreamed of and would open up lands in the interior for future settlement. The idea of launching such a major expedition had been mooted as early as the autumn of 1756 by Loudoun, who had written that 'there is no method of carrying on War with Success in this Country, but by striking at the Root of the Evil at once, by making your Attempts on Quebec, by the River St Lawrence'.[14] His views were echoed by Governor Pownall of Massachusetts, who argued that as long as the war remained a struggle in the Ohio Valley and on Lakes George and Champlain 'we are still engaged in a petty skirmishing War, from the State of which 'twas always plain and experience now proves we shall ever be Inferiour and Beat by the French'.[15] If the British instead resorted to a regular war on the St Lawrence, the superiority of British arms must tell. Once Quebec had been captured, the rest of Canada could not resist for long. Quebec was the centre of the French presence in North America. It was the political capital of Canada. It was here that the governor and council met. It was the seat of the colony's Roman Catholic bishop. Its capture would thus severely disrupt the functioning of the French colonial regime. It was the largest settlement in Canada, with a population in 1759 of approximately 8,000. Montreal, the second largest settlement, had a population of only 4,000. Indeed, it contained almost an eighth of the population of all Canada. Perhaps most importantly, its strategic location meant that if it was captured the rest of Canada would surely fall, for Quebec controlled access to the St Lawrence and thus to Europe. With Quebec in British hands, Montreal and the Canadian interior would be isolated from European aid and could be picked off by the British at will.[16]

This meant that the campaign was a new departure in the war in North America: it was about the future control of the continent. Indeed, Pownall summed up these sentiments neatly. He pointed out that 'we have chang'd the Point and brought it to its true Issue... – whether We as Provinces of Great Britain or Canada as the Province of France shall be Superiour in America'.[17] This significance did not go unnoticed by France's Canadian colonists, the *habitants* of New France. To them the expedition was no less than a conquest by a hostile power. Indeed, the Seven Years' War in French Canada is simply termed *La Guerre de la Conquête* – The War of the Conquest. Canadians suspected that a British conquest would at the very least rob them of their religion and government; at the worst they could suffer like their Acadian counterparts and be driven from their lands and forced to become refugees.

For 150 years Quebec had served as a barrier to British expansion and as a threat to the security of the British colonies. Now one man in particular determined that the main goal of the war should be the conquest of Quebec. That man was William Pitt. Pitt's support for waging war in North America was motivated, at least in part, by political calculation. Pitt had built his popularity by opposing the expenditure of vast sums of money on continental wars. To the ordinary inhabit- ants of Britain, the Seven Years' War in Europe meant little. British victories would be lauded, but in its early years the war simply meant higher taxes – particularly higher excise taxes on beer and cider – which were very unpopular. Then, as fears of French invasion grew, came the 1757 Militia Act. The Militia Act revived the English militia, which had fallen into neglect. However, the militia was not to be a part-time amateur army, but rather a professional army drawn from the ranks of the

English citizenry. Men were chosen by ballot from the adult male population in each county. Those chosen were required to serve for three years, although they were promised that they would not be sent overseas. They could pay for a replacement, which most chose to do, but the poor could not afford the cost. For those middling landowners or artisans who were selected, the payment of a replacement essentially became another onerous tax. As a result, when magistrates tried to enforce the act, there were sizeable riots across most of England.[18]

By the summer of 1757 there was substantial hostility to the war across Britain. The landed and mercantile elites resented the high taxes, the labouring poor the demand for militia service. This opposition was further fuelled by a perception that the war was being fought largely in defence of George II's electorate of Hanover. William Pitt's great strategy when he came to power was to convert the war into a war for empire, to be fought not in Germany but across the oceans of the world and in North America, to be fought for the benefit of British commerce and the British 'empire'. However, to most ordinary Britons the concept of 'empire' meant little more than being able to buy more 'exotic' goods like sugar, tea and coffee in the local store. Even to the merchants of Britain's port towns, the possible conquest of Canada was of limited importance. Compared to the West Indies, to West Africa and to India, where the British were also making territorial advances against the French, Canada was little more than a barren wasteland with only a few greasy furs to tempt merchants.[19]

Pitt's 'genius' was to tap into popular opinion to build support for an overseas war – to launch a 'great war for empire' against the French. Money would be spent on equipping British expeditions, not on supporting continental allies. (Once in power, Pitt, despite his rhetoric, soon found that his German allies were essential to the war effort, and most of the subsidies continued.) The benefits of war, Pitt argued, would be seen by all Britons, not just the king's German subjects. Pitt realised that Britain had several important advantages in waging an all-out war against the French in the colonies, advantages that he was determined to utilise to the utmost. The first of these was simply Britain's ability to raise money to fight the war. The 'financial revolution' which had taken place from the late seventeenth century and continued through the first half of the eighteenth century allowed the British government to borrow huge sums during the Seven Years' War to fund the campaign. These loans were secured on future tax revenues of the country. With the prospect of secure interest payments on loans to the government, many merchants and bankers invested their surplus capital in government loans. Lending to the government was facilitated by the creation of the Bank of England, established in 1694, which could administer these loans. Tax revenues paid on land and excise revenues on trade were sufficient to guarantee substantial loans. Ably administered by the Duke of Newcastle, the exchequer's regular annual income was sufficient to allow government debt to rise to £137 million by the end of the war, with interest rates of less than 5 per cent per annum. In contrast, although French trade had grown even faster than British trade in the first half of the eighteenth century, the French government was able to raise much less money and had to pay much higher interest rates, averaging nearly 10 per cent and ranging up to 14 per cent.[20]

The ability to raise such substantial funds was central to the British war effort. First, it allowed the British to subsidise their continental allies. The 'Army of Observation' which fought in Hanover was composed not principally of British troops, but their German allies and British mercenaries. Subsidies were essential in maintaining these allies. In particular, substantial subsidies to Frederick of Prussia allowed him to continue the war, and encouraged him to continue fighting even when all hope of victory seemed lost. In July 1757, the French decisively defeated the British army, under the command of the Duke of Cumberland, at the battle of Hastenbeck. Cumberland was compelled to sign the humiliating Convention of Klosterseven, removing his army from the field while the French occupied most of the Netherlands. Meanwhile, the Austrians defeated Frederick at the battle of Kolin, while the Russians occupied Berlin. Substantial British subsidies enabled Frederick to continue the war. Had Frederick decided to make peace at this point, the British would probably also have had to come to terms with the French. It is probable that had peace been made at this point the British would have been compelled to recognise French possession of the Ohio Valley and possibly return Nova Scotia.[21]

The second crucial long-term structural advantage was the development of the Royal Navy. The construction of large and dedicated naval dockyards at Chatham and Portsmouth in the early eighteenth century had allowed British naval construction to advance substantially. Large numbers of naval vessels could be built relatively quickly. Before the mid-eighteenth century, British vessels had had no superiority over French vessels in their construction. However, during the early 1750s the First Lord of the Admiralty, George Anson, introduced several new ship designs, and these arguably gave the Royal Navy a slight advantage. Most important of these was the two-deck seventy-four-gun warship. This was large enough to engage in battle with any French vessel, but had a shallower draught and was more manoeuvrable than larger vessels. Anson also introduced several new types of frigate, increasing their firepower. Indeed, frigates, with a shallower draught and greater manoeuvrability than men-of-war, would play an important role on the St Lawrence.[22]

More important than design advantages, by the late 1750s the Royal Navy had a clear numerical superiority. During the first half of the eighteenth century the British had invested heavily in the construction of new naval vessels. By 1758 the Royal Navy had 275 ships in commission, with a further forty-nine being built, compared to France's meagre seventy-two. Equally important, Anson had undertaken a thorough reform of the naval officer corps, making it easier to gain promotion through proven ability rather than through purchase alone. In contrast, the French navy was particularly poorly officered. A French naval career was viewed as unattractive and good officers were few and far between. French seamen were equally difficult to find, as the French merchant marine was substantially smaller than the British and France lacked the British 'maritime tradition'. Consequently, French ships were less well commanded and manned than British ships. The British also had an important superiority over the French in their provisioning of the navy. The development of the contracting system around the world, where local suppliers were given a regular contract to provision British ships, meant that the Royal Navy was kept supplied with fresh provisions and provisions of a generally high quality. Consequently, when it came to battle, a far higher percentage of British crews were fit and functional than their French counterparts. Numbers, design, better officers and fitter crews all served to give the British an important superiority in the war at sea.[23]

The real importance of British naval superiority told in operations off the French coast. British warships operating out of Gibraltar effectively prevented French warships and supply ships from leaving the Mediterranean. Meanwhile, the British Atlantic fleet under Admiral Holmes kept the French Atlantic fleet blockaded in port. Naval superiority had a very direct impact upon the war in North America. In 1755, even before an official declaration of war, the Royal Navy had begun to seize French merchantmen around the world and threatened French supply lines. By the end of 1755 the navy had captured nearly 300 French merchantmen, including sixteen provision ships bound for New France, and over 8,000 French mariners. By 1757, despite a string of French military victories on land in Europe and North America, Canada was desperately short of supplies.[24]

The French also felt unable to send reinforcements to North America for fear that they would be captured in the North Atlantic. Without reinforcements from France, Canada's military power was slowly ground down by the British military machine. In addition, colonial regiments were not always raised to full strength because there were not the supplies needed for them. For the French military, maintaining supplies and conserving supplies became an essential part of their strategy. Within Canada, troops were dispatched later in the campaign than officers would have liked, to ensure that supplies could be maintained and their wastage lessened. During 1759 the shortage of supplies experienced by the French in Canada, a consequence of the long-term development of British naval power, would dramatically shape the nature of the campaign.

While Pitt was able to argue for a vigorous expansion of the war into North America, to drive the French from the continent, the French drew opposite conclusions. As war commenced, French strategy depended upon winning major land victories in Europe while simply holding the British at bay in North America. Any losses in North America would be traded for gains in Europe. French strategy thus depended upon winning decisive victories in Europe before they suffered too many losses in North America. In Europe matters looked very hopeful. The French had assembled an alliance with the Russians and Austrians who opposed Britain's only ally, the Prussians. It seemed unlikely that Britain's small 'Army of Observation' in George II's electorate of Hanover and the Prussian army would be able to hold off the French alliance for any great length of time.

In North America, French Canada was dwarfed by the British mainland colonies. French hopes for victory lay in using Canada's limited resources on the St Lawrence and Hudson rivers against the main British and American provincial armies, while encouraging their Native American allies to paralyse the frontier of the British colonies to the south. In 1756, Canadian governor Vaudreuil outlined French military policy. He declared that there was no possibility 'of managing the English. Their enterprises are carried to excess, and… they are making new and greater efforts against this Colony.' The only opportunity to halt the British advance, he believed, was 'to carry the war into their country… [by] sending parties of Indians into the English Colonies'. He concluded that 'nothing is more calculated to disgust the people of those Colonies and to make them desire the return of peace'.[25]

Vaudreuil and his fellow Canadians still assumed that they would receive assistance from France in their struggle. The ministry in Versailles, however, felt differently. France's resources were stretched in Europe, and ministers feared that the Royal Navy would intercept any aid that might be sent. Canada would have to fend for itself. Instead of attempting to relieve the French colonies and to stem the British tide in North America, French ministers proposed that France should instead attempt an invasion of Great Britain and consolidate their position in Germany. No reinforcements and few supplies could be spared for North America. Any losses in Canada would be recompensed by gains in Europe. To the British, then, the struggle for Germany was being fought in Canada; to the French, the struggle for Canada was being fought in Germany. Although aware that the British were planning to launch a major expedition against Canada, most Canadians doubted that it could ever succeed. Quebec's mariners all maintained that the St Lawrence was extremely difficult to navigate. A large fleet would never be able to reach Quebec.[26]

Indeed, this was far from the first British attempt to seize Quebec. In 1690, during King William's War, or the War of the League of Augsburg, Sir William Phips had headed a three-pronged campaign against Quebec. This campaign was funded and equipped not by the government in London, but by the colonies of New England. In the summer of 1690, 2,300 men had sailed from Boston to Quebec, while an over-land expedition attacked up Lake Champlain, a plan very similar to that being discussed for 1759. Phips had delayed in Boston, vainly hoping for assistance from London, and it was mid-summer before his expedition departed. It suc-cessfully navigated the St Lawrence, no mean feat in itself, but he did not reach Quebec until October. In desperation, knowing that winter was about to freeze the St Lawrence, Phips's fleet bombarded the city while his men attempted to make a landing. The resulting attack was chaotic and the expedition was abandoned.[27] Plans for an attack on Quebec were revived in 1711 when another major expedition was launched, commanded by Admiral Sir Hovendon Walker. This time the major participants were not colonial forces but British regulars, including some veterans from the Duke of Marlborough's campaigns in Europe. Walker assembled a force of almost sixty vessels and over 12,500 men, half the population of all Canada. However, once more, the expedi-tion started late in the year. It was beset by bad weather and foundered, literally, in the St Lawrence River. Once more the expedition was abandoned.[28] Plans for yet another expedition were mooted in 1745 following the capture of Louisbourg. New Englanders mustered their troops and waited anxiously in the spring of 1746 for ships, supplies, and reinforcements from Great Britain. None came. The British were distracted by the Jacobite uprising and war in Europe. Without British naval power, New Englanders were reluctant to attack the bastion of French power in North America, and plans for the attack were postponed and would not be revived before the Treaty of Aix-la-Chappelle was signed in 1748.[29]

To many Canadians, the failure of these expeditions provided evidence that the colony was protected by divine providence. Even at the start of the Seven Years' War, British forces had been routed and defeated where they should have won victories. A nun in the General Hospital in Quebec summed up the feeling of many Canadians: 'During the first attacks of our enemy... every where they appeared, they were beaten and repulsed with considerable loss... our warriors returned crowned with laurels... It was miraculous; their small numbers, without heavenly aid, could not so completely have accomplished it.'[30] With God's protection, they believed, Canada would survive. This fervent belief was reflected in the way the residents of Quebec commemorated their earlier escapes. After Phips abandoned his siege of the city in 1690, to thank the Virgin Mary for her protection, the church of Ste Genevieve was renamed Notre Dame de la Victoire to commemorate the victory. Every year, on the anniversary of the expedition, residents would congregate for a celebratory Mass. When Walker's fleet was wrecked in 1711, the inhabitants again flocked to the church to give thanks and it was renamed Notre Dame des Victoires.[31]

While Canadians may have felt confident in God's protection, they were less confident in their own governors. There were severe shortages of foodstuffs throughout the colony and in December 1758 rumours of a reduction in civilian rations caused widespread discontent. This discontent grew as throughout the winter the Intendant, François Bigot, had continued to throw lavish balls and parties in his palace while the people starved. Finally, on 2 January 1759, a mob of 400 women assembled in the town and rioted in the snowy streets. Bigot's actions caused many Quebecers to wonder whether they still merited God's protection. Such concerns intensified over the winter, when a brothel was established in the city. So worried was the bishop of Quebec at the growing immorality of his flock that in April he called for a day of public prayer and fasting, to ask for God's forgiveness and beg for his protection in the coming campaign.[32]

If Canadians were concerned about their ability to resist the British, and placed their trust in divine providence, Pitt had every reason to be confident that this expedition could succeed where previous expeditions had failed. The British forces attacking Canada had a decisive numerical advantage over the French and Canadian forces. In North America they would send out three separate expeditions against the French strongholds of Quebec, Montreal and Fort Niagara. Each would be an independent operation, but together they would form part of the overall scheme for the conquest of Canada. These expeditions would see a substantial commitment of about 30,000 British regular troops to North America. They would be supported by an even greater number of provincial troops raised in North America, a substantial proportion of the Royal Navy, and by millions of pounds of British gold.[33] If the seaborne invasion along the St Lawrence failed, an overland expedition up Lake Champlain and the Richelieu river might yield fruit. If that failed, there was always the possibility that the expedition against Fort Niagara could advance down the St Lawrence to strike into the heart of Canada. These three expeditions would force the French to divide their meagre forces. Each one of them should be victorious, since British troops were better equipped, better trained and better prepared than for any previous expedition. Most importantly, at Louisbourg British troops had gained experience in conducting combined operations with the Royal Navy and in launching amphibious assaults.

As British troops sailed into the St Lawrence River in the summer of 1759, the experience of years of warfare in North America shaped their expectations. Decisions already made in

London and Paris would influence their chances of success; so would pure chance, and many Canadians desperately hoped that once more fortune would favour them. However, they soon found that their luck was now deserting them.

2

Two Armies

While the Canadians may have hoped that divine providence and luck would again determine the contest for Quebec, Pitt and his ministry were determined that luck would play as small a role as possible. To that end, Pitt did everything he could to ensure that the troops and commanders would be adequate for the task ahead. The French ministry, on the other hand, did little to change the disposition of their troops in Canada or even to offer them substantial support. While not perhaps relying on fate alone, they hoped that the skills and courage of the Canadians, honed by years of warfare against the British colonies, would be sufficient to fend off any army that might be thrown at the colony.

The first task for Pitt was the selection of the commanders for the expedition. Jeffery Amherst, the commander of the successful expedition to Louisbourg, hoped that he would lead the expedition, for as he confided to a friend 'Quebec is everything.'[1] However, Pitt wanted a commander who was

prepared to take some risks, for it would be a difficult assign-
ment. Amherst was a meticulous planner with a great eye
for detail. He was not an innovative strategist or risk-taker.
He would not lose out altogether, for he would be commander-in-chief and would lead the southern thrust into
Canada along Lake George and Lake Champlain. From here
he would be able to remain in constant contact with the colonial governors and armies. The army on the St Lawrence, by
comparison, would be isolated and cut off. The command of
the Quebec expedition would go to a young colonel who
had risen to prominence during the Louisbourg campaign of
1758, James Wolfe. He would have complete and independent
command of the expedition, holding the rank of brigadier-
general. However, when his army and Amherst's joined, as was
expected, Amherst would have overall command. Wolfe was
something of a prodigy. When he received his appointment
he was only thirty-one. Born into a relatively humble family,
his father had spent his life in the army, reaching the rank of
lieutenant-general. Wolfe hoped to follow in his footsteps. He
had joined the army at the age of fourteen and rose rapidly
in rank. By eighteen he was a major, and at thirty he was
appointed colonel of the 67th Regiment.[2]

Wolfe demanded, as was customary, that as commander he
should have some influence in the appointment of the officers to serve under him. Wolfe seems to have been allowed the
appointment of two of his three brigadiers: Robert Monckton,
the second son of John Monckton, Viscount Galway, and James
Murray, son of Lord Elibank. Both Monckton and Murray
had distinguished service records and both had already served
in North America during the war. Both were known to
Wolfe from the Louisbourg expedition. The third and final
brigadier was not known to Wolfe. He was George Townshend,
the eldest son of Viscount Townshend. He had pursued an
active political as well as military career, and had been the

author of the 1757 Militia Act. In June 1757 Townshend had sought a place in Pitt's government, but Pitt had turned him down. His commission seems to have been, at least in part, compensation for his exclusion. His background almost certainly affected his relationship with Wolfe, who often placed him in positions of little importance and responsibility.[3]

At the end of the Louisbourg campaign Wolfe had returned to England with hopes of securing what he saw as a more rewarding commission to serve in Germany. As soon as he arrived, he received the news that he was to return to North America. He was to command 12,000 troops, with orders to make every attempt possible to seize the city of Quebec and hold it over the winter if necessary. Pitt believed that the French could muster a similar-sized army to Wolfe's in Canada. However, Pitt and his ministers felt certain that the planned three-pronged invasion of Canada, including attacks via Niagara and Lake Champlain, would force the French to divide their forces. Wolfe was expected to face, at most, 8,000 men, most of whom would be undisciplined militia and not regulars. Wolfe would have a larger and more professional force; he faced a difficult but not an impossible task.[4]

Wolfe's army was to consist almost entirely of regular troops. Ten battalions of regulars, who had all served for some time in North America, would form the main contingent. They included the 15th Regiment, or Amherst's Regiment (it was a traditional practice in the British army to name a regiment after their commanding officer, even though he would often not be present with the regiment), the 58th or Anstruther's, and the second and third battalions of the 60th or Royal American Regiment, all of whom were in winter quarters in Halifax, the principal port in Nova Scotia. They would be joined by the 28th Regiment, or Bragg's, which were garrisoned in Louisbourg; the 35th Regiment, or Otway's, which was garrisoned in Annapolis, Nova Scotia; and the 43rd Regiment, or

Kennedy's, which had spent the previous two years on garrison duty on the Nova Scotia frontier. Some of the regiments would be joining the expedition from further south. The 48th Regiment, or Webb's, and the 78th (Highland) Regiment, or Fraser's, had both been in winter quarters in New York, while the 47th Regiment, or Lascelles's, which had been in Nova Scotia since 1750 and had participated in the siege of Louisbourg, had gone into winter quarters in New Jersey. Accompanying them were three companies of Grenadiers, drawn from the garrison at Louisbourg and popularly termed 'The Louisbourg Grenadiers'.[5]

While these troops were all regular regiments, a substantial number of men from the American colonies were also involved in various ways in the expedition. There were six companies of rangers, who were all American colonists, serving in Wolfe's army. These ranger companies would play a central role in the campaign. While no provincial troops (troops raised by and paid by the assemblies of the individual colonies) directly participated in the campaign, 2,500 Massachusetts troops played an important role by garrisoning British forts across Nova Scotia, especially Halifax and Louisbourg. This released the regular troops for service on the Quebec expedition. In addition, the two Royal American battalions were largely made up of troops who had been enlisted in Britain's North American colonies. Indeed, the Royal American Regiment had been created specifically to allow the foreign-born residents of Britain's colonies, particularly German colonists, to enlist in the British army and serve under officers of their own nationality. Finally, the provincials also composed 40 per cent of the army under Amherst which was to attack towards Montreal from the south.[6]

Wolfe and most of the other British officers were grateful for the absence of provincial forces, for they believed that provincial forces were inherently inferior to regulars. This preconception was so strong that even though the rangers would prove themselves useful, Wolfe initially dismissed them as 'the worst soldiers in the universe'. He complained to Monckton that 'the Pow-wow & paint, & howl operates too strongly upon the Rangers – either they must make themselves useful in their way, or I shall leave 'em to while away the Campaign in their Present Posts'.[7] Wolfe's preconception was based upon the provincial troops' lack of training and discipline. Each company in the British army contained a cadre of troops who had served for many years, and all British troops had experienced months if not years of training and drilling. Most of the men in the British army were career soldiers. It was their length of service and the development of strong bonds of comradeship that made regular units more cohesive and more disciplined. Many provincial troops, by contrast, had enlisted for one single campaign rather than for many years of service, and their companies did not contain large numbers of seasoned veterans. The primary purpose of training and discipline in the regular army was to ensure that the ranks would not break in battle. Combat on European battlefields called for the two armies to close as near as possible before discharging musket shot directly at each other. As the effective range of the musket was only, at most, 200 metres, armies needed to get to very close range. In addition, firing and reloading the musket under combat conditions required men to hold their nerve. Speed of fire was very important. A well-trained soldier could fire up to five shots a minute, but a poorly-trained soldier might flounder, especially under fire. This was the purpose of military discipline, and here the provincial troops looked a sorry lot.[8]

Trained in this manner, primarily to ensure that they would not break under fierce fire, many contemporary observers viewed the rank and file of the British army as little more than automaton cannon fodder. They dismissed the men as 'the scum of the earth'. Forced and coerced by the press into the army, they were viewed as the lowest of the low. In reality, most men were volunteers, as an act of Parliament was required to impress men. As this was very unpopular it was rarely enacted, and indeed in 1757 such an act had prompted widespread opposition and a deep political crisis. Nor were most troops from the very lowest levels of society. Many were skilled or semi-skilled workers, such as weavers and shoemakers. Most regular regiments had recruited men after their arrival in North America and consequently the ranks were surprisingly diverse in their ethnic backgrounds. In some cases they had even enlisted French deserters, frequently Germans who had been serving in the French army, but on occasion even residents of Quebec.[9]

The previous experiences of all these troops made the force being prepared for the Quebec expedition rather different in quality from previous British expeditions to North America. All the troops who accompanied Wolfe had already served in North America and consequently were accustomed to American conditions. This had not been the case on previous expeditions. The men who accompanied General Edward Braddock, for instance, on his ill-fated expedition in 1755, had all been transported directly from Britain. It was not simply in their prior experience that Wolfe's men differed from previous expeditions, but also in their training and equipment. Four years of warfare in North America had allowed British officers to modify the training and equipment of their troops. Traditionally, British troops were provided with the standard-issue flintlock musket, popularly nicknamed 'Brown Bess'. For service in America, where troops often had to cross deep ravines and ford rivers, this was, in the words of one soldier, 'heavy and inconvenient'. Many of the troops on the Quebec expedition, particularly the light infantry, were not issued with the standard musket, but instead received lighter French arms. A few were even equipped with rifles for sharpshooting and skirmishing. Most carried fixed bayonets and many also carried tomahawks, which were useful both for fighting and as general cutting implements. Training had also been modified and Amherst had introduced a new training regimen designed to prepare troops for conditions in North America. George Augustus, Viscount Howe, had also realised the importance of light infantry in American conditions, and by 1759 most British regiments contained a company of light infantry. All these changes meant that British troops were better equipped in 1759 to wage warfare in North America than they had been at any time previously.[10]

These troops were supported by a substantial band of auxiliaries. Three hundred provincial troops served as pioneers to assist in some of the manual work of the campaign. Civilians served on many of the ships which provisioned the expedition, venturing ashore to sell goods to the troops. It was not only men who served alongside the army; several hundred women also accompanied the expedition. The wives of soldiers were allowed to accompany the army on many of its campaigns and perhaps one man in six was married. The status of unmarried partners, or 'artillery wives' as they were popularly known, was less clear, but they were also allowed to accompany the army on many expeditions. When accompanying the army and eating the army's provisions, women were expected to serve the army as much as their husbands. They were attached to their husband's company and worked as cooks and washerwomen, and were vital to the performance of the army. Wolfe, however, conscious of the difficulty of procuring fresh supplies in Quebec, tried to limit the number of women who accompanied the expedition. 'Artillery wives' in particular would not accompany the expedition.[11]

It is difficult to determine the exact number of women who accompanied and served in Wolfe's army. If all married men had been accompanied by their wives, this would have

resulted in between ten and fifteen women for each company. However, when on campaign the army made desperate,
although not always successful, attempts to limit the number of
women present. The captain of each company had the discre-
tion to select only a few of the soldiers' wives to accompany
the expedition, generally favouring those who did not have
children. Wolfe ordered captains to limit the number of women
to just three for each company of seventy men, and four for
a company of 100 men. Since he was forced repeatedly to
reissue this order, it seems that many companies did not abide
by these regulations. Indeed, many women who had been left
behind in Boston may have managed to board one of the many
supply ships bound for the St Lawrence in a desperate attempt
to rejoin their husbands. As each battalion consisted of ten
companies, and as there were ten battalions, plus the grenadiers,
rangers and pioneers, this suggests that the number of women
accompanying the army may have exceeded 500. Indeed, an
investigation of the garrison which remained in Quebec over
the winter revealed that there were 569 women in the garrison.
Mostly invisible in military records, they nevertheless played an
important role washing the soldiers' uniforms and preparing
and cooking their food.[12]

The most important job that women undertook in the
army was in staffing the hospitals, such as those at Chelsea
and St Guy's. In these hospitals women could hold an official
rank in the army as matron, and there were occasions when
women could command men. When on campaign the army
was accompanied by a field hospital, which would generally
be located several miles to the rear of the army. During the
Quebec campaign the field hospital was initially on board a
ship especially equipped for the purpose in Boston. Following
the arrival of the army on the St Lawrence, the hospital was
transferred to quarters on the Île d'Orléans. The hospital was
staffed by two male surgeons, one apothecary and ten mates,

accompanied by several female nurses. In addition, following a battle when there were many wounded to be tended to, women from all the companies of the army were expected to care for the sick. This was a thankless and back-breaking task, which often exposed the women to disease and sickness. However, although a few women were reluctant to accept such tasks, most accepted this as a necessary consequence of their being allowed to accompany their husbands.[13]

The women who officially accompanied the army generally shared the same conditions as the men. Indeed, in many cases they shared the same quarters, and in some cases the same tents and even the same beds. When on campaign, as on the St Lawrence, they received the same rations as men, or, when rations became short, two-thirds of the ration. Eighteenth-century sensibilities meant that women did normally share the same fierce discipline as their husbands, and for this reason they were the scourge of many an officer who sought to restrain their excesses, particularly in selling the troops a dram or two (or more) of rum. However, the threat of being beaten out of camp and excluded from rations, especially when on a campaign such as that of 1759, was normally sufficient to force any recalcitrant women to obey orders. The women who unofficially accompanied the army were forced to find their own quarters wherever they could, although it seems that many company captains would willingly turn a blind eye to the presence of the wife of one or two of his men, as long as they assisted in cooking and laundering. That Wolfe was forced so frequently to issue orders limiting the presence of women attests to their ability and tenacity in reaching the army on board one of the many civilian supply ships which sailed to the St Lawrence from New England.[14]

These supply ships felt safe in sailing to the St Lawrence, because the expedition was accompanied by a formidable fleet, which had to be assembled on both sides of the Atlantic.

Forty-nine warships were assigned to the expedition, including the ninety-gun *Neptune*, the flagship of the admiral. While many of these ships were smaller vessels such as frigates and sloops, which had greater manoeuvrability in the shallow waters of the St Lawrence, they ensured that the Royal Navy had control of the sea. In addition to the warships, there were over 160 transports for the troops and artillery, requisitioned in England and in Boston, New York and Philadelphia. Another fifty whaleboats and forty sloops or schooners had been acquired to act as landing craft and to patrol the shallow waters. Finally, there were assorted supply ships, which joined the fleet at various times, sailing mainly from New England. Altogether these ships were manned by around 13,000 sailors – more men than in Wolfe's army.[15]

The fleet was essential to the expedition. Indeed, Wolfe's instructions from the king specifically stated that 'the Success of this Expedition will very much depend upon an entire good Understanding between our Land and Sea Officers'. Consequently, Wolfe was to ensure that he consulted the admiral of the fleet on all military matters.[16] Indeed, the Quebec campaign was in all aspects a combined operation of army and navy. The navy would not only land Wolfe's men, but it would also provide support for the landings, maintain communications, provide supplies, and allow Wolfe to move his men around the St Lawrence. Wolfe was fortunate to have some excellent naval officers on the expedition. Rear-Admiral Sir Charles Saunders commanded the fleet. He was an experienced officer and was assisted by second-in-command Rear-Admiral Philip Durell, who had served in North American waters during the previous year. Third in command was Rear-Admiral Charles Holmes. While Wolfe had reservations about Durell, reflected in repeated complaints about his performance, he developed an excellent working relationship with Saunders. Indeed, at the end of the expedition Townshend wrote to Pitt 'acknowledging how much we are indebted for our success to the constant assistance & support received and the perfect Harmony & Correspondence which had prevaild throughout all our operations'.[17]

With 12,000 soldiers and 13,000 sailors assigned by Pitt, this should have been a force to be reckoned with. However, it soon became clear that Wolfe would not have this number of men, as neither the fleet nor the battalions assigned to the expedition were at full strength. Pitt had decided to assign to the expedition regiments already stationed in North America. Consequently, they had already suffered substantial attrition through combat, disease and desertion. The regiments which had been garrisoning Louisbourg had suffered particularly badly, loosing 1,558 men over the winter, mainly from disease and in particular from scurvy. While officers had tried to find new recruits in North America, few men came forward. Four years of warfare had seen most potential recruits already join the ranks, while the economic boom that had begun to grip the British colonial port cities from 1757 onwards meant that there was little economic incentive for men to enlist in the British army. Lascelles's Regiment, for instance, required 404 men to return to full strength, but struggled to recruit ninety-seven. Some of the regiments in Louisbourg were so desperate for recruits that they were even prepared to enlist former soldiers from the French garrison in the town. In particular, 131 men from the French *Voluntaire Étranger* regiment, the eighteenth-century Foreign Legion, were recruited en masse into the British army. As a result, some former French residents of Quebec served in the British army in the campaign against their birthplace.[18]

Most of Wolfe's regiments were under strength by about 30 per cent as they prepared to embark for Quebec. Further troops were lost because Rear-Admiral Durell, who had wintered with a squadron in Halifax, had been unable to impress civilian seamen to man his ships. Much to his disgust, Wolfe was forced to provide him with some of his men to complete his squadron. By the time Wolfe assembled his force in Louisbourg at the beginning of June 1759, instead of the 12,000 men he had been promised, he found he had only 8,205. Despite the small size of his force, as Wolfe prepared to sail from Louisbourg to Quebec, he was not disheartened. He realised that much depended upon Amherst's expedition forcing Montcalm, who commanded the French troops in Canada, to divide his force. However, numbers alone did not tell the whole story. Montcalm's army, while comparable in size to Wolfe's, was rather different in composition.[19]

Montcalm had at his disposal eight battalions of regular troops sent from metropolitan France, or *troupes de terre*. These units had been dispatched to Canada on various occasions between 1755 and 1757. They were regular French metropolitan regiments and were expected to return to France once the war was over. They were, for most purposes, the equivalent of the British regular battalions that were serving with Wolfe, and were generally well led and equipped and highly trained. When shipped from France, each of these battalions had contained between 500 and 600 men. By 1759, after service in several campaigns, this number had dropped towards 400 men per battalion. Each battalion was therefore considerably weaker than a British regular battalion. To maintain their numbers, like their British counterparts, French officers were prepared to accept a wide range of men as potential recruits, and these included many of the deserters from the British army.[20]

In addition to the *troupes de terre*, Montcalm also had at his disposal the *compagnies franches de la Marine* or *troupes de la Marine*. These were the regular garrison troops of New France. While they were commonly termed the *troupes de la colonie* or provincial troops, unlike the provincial forces in the British army, the troops were not colonists but were recruited in metropolitan France. They were, however, expected to spend their entire military service in Canada. The men were encouraged to develop close ties with the colony and to marry Canadian women, and were offered land grants and bounties to settle in Canada after their terms of enlistment expired. The *troupes de la Marine* were, in the main, commanded by Canadian officers. Few French officers were willing to endure the arduous service thousands of miles from home; on the other hand, Canadians saw service in the officer corps as a route to respectability in the colony. This was particularly important as the French officer corps was still largely reserved for the old nobility, the *noblesse de l'épée*. Indeed, in 1758 the Marshall de Belle-Isle had sent a circular letter to all infantry colonels urging them to give preference to nobles and not to give a commission to a commoner as long as there was a noble who desired it.[21]

The *troupes de la Marine* were also frequently billeted among the *habitants*. This could have been a heavy penalty, and similar attempts to billet British troops among the population of the British colonies provoked bitter opposition. However, in Canada it was warmly welcomed by the *habitants* because the troops were allowed to assist them in their farm work, in chopping firewood, clearing land and, most importantly, harvesting. In a society which suffered from a chronic labour shortage such additional hands were most welcome. While being regular forces, the *troupes de la Marine* consequently had strong ties and commitments to the colony that were lacking amongst the *troupes de terre*. In theory, the *troupes de la Marine* comprised forty companies of sixty-five men each, or over 2,500 men. However, by 1759 service during the war had left its mark, and the ranks were severely under-strength, and the total number available for service was probably around 1,000 men.[22]

While the *troupes de terre* and the *troupes de la Marine* were both regular units, they differed greatly in their command structure. The *troupes de terre* had a standard officer corps and command structure identical to other French regiments. The *troupes de la Marine*, on the other hand, were not organised into regiments but served as independent companies (*compagnies franches*). Indeed, they did not even come under the same authority as the *troupes de terre*, being under the jurisdiction of the Ministry of the Navy, which had responsibility for the administration of the colonies, rather than the Ministry of War. As a result, they were in general slightly less disciplined and efficient than the regular battalions, although their local knowledge and experience made them better frontier and irregular fighters.[23]

The final element of the French forces was the Canadian militia. The militia was by far the most numerous of the forces available to Montcalm and played a central role in the colony's defence. Militia service was expected of each adult male in Canada. The men received no pay and even had to provide their own muskets. However, they were able to buy these at cost, and after militia duty they might be kept and used for hunting and other purposes. Not surprisingly, these muskets were eagerly sought after. Because many Canadians were frequent hunters, they were often relatively good marksmen. This skill was further honed in militia training. This focused on individual skills in shooting, and not on mass drill and discipline. As a result of this training and their personal experiences in hunting, the skills of the militia were very different from those of regular troops. The militia could be used very effectively as skirmishers or to launch small-scale raids on outposts; their use in regular combat was much more limited. They also served a further central purpose, as labourers and workmen to construct fortifications and move supplies. Indeed, the militia provided the principal means of moving military supplies around the colony.[24]

The Canadian militia was very different from its British colonial counterpart. In most years, the captain of the militia in each parish would select the number of men required for service, and consequently only a proportion of the adult male population would serve. Such service was typically only for a short campaign, a few weeks or months at most. However, in 1759, with the very future of Canada under threat, most adult males volunteered for service. Even the students at the Jesuit college in Quebec volunteered, forming themselves into a militia company which became nicknamed the *Royal-Syntaxe*. One report even maintained that 'old men of 80, and children of 12... [&] 13 were seen coming to the camp, who would never consent to take advantage of the exemption granted to their age'. Ten thousand militia eventually reported for service, representing one in six of the total Canadian population and over half the total adult male population. This was indeed total war for the colony. Numbers alone, however, could not always overcome its indiscipline and Montcalm fretted that the militia would never be able to oppose British regulars in battle. The militia tended to drift away from the army, especially during times when labour was needed for the harvest. In combat, the men were difficult to form into ranks and lacked order. Their firing was slow and often irregular. To what use Montcalm could put them remained to be seen.[25]

If the militia were disorderly and difficult to command, they posed little problem to French commanders compared to their Native American allies. Nearly 2,000 Native American warriors joined the French during the Quebec campaign, and many others offered support to the campaigns on the Great Lakes and in the Ohio Valley. The largest contingents who arrived in Quebec came from the Ottawa and Iroquois, whose homelands were nearby, but there were also smaller numbers of Potawatomis from the Illinois country, Mi'kmaqs from Nova Scotia, and Foxes and Crees from the Great Lakes. Native American warriors could be extremely useful for harassing enemy troops and gaining intelligence of enemy troop movements. In particular, the deployment of Native American

warriors with French militia or *troupes de la Marine* proved particularly valuable. This practice had been developed during the
previous decades of frontier warfare against the British. Indeed,
during the Quebec campaign Canadians and Native Americans
serving alongside each other would cause substantial problems
for British commanders and would be an important feature
of the campaign. Indeed, as Montcalm realised, the mere sight
of Native American warriors was often enough to inspire fear
even amongst the stoutest of British regulars. He commented
in his journal that 'it is good that the enemy can see them on
the shore; because they inspire great fear as all the deserters will
attest'.[26] Fear could also be useful in keeping French regulars in
order. The governor of Canada, Pierre de Rigaud de Vaudreuil,
wrote to Nicolas-René Berryer, the minister of the Marine
and Colonies, that 'as nothing is more dangerous than the
desertion of the soldiers... I saw the necessity of employing
Indians'. Any soldier who might be tempted to desert would
risk losing his scalp.[27]

While Native American warriors played an important role
in irregular combat, in regular combat Montcalm discovered
that they could be difficult, if not impossible, to direct. In part
this was because Montcalm had to rely on only a few interpret-
ers, often former *coureurs de bois* or officers in the *troupes de la
Marine*. As one French officer noted: 'These Officers, some by
nature unpolished and in some points partaking of the character of the Savages whose morals & manners they imitated,
wanted to be not only independent, but to make themselves
of consequence, by instilling their sentiments into the minds of
the Savages whom they made to say only what they thought fit;
there not being any other persons who understood, or could
explain their language.' Perhaps most importantly, French
officers were particularly frustrated at the tendency of Native
American warriors to disperse before a battle was over, especially if there was the prospect of heavy casualties.[28]

This behaviour, which so infuriated French commanders, reflected traditional Native American war practices. Native American warriors did not regard death in battle as heroic or valiant. Casualties in war were to be avoided whenever possible. Consequently, even when about to win a victory, Native American warriors might leave the battlefield if they believed that losses would be too heavy. If such beliefs were infuriating to French commanders, other traditional practices proved even more unpalatable. The Native American treatment of prisoners, and in particular the practice of scalping and the mutilation of the dead, horrified European commanders like Montcalm. What Europeans saw as cruel and barbaric in fact had a religious connotation for most Native American peoples. Practices such as eating the flesh of dead warriors were religious customs amongst the Iroquois, for instance, which allowed the living to partake of the courage and strength of the dead warrior. Such practices, however, sat very awkwardly alongside European concepts of limited warfare. These concepts, however, would be sorely tested during the Quebec campaign and practices such as scalping became common not just amongst Native American warriors.[29]

French officers, unlike their Canadian counterparts, tended to dismiss the role which Native Americans could play in the conflict. They were equally dismissive of the role of Canadian troops. Frequently, French officers derided the indiscipline and timidity of the Canadians. Indeed, following the capture of Fort William Henry Montcalm wrote, 'I must say in truth that the Colonial troops and the Canadians had behaved very indifferently... the Commandant has been obliged to fire on some of them who were abandoning their post.' This attitude created deep tensions and animosities in the French establishment, which reached to the top of the command structure. Indeed, the different attitude to Canadian troops was fundamental to the differences between Montcalm and the governor, Vaudreuil.[30]

Montcalm appreciated that the use of Native Americans, militia and *troupes de la Marine* as irregular units had made a great contribution to Canada's struggle in the early years of the war and in previous wars. Yet he believed that the campaign which he faced in the summer of 1759 would be markedly different from previous campaigns. He argued that 'the nature of the war in this Colony has radically changed. In days of yore, the Canadians thought they made it; it consisted of excursions like hunting parties; now, of regular expeditions. Formerly the Indians formed the basis; now the accessory; other views, other maxims are therefore necessary'.[31] To combat the British invasion, Montcalm argued that Canada would need to resort to regular tactics and to maintain an army in the field throughout the summer months, not just for a few weeks. Raids against the colonial frontier to the south had served the Canadians well, but now they would not stop Wolfe's army. However, with few regular troops at his disposal Montcalm had to find the best way of using the available manpower. Consequently, at the end of 1758 he drew up plans to strengthen each of the regular companies with fifteen militiamen. He hoped that the presence of these woodsmen would improve the regulars' ability to fight in the woods, while service alongside the regulars would ensure that the former militiamen improved in discipline. However, in September 1759 their presence amongst the regulars would prove fatal.[32]

The contribution of the militia and the *troupes de la Marine*, and the role that irregular warfare should play in the defence of Canada, were the main sources of tension between Montcalm and Vaudreuil. This tension was exacerbated by the awkward command structure which existed in New France. As governor of New France, Vaudreuil was commander-in-chief of the colonial forces. Montcalm, as lieutenant-general of the Crown, was commander of the *troupes de terre*. Such a blurred command structure was not uncommon in the French army, where many a compliant general appointed for political purposes was given the title but directed by a reliable mentor.[33] Montcalm was the experienced military commander and tactician; Vaudreuil possessed an intimate knowledge of Canada, the Canadian people and their Native American allies. Eventually these disputes became very public. Following the capture of Fort William Henry in 1757, Vaudreuil bitterly attacked Montcalm for his failure to press the advantage by continuing his advance. By 1758, the disputes had become so bitter that they threatened to paralyse the French command. Vaudreuil saw no reason to abandon Canada's traditional reliance on small-scale raids to paralyse the British colonial frontier. He believed that greater reliance should be placed on the *troupes de la Marine* and colonial militia. Indeed, in November 1758 Vaudreuil had even written to Versailles suggesting that the regulars should be withdrawn as soon as possible. He maintained that 'besides costing a great deal, they will always foster a spirit of division; their manner of waging war being accompanied with less hardship than that of the Colony, would insensibly be adopted; the introduction of baggage and provisions in the campaign proceeds from the officers of those troops; 'tis most pernicious to the fashion of bush fighting; is an obstacle to the change of camp from one moment to the other and thereby prevents frequent detachments'.[34]

Not only did Montcalm and Vaudreuil disagree over the methods of waging war; they also disagreed on fundamental elements of strategy. Vaudreuil believed that Canada could not survive without its dependent territories, in particular the Great Lakes and Ohio Valley. Without their Native American allies who inhabited the region, it would be difficult to raid the British frontier to the south; without the region's fur trade, Canada would have lost its economic *raison d'être*. He therefore believed that every inch of Canadian soil should be defended. Montcalm, on the other hand, believed that there was no hope of defending Canada if Quebec fell. Rather than defend Canada on all sides, he believed that Canadian defences should be contracted and the main armies should concentrate on the defence of Quebec. The disputes between the two caused much disgust, both in Canada and France. When, in the autumn of 1758, Montcalm wrote to Versailles requesting that he be allowed to return to France, he was simply informed that his presence in Canada was too essential for him to leave. However, he was promoted to lieutenant-general, and Vaudreuil received orders that Montcalm was now to control all military matters and he all civil matters. During the spring and summer of 1759, the two were able to patch up some of their worst disputes, but there was still a strong element of tension between them and a willingness to blame the other for any failure. This certainly did not assist in the defence of Quebec.[35]

Another reason for Montcalm's disgust with Vaudreuil and with all things Canadian was what he perceived as the rampant corruption in Canada. He was particularly incensed by the Intendant François Bigot's engrossing of military supplies and his rampant profiteering. Bigot had amazing powers. As Intendant he had control of royal finances and oversaw the purchase and distribution of supplies for the troops and for the various military posts, and he directed the importation of supplies from France. However, Bigot often used these powers for his own benefit rather than for the colony. Supplies collected for the use of the army disappeared into private hands before being repurchased. When supplies of foodstuffs grew low, Bigot sent inspectors to buy up all they could find at a fixed low price. If the farmers wanted to eat they would have to buy their grain back from the Intendant at market prices. Not surprisingly, this caused Canadian farmers to hide foodstuffs and refuse to sell them to the Crown. Indeed, the critical shortage of supplies which was experienced in

Canada in 1759 seems to have been not only the result of poor harvests, but also the consequence of many farmers hiding their foodstuffs. Montcalm railed at this corruption and wrote to the Marshall de Belle-Isle in Paris that 'Bigot appears occupied only in making a large fortune for himself, his adherents and sycophants. Cupidity has seized officers, store-keepers; the commissaries also… Everybody appears in a hurry to make his fortune before the Colony is lost, which event many, perhaps, desire, as an impenetrable veil over their conduct.' While Montcalm probably overstated the extent of corruption in Canada, and misunderstood the nature of the colonial system, the machinations of some officials certainly hampered Canada's war effort.[36]

Bigot's machinations certainly helped to ensure that supplies were scarce. The large numbers of militia and Native American warriors who turned up for the defence of Quebec further exacerbated this shortage. Montcalm fretted about the number of mouths he had to feed and whether the contribution of the Canadians and Native Americans to the city's defence merited their consumption of supplies. Montcalm also fretted about how many troops he should send for the defence of Fort Ticonderoga and Fort Niagara. Ultimately he decided to send 2,500 men, including three battalions of regulars, to Ticonderoga under the command of Brigadier-General François-Charles de Bourlamaque. An additional 500 men, mainly *troupes de la Marine*, would be sent to join the men already on the Ohio and at Fort Niagara. This would leave Montcalm with five out of the eight battalions of regular troops to assist in the defence of Quebec. They would be joined by the remainder of the *troupes de la Marine*. The militia would also join them, but only when the British fleet finally appeared in the river. In total, Montcalm would have at Quebec about 1,600 *troupes de terre*, about 600 *troupes de la Marine* and 10,000 militia.[37]

Montcalm also realised that he had to make every possible use of Quebec's natural defences. The city of Quebec itself was in a naturally defensive position. The city was in two halves divided by a steep cliff. Nestling at the foot of the cliff, along the shore of the St Lawrence, was the lower town. The lower town was home to most of the city's merchants and crafts-men. It could only be attacked directly from the river, or through the upper town. To prevent a landing many of the warehouses which fronted onto the river had been demolished and replaced with batteries. Consequently, it seemed unlikely that Wolfe would assault the town directly. However, in case he did attempt such a rash act Montcalm closed off many of the streets between the upper and lower town and left only one steep and narrow passage connecting the two.[38]

The upper town had a commanding position on heights towering over the river. Here were all the principal build-ings of the town, including the palaces of the governor and Intendant, the Jesuits' college and the cathedral. On the river side, the upper town was protected by a steep cliff and by the lower town. An assault from that quarter was highly unlikely. On the land side, however, it was more vulnerable to attack from the open ground to the west, commonly called the Plains of Abraham. Over the many years since Quebec's foundation, a network of fortifications and redoubts had been built to protect the city on its landward side. These were sufficiently substantial to prevent the city being taken by a surprise assault or in a raid, but they were incomplete and would not prevent a determined enemy from taking the city by storm. Montcalm attempted to improve these defences, but by the time of Wolfe's arrival, the city was still vulnerable to an attack from the west. There were also several suburbs which lay outside these defences. Although Montcalm took steps to protect them with stockades and embankments, these would offer only limited resistance to a determined attacker.[39]

To attack the city by land, the British first had to get to the Plains. A landing to the west of the town was considered unlikely. In part, this was because of the terrain. Steep cliffs made landing difficult except at a few coves. More importantly, to land west of Quebec the British would have to get their ships and landing craft past the town. As the shoreline bristled with French batteries and the river was less than a mile wide at the city, it was felt unlikely that the British would attempt to get upstream of the city or, if they did try, that they would succeed. Montcalm thought it was more likely that Wolfe would attempt a landing to the east of the town, along the low-lying shoreline which stretched for about six miles out to the mouth of the river Montmorency. To protect this shoreline, in the two months before Wolfe's arrival Montcalm organised the construction of an extensive network of batteries, entrenchments and redoubts from the Montmorency river to the St Charles. It was along this shore, called the Beauport shore, that he would garrison the bulk of his troops, and in the middle of the line, in the village of Beauport, that he made his headquarters.[40]

In addition to these measures, Montcalm called a council of war of his leading officers to consider what other actions could be taken to prevent the British fleet approaching the city. The council suggested that all the navigation markers on the St Lawrence, particularly the lighthouses constructed on the Île d'Orléans to mark the narrow passage known as the Traverse to the east of the island, should be destroyed. The council also ordered the construction of a number of floating batteries. These were large floating platforms that carried as many as twelve guns of different calibres. While not very manoeuvrable, they could challenge any small vessel that ventured too close. Montcalm also ordered the construction of six gun-boats, each carrying a substantial twenty-four-pounder cannon, and eight rafts carrying an eight-pounder. While these vessels would not be able to challenge British warships, they would prove to be very important in the campaign. The British only controlled the parts of the river where they had warships stationed. Supplies and men could only be transported with a naval escort. This would hamper many of Wolfe's operations.[41]

The two French frigates which were marooned in Quebec with the approach of the British fleet were ordered upstream to station themselves just above Quebec to prevent a British landing above the town. This was probably an unfortunate decision. Admiral Holmes had to send small craft ahead of the main fleet to sound the channel. Had the French frigates been stationed at the narrow Traverse, they would have forced Holmes to send up some of his warships into uncharted waters. While the French frigates might ultimately have been sacrificed, they would certainly have slowed the British fleet's approach.[42]

The decision to keep the two frigates above Quebec reflected French concerns about preserving their supply lines. To ensure that provisions could be transported by land as well as water, in case British vessels managed to pass Quebec, carts and wagons were constructed and bridges were thrown over the rivers Cap Rouge and Jacques Cartier to the west of Quebec. A series of ovens was also built around Cap Rouge and Jacques Cartier for baking bread for the army. Ironically, these decisions, which were designed to protect the French supply lines in case Quebec should be besieged and the army need to retreat westwards, had the effect of making the supply lines more exposed to any British attack to the west of Quebec and left the city with a dangerously low stockpile of supplies.[43]

These activities had several consequences for civilians in Quebec. For all Canadians, this was total war. Far more than was imaginable in Britain, or Britain's North American colonies, by the spring of 1759 all Canada was geared for war. The most noticeable consequence was the almost complete absence of adult men from late April onwards. Nearly all adult men offered their service in the militia. Not only were the services of men utilised, even women, children and old men helped in the movement of supplies and construction of wagons, bridges and fire-ships. All Canadians endured the chronic shortages of provisions and supplies. As news of the pending arrival of the British fleet reached Quebec, civilians along the St Lawrence prepared to evacuate their homes. Most had already hidden their personal property and livestock and now retreated to prepared encampments deep in the woods, where it was hoped the British would be unable to find them. The women and children in the city of Quebec also prepared to evacuate. Many headed upstream to the town of Deschambault, while others found shelter in some of the smaller towns around Quebec like Charlesbourg.[44]

Few Canadians were reluctant to volunteer their services, for most feared the prospect of conquest by the British. The years of continual conflict with the British colonies had bred lurid tales of what could be expected if the British ever entered Quebec. Some of these were more fantasy than reality, but the civilians of Canada had every reason to fear the results of conquest by the British. They did not have to look far to see an example of what such a conquest might bring. Indeed, as they prepared to fight the British they were joined by a contingent of Acadians who had struggled to Quebec to join them. The fate of the Acadians provided ample evidence of what might await Quebec. The Acadians had had the misfortune to live in territory disputed by Britain and France. At the Treaty of Utrecht in 1713, the French had ceded Nova Scotia to Great Britain and many French-speaking settlers now found themselves in British territory. When war broke out in North America in 1755, British officials wondered what should be done with the French *habitants* who remained there. The Board of Trade ruled that unless the Acadians took an oath of submission to the Crown they should be treated as rebels and dealt with appropriately. In the autumn of 1755, the governor of Nova Scotia implemented this policy. When the Acadians refused to swear the oath, they were rounded up and forcibly deported from their homeland. In total almost 6,000 Acadians were removed from their homes and resettled in the British North American colonies. The operation to round up and deport Acadian civilians soon extended far outside Nova Scotia's recognised boundaries. Following the fall of Louisbourg, Amherst sent Wolfe with three battalions of regulars to destroy all the settlements along the coast of Miramichi Bay, Chaleur Bay and the coast of the Gaspé Peninsula to the north. There could be little military justification for the actions, as these settlements were isolated farmsteads and hamlets which contributed little to the French war effort.[45]

British actions against the Acadians were, even in eighteenth-century terms, of a dubious morality. By the middle of the eighteenth century there was a general feeling in Europe that warfare was becoming more regulated and restricted. There were now available a considerable number of general discussions on how nations should wage war. Most notable amongst these was *Le Droit des Gens ou les Principes de la Loi Naturelle* by the Swiss writer Emmeric de Vattel, published in London in 1758.[46] Vattel's work was quite specific in defining the rights of civilians in war:

> Women, children, feeble old men, and sick persons come under the description of enemies; and we have certain rights over them, inasmuch as they belong to the nation with whom we are at war, and as, between nation and nation, all rights and pretensions affect the body of the society, together with all its members. But these are enemies who make no resistance; and consequently we have no right to maltreat their persons or use any violence against them, much less to take away their lives.

This is so plain a maxim of justice and humanity, that at present every nation in the least degree civilized, acquiesces in it.[47]

Vattel's work reflected the thinking common in Europe at the time of the Quebec campaign that civilians must be protected from the worst horrors of war. Rules and regulations of warfare governed the conduct of armies in many other ways. Prisoners should be exchanged, subject to an agreement not to serve again in the campaign. Officers captured in battle could expect a treatment markedly different from their men; indeed, many were kept on parole with little restraints on their freedom until an agreement could be made for their release. Similarly, the wounded were offered a degree of protection. Hospitals and wagons transporting the wounded were protected. Clearly, the civilians of Acadia were not protected in this manner. Their homes and settlements were destroyed, and many perished in the flames or from starvation. As straggling survivors from Acadia arrived on the St Lawrence to assist in the defence of Quebec, tales of British atrocities spread widely. As Wolfe's army prepared for its ascent of the St Lawrence, and Montcalm made preparations to defend Canada, the Canadians wondered what fate the summer held for them.

The residents of Quebec were not alone in wondering what the summer would hold. In London, much political capital rested on the fate of the expedition. When the ministry had drawn up their plans for Wolfe's expedition, they had presumed that he would have with him 12,000 regulars to combat a smaller French army of at most 8,000. Amherst's army, Pitt confidently presumed, would cause Montcalm to dispatch many of his regular forces to Fort Ticonderoga. Montcalm, however, had concentrated the bulk of his forces around Quebec and dispatched few men to oppose Amherst. Now, as Wolfe's expedition approached the St Lawrence, his army was outnumbered by the French. While Wolfe's army consisted solely of regulars, Montcalm had the advantage of terrain and prepared positions. Wolfe and his fellow officers realised that they faced a difficult task. Just how difficult that task would be became apparent when the British expedition finally landed outside Quebec.

3

Beginnings

On 14 February 1759, fifty-nine transports, eight warships and seven ordnance ships sailed from Portsmouth, bound for America. Three days later, a smaller convoy departed carrying General Wolfe. The expedition had begun. The ministry's plan called for the fleet to rendezvous at Louisbourg on 20 April. There, the fleet and transports would re-provision before setting sail for the St Lawrence on 7 May. Such a schedule was extremely optimistic. Indeed, news of their involvement in the Quebec expedition did not reach many of the British troops in North America until early April. Troops, supplies and transports had to be collected from across the eastern seaboard, from Louisbourg at the tip of Cape Breton Island to Philadelphia almost a thousand miles to the south.[1]

As the troops departed, they left behind them their wives, mistresses and children. Some of these women and children had followed their husbands from Britain; others were the result of more recent liaisons during the troops' sojourn in

America. This created an unexpected problem. The women and children began to move to the port cities in search of work to support themselves during their husbands' absence, for they would receive no support from the army. Worse still, if their partners were wounded or killed they would be destitute. In New England, where large numbers of troops had spent the winter and where there was already a substantial number of poor, the influx of women into Boston created tensions. In mid-May, acting governor Thomas Hutchinson wrote to General Amherst asking for advice. He wrote that 'the Regiment has left behind them a number of Women & Children which must immediately come to the Town for their support... If the Town is forced to bear the charge of these women & children I am afraid it will cause a great deal of discontent & grumbling.' Eventually it was agreed, under pressure from Amherst, that the women would be supported by the poor rate where necessary until a more permanent solution was found.[2]

This problem resolved, the assembling of troops and supplies proceeded remarkably smoothly, thanks in no small part to Amherst's meticulous attention. Across the eastern seaboard ships loaded provisions and troops and prepared to sail. The greatest delay to the expedition came from the bad weather. Unusually strong northerly and north-easterly winds drove the melting ice from the Gulf of St Lawrence against the Cape Breton coast and into the harbour at Louisbourg. The harbour was so packed with ice that few ships were able to enter the port. Consequently, Saunders had to abandon his plans to rendezvous the fleet at Louisbourg and instead headed to Halifax to the south.[3]

With the expedition delayed, Saunders dispatched Rear-Admiral Durell with a squadron to patrol the Gulf of St Lawrence, to prevent any French supply ships from reaching Canada. Unfortunately, Durell was late reaching the river.

The heavy ice around Louisbourg slowed his journey. It was not until 5 May that he was able to get out of port. This was unlucky for Durell, for the supply ships, arriving directly from France, were able to take a more northerly route, closer to the Île d'Anticosti, avoiding the worst of the ice. In the first two weeks of May, before his fleet was able to take up station in the St Lawrence, sixteen supply ships slipped into Quebec, providing the equivalent of eighty days' provisions for Canada's entire population. Wolfe would not quickly forget this failure.[4]

These supply ships also brought to Canada the first confirmed reports of the coming British assault. Throughout the winter there had been only vague rumours of the planned attack. For instance, British prisoners taken on the New York frontier had reported plans for an assault by 60,000 men. While these reports were obviously exaggerated, it was evident that the British were planning a major expedition against Canada. Yet it was not clear where that campaign would be fought. Montcalm and Vaudreuil bickered over how to defend the colony from the British onslaught, and over whether the major attack would be from the south along Lake George and Lake Champlain or from the east along the St Lawrence River. The attack up the St Lawrence seemed in many ways the least likely. It would take a massive combined naval and land operation to seize the city of Quebec; if the city was not taken, British troops would have to retreat before the harsh Canadian winter set in, as they had done in 1690. Moreover, Canadian pilots repeatedly uttered assurances that the St Lawrence was difficult to navigate; a large British fleet would never get upstream to Quebec but would be wrecked on the rocks and shoals, as had the last British expedition which attempted to enter the river in 1711. Vaudreuil doubted that the British would risk such an expedition, when they could equally well attack overland. As late as the beginning of April he had argued, 'I do not presume that the enemy will undertake coming to Quebec.'[5]

The supply ships from France, however, brought chilling details in the form of a copy of an intercepted letter from Amherst to the ministry in London, providing all the particulars of the coming campaign. The letter provided indisputable evidence of the coming onslaught. Both governor and general began to make preparations for the defence of the colony. Around Quebec, entrenchments were begun, but the work proceeded at a surprisingly leisurely pace. In part, this was because many still doubted that a major expedition would attempt to sail up the river and if they did that it would take many weeks – in part because the shortage of supplies meant that the militia, the main source of manpower, could not be mustered too quickly to begin the construction of the defences.[6]

Canadian officials also believed that Versailles would send them some assistance, even if only an additional battalion or two of *troupes de terre*, and certainly plenty of supplies and materiel. The previous autumn, Montcalm had dispatched Louis-Antoine, Comte de Bougainville, to France. He was to give the ministry full details of Canada's plight. Once the ministry knew of Canada's dire straits, Canadians were sure that it would send aid. On 14 May, Bougainville arrived back in Quebec. He brought distressing news: Versailles had all but abandoned Canada. Despairing of winning a victory in North America, the French now planned to strike closer to home. The French ministry planned an expedition to invade Britain. All ships and all resources were to be channelled into this enterprise.[7] The Marechal de Belle-Isle provided Bougainville with a letter to give to Montcalm. In it, he bluntly informed the general:

> I am very sorry to have to inform you that you must not expect to receive any Military reinforcements. Besides augmenting the scarcity of provisions which you have only too much experi-

enced up to the present time, it would be much to be feared that they would be intercepted by the English on the passage… As it is to be expected that the entire efforts of the English will be directed against Canada, and that they will attack you at different points at once, it will be necessary that you… confine your plan of defence to those which are most essential and most connected, in order that being concentrated on a smaller extent of country, you may be always enabled mutually to help each other. However trifling the space you can preserve, it is of the utmost importance to possess always a foothold in Canada, for should we once wholly lose that country, it would be quite impossible to enter it again.[8]

Any lingering hopes Quebecers still held that the British would not arrive were soon quashed. On 23 May, the beacons along the Côte du Sud were lit to announce the arrival of a British fleet in the St Lawrence River.[9]

The news that the British had finally arrived created concern, but not full panic in Quebec City. Citizens began to hide their valuables in cellars or to send them away to friends further up the river. Some of the wealthier inhabitants departed for Montreal, while others tried to secure a passage to France. Along the St Lawrence Vaudreuil had originally planned a staged evacuation of the civilian population, but the local *habitants* did not initially believe that a British attack was impending and refused to cooperate. Now that the British were in the river, the evacuation would have to be hasty. On 24 May, Montcalm sent several detachments of *troupes de la Marine* to force the evacuation of villages and to ensure the secreting of all supplies and livestock in the woods.[10] The haste with which the evacuation was conducted, particularly from the Île-aux-Coudres and the Île d'Orléans, was unfortunate. One French eyewitness recorded in his journal that it 'caused much greater injury to thousand of Inhabitants, than ever the

Enemy could have inflicted upon them. Numbers of Families were ruined by these precipitate measures – three fourths of the Cattle died… besides several of the Inhabitants, Women and Children… [who] unhappily perished, in consequence of their being collected at one of the extremities of these Islands, without any means having been previously taken of providing food for their sustenance, Boats for their conveyance, or places to which they could retire.'[11]

Quebecers held their breath, yet the expected invasion never came. The British ships sat in the St Lawrence over 100 miles below Quebec. For this was not the invasion fleet, but Durell's squadron sent to prevent French supplies getting to Quebec. In some ways the delay was unfortunate, for Quebecers once more relaxed in their preparations. One French soldier commented that 'this prevarication was very prejudicial to the Colony. If the English had appeared soon after the first moment of alarm, Surprise, Courage & enthusiasm would have supplied the absence of those works which did not then exist; and the ardour which prevailed at that time would have been the mere presage of Victory – the delay on the contrary, gave time for that ardour to cool; the Canadians being by nature impatient, and eager for the speedy decision of all matters of great interest.'[12]

Indeed, the British force had not begun assembling in Louisbourg until mid-May. Even this late in the season, bad weather still hampered the preparations. On 29 May, one soldier recorded in his journal that 'the harbour was so full of shoals of ice that no boats could go from the ships to shore'.[13] Some foolhardy men even attempted to walk over the ice from their ships to the shore. Wolfe, who had only arrived himself in Louisbourg on 14 May, tried to make some use of the delay by ordering as many troops as possible ashore to exercise and prepared for the coming campaign.[14]

On 4 June, the fleet finally began to depart from Louisbourg. As the troops prepared for their departure, many had mixed feelings. For those troops who had been serving on garrison duty, the campaign offered the prospect of a welcome release. Captain John Knox, whose regiment was one of those previously confined to garrison duty, confided in his journal that 'we are now about to depart from his Majesty's Province of Nova Scotia, where the forty-third regiment have had the misfortune to undergo an inglorious exile of twenty-two months and upwards, separated not only from the busy active world, but likewise from those scenes of honour, in which I can venture to affirm, every man, both commissioned and private, most ardently wished to have shared'. As the ships departed, he reported that 'the soldiers of each ship they gave three cheers, expressive of their joy at being released from their tedious and slavish exile; thanking God they were at last going to join the army'.[15] For many soldiers, however, such outward expressions may have been as much bravado as a reflection of true feeling. Some troops viewed the prospect of the coming campaign with dread. They knew they faced a difficult campaign and that many of their number would not return. One trooper recorded in his journal: 'I hear a Lieut. on board one of the men of War has shot himself – for fear I suppose the French shou'd do it.'[16]

After its departure from Louisbourg, the expedition made swift progress. On 9 June, the expedition reached the mouth of the St Lawrence and began to proceed slowly upstream. From the shore, the few remaining *habitants* and militia watched with unease as the leading vessels entered the river. Then, to their surprise, the ships hoisted the French colours. Jubilant that French ships had arrived in the river bringing men and aid, the local pilots hastily paddled out into the river. Scrambling aboard the ships, their delight soon turned to horror when the French colours were struck and the Royal Navy ensign raised. They had been tricked. Now the British had pilots to navigate the river. Saunders ordered that a French pilot be put on board each of the lead warships. Most were unwilling but had little choice. The pilot on board the *Goodwill* 'gasconaded at a most extravagant rate, and gave us to understand it was much against his inclination that he was become an English Pilot. The poor fellow assumed great latitude in his conversation; said, "he made no doubt that some of the fleet would return to England, but they should have a dismal tale to carry with them; for Canada should be the grave of the whole army, and he expected in a short time to see the walls of Quebec ornamented with English scalps." Had it not been in obedience to the Admiral, who gave orders that he should not be ill used, he would certainly have been thrown over-board.'[17]

The progress of the fleet up the St Lawrence was surprisingly speedy. This was largely thanks to Durell, who had made use of his stay in the river to send out small vessels to sound the channel. By the time the main fleet arrived, his men had already sounded and charted most of the St Lawrence as far as the Île d'Orléans, almost to within sight of Quebec City. On 18 June the main fleet arrived in the St Lawrence, where it anchored off Bic and waited for stragglers to arrive. News of the arrival of the main fleet reached Quebec City on 20 June. However, the city's residents had been anticipating the fleet's arrival for weeks. There was still no undue concern, for their mariners assured them that it would take the British weeks to navigate the narrow 'Traverse' between the Île d'Orléans and the Côte du Sud. Divine providence had protected the city before and surely it would do so again. However, less than a week later, on 26 June, the British fleet appeared in sight of Quebec. Now for the first time there was a palpable sense of panic and despair.[18]

As the British fleet approached, Montcalm finalised the disposition of his army. The French army he assembled at Beauport consisted of nearly five battalions of *troupes de terre*, all the *troupes de la Marine*, several parties of Native American warriors and most of the militia. The second battalion of Royal Roussillon, the militia of Montreal and Montcalm's Native American allies were on his left, close to the river Montmorency, under the command of Brigadier François-Gaston, Chevalier de Lévis. The right wing, close to the St Charles River where Montcalm perceived the threat was less, was composed of the militia of Quebec and Trois Rivières, and part of the *troupes de la Marine* under the command of Governor Vaudreuil. The greatest strength of the line was placed in the centre around the village of Beauport, under Montcalm's own command. He commanded four battalions of the *troupes de terre,* the battalions of La Sarre, Languedoc, Guyenne and Béarn. From the centre, the troops could be sent to assist either wing in case of attack. To protect the city of Quebec, Montcalm left a garrison of 800 militia, 110 *troupes de la Marine* and 700 seamen who manned the artillery batteries.[19]

Montcalm convened a council of war to consider what additional measures should be taken for the protection of the city. The council reached some unsettling conclusions. They presumed that any British bombardment would quickly set the lower town on fire. If this happened, all the troops manning the batteries were to evacuate the lower town and not attempt to put out the fires, since as long as the fires were burning the British could not make a landing. Once the fires had burned themselves out, the lower town should be reoccupied and the batteries quickly re-established. For the townspeople who remained, this was chilling news.[20]

On 26 June, as they watched from the heights of the city, or from the Beauport shore, the Canadians and French troops saw the British fleet come into view. Now Wolfe finally had to commit himself to action. It had been difficult for Wolfe to make many advanced plans, as he knew comparatively little about Quebec itself. For most European towns and fortresses Wolfe could have obtained detailed maps and plans, but not for Quebec. He was forced to rely on reports from the British engineer Patrick MacKellar, who had been captured by the French at Fort Oswego in 1756 and held prisoner for some time in Quebec. Now he accompanied the expedition and provided Wolfe with a detailed report and map of the city's defences. His original information was at best sketchy; by 1759 it was also considerably outdated.[21] However, based on MacKellar's advice, Wolfe had already determined a plan. Before his departure from Louisbourg he outlined his plans to his uncle:

> The town of Quebec is poorly fortified, but the ground round about it is rocky. To invest the place, and cut off all communication with the colony, it will be necessary to encamp with our right to the River St. Lawrence, and our left to the river St. Charles. From the river St. Charles to Beauport the communication must be kept open by strong entrenched posts and redoubts. The enemy can pass that river at low water; and it will be proper to establish ourselves with small entrenched posts from the point of Levi to La Chaudiere. It is the business of our naval force to be masters of the river, both above and below the town. If I find that the enemy is strong, audacious, and well commanded, I shall proceed with the utmost caution and circumspection, giving Mr. Amherst time to use his superiority. If they are timid, weak, and ignorant, we shall push them with more vivacity, that we may be able before the summer is gone to assist the Commander-in-Chief. I reckon we shall have a smart action at the passage of the river St. Charles.[22]

Wolfe planned to land on the Île d'Orléans to provide a secure base of operations. Then he would cross his army over to the Beauport shore and advance on Quebec from the east. The great battle, he suspected, would occur on the banks of the

St Charles River. On 26 June, the fleet arrived at its anchor off the Île d'Orléans. However, it was late in the day so rather than landing his men at night Wolfe dispatched a small party of rangers to secure the main landing and waited until daybreak. This proved fortunate for Wolfe, since Vaudreuil had sent a large party of Canadians and Indians to harass any British troops landing on the island. When the troops did not disembark immediately, Vaudreuil assumed that the main landing would take place the following day on the Beauport shore, and recalled the party. On 27 June, the British landing began in earnest at St-Laurent without interruption. At the first opportunity, Wolfe and MacKellar proceeded to the western point of the island, from where they could get their first good view of the French defences. As he stared across the Basin, Wolfe's heart sank. The shoreline was bristling with guns and entrenchments. Thomas Bell, his aide-de-camp, reported that 'we saw the Town; 4 Batteries along Beaupt Entrenchments here & there, with 5 Encampments'. A direct attack on the Beauport shore was impossible.[23]

As Quebecers watched the British secure their landing on the Île d'Orléans, they were more than a little concerned. Virtually nothing had been done to impede the progress of the British fleet up the river, not even to harass the many small landing parties which went ashore to gather fresh food and water. As one Quebec resident confided, a 'neglect of prudential measures was also observed in not having kept upon the South Shore 3 or 400 Savages, who remained in Quebec, where they did nothing but create disturbances and who might with the greatest ease have destroyed vast numbers of the English left upon the Shore'.[24] In part, this was the result of Montcalm's failure to appreciate the potential of irregular forces in opposing the British, and in particular his failure to appoint effective officers to command those expeditions which were sent out.

Although the French had failed to mount a serious challenge to the expedition so far, Mother Nature now intervened. The troops had no sooner finished landing than a fierce storm blew up. A strong easterly wind caused many ships to break their anchors and drove several onto the shore. Many of the smaller boats foundered and sank. Many others would have to return to Boston for repairs. It was only thanks to the skill and bravery of the crews that the fleet did not suffer more damage. As the wind died down the fleet was left in great confusion.[25]

That evening, the French tried to profit from this disorder. From the moment that the French had first known that the British were sending a fleet against Quebec, plans had been made to destroy the fleet with fire-ships. For this purpose Vaudreuil had requisitioned eight of the merchant vessels that were in the city. Filled with pitch and turpentine, they were to be sailed into the midst of the British fleet as soon as it arrived in the Basin of Quebec. The French hoped that in the confined space of the Basin the fire would spread quickly between the crowded ships, causing havoc. In addition to the large fire-ships, 120 smaller fire-rafts or *radeaux* were built. These were simply floating platforms on which wood and other combustible material could be placed. Unlike the fire-ships, which would be sailed into the British fleet, the *radeaux* would simply be allowed to drift with the current into the fleet. With the British fleet crowded in the Basin and now in such disorder, a council of war decided the time was right to dispatch the fire-ships.[26]

Late in the evening, the fire-ships left the quayside and navigated downstream. There were already bad omens. While meeting to coordinate their actions, the captains of the fire-ships had argued about the plans for the attack. Now, as the ships neared the British fleet, fear seems to have got the better of some of them. Quebecers watched in horror as, still at a great distance from the British fleet, their crews set the ships on fire and hurriedly jumped over board. The British ships closest to the fire-ships hastily cut their anchors and moved out of the way.[27] Meanwhile, a flotilla of small boats grappled the fire-ships safely onto the shore. Captain Knox, who watched the French fire-ships from the British camp on the Île d'Orléans, recorded in his journal that:

> They were certainly the grandest fire-work (if I may be allowed to call them so) that can possibly be conceived, every circumstance having contributed to their awful, yet beautiful appearance… the blaze of the floating fires, issuing from all parts, and running almost as quick as thought up the masts and rigging; add to this the solemnity of the sable night, still more obscured by the profuse clouds of smoke, with the firing of the cannon, the bursting of the grenado's, and the crackling of the other combustibles; all which reverberated thro' the air, and the adjacent woods, together with the sonorous shots, and frequent repetitions of *All's well*, from our gallant seamen on the water afford a scene, I think, infinitely superior to any adequate description.[28]

Montcalm and his officers watched the fire-ships from a vantage point near Beaumont church on the south shore. He was outraged at their failure. The next morning he wrote 'Our dear fire-ships. That epithet is very fitting, because they cost 15 to 18,000 francs… left yesterday evening. They were set on fire three leagues from the enemy…[and] most certainly effected only a few bad jokes.'[29] The residents of Quebec were even angrier. As the captains of the fire-ships returned to the city, they were greeted with cries of treason and an angry mob assembled at the Château St Louis. It was only with difficulty that Vaudreuil prevented the mob from placing all the captains in a ship, setting it on fire and floating it again downstream.[30]

It was now apparent to all that the British fleet had safely arrived in the Quebec Basin. Consequently, Vaudreuil felt that it was necessary to place restrictions on the civilian population. All non-essential personnel were ordered to leave the city and for the first time, on the evening of 29 June, the gates of the city were closed to prevent a surprise attack. Church bells were to be silenced, even for burials and baptisms. In future, they would be rung only briefly to mark the closing of the gates at 10 p.m. or to raise the alarm of a British attack on the city.[31]

With the French fire-ships destroyed, Saunders felt sufficiently confident to advance some of his warships further into the Basin and to send out small craft to sound the river to determine whether his warships could support a landing on the Beauport shore. As these craft advanced, it became clear that to guarantee their safety the army would need to secure both the point of the Île d'Orléans and Pointe-Lévy on the south shore. From either of these positions the French could erect batteries that would force any British ships to withdraw. On the evening of 29 June, Wolfe dispatched Monckton with Amherst's Regiment, Fraser's Highlanders and two companies of rangers to secure the Pointe-Lévy. Landing near Beaumont, Monckton encountered determined opposition from a unit of local militia under the command of Sieur de Charest. However, fearing that the British would soon surround his small detachment, de Charest withdrew. The sudden French withdrawal surprised the British. One officer confided in his journal, 'we were surprised that they should so quietly give up this important post'.[32] With the landing site secured, Monckton's men took up position in the church at Beaumont and secured Pointe-Lévy and the nearby heights at the Pointe-aux-Pères.

Now that the south bank was secured, Wolfe spent 1 and 2 July reconnoitring from Pointe-aux-Pères to the west as far as the Etchemin river. From here he was able to examine closely the defences of the city and investigate possible landing sites to the west of the city. The shore to the west of the city was steep and wooded, but there were several weakly defended coves. A landing here might be possible. Wolfe also determined that the heights above Pointe-aux-Pères would make an excellent location for batteries. From here the British could bombard the city of Quebec, less than one mile distant across the river. He immediately ordered Monckton to begin construction of a series of batteries aimed at the city.[33]

The following day, 3 July, Wolfe met with Admiral Saunders to determine where the army should attack. Saunders informed Wolfe that his men had established that the waters off the Beauport shore were too shallow to allow the fleet to support a landing. This disappointed Wolfe. However, both Wolfe and Saunders agreed that they should now investigate the possibility of landing to the west of the city. Consequently, Wolfe ordered Murray to take a detachment along the south shore as far as the Chaudière river to examine once more the landing sites to the west of Quebec. While Murray was finding a landing site upstream, Townshend was to prepare his forces on the Île d'Orléans to make a diversionary landing at the east end of Montcalm's line at the Falls of Montmorency. When Murray returned, he informed Wolfe that a landing about three miles west of Quebec was feasible. Wolfe ordered immediate preparations for the landing and directed the construction of rafts and bateaux.[34]

The residents of Quebec watched all this activity with more than a little concern. As it became apparent that the British were establishing batteries at Pointe-aux-Pères, the city's sense of unease became intense. Townspeople complained that Montcalm and Vaudreuil had done little to secure the point. Why, they murmured, had they not established a redoubt or battery there to protect it? However, it made little strategic sense to secure the point. With the British naval presence, any troops posted there would soon have been isolated and out of supply, and have fallen easy prey to the British. Montcalm could not risk losing so many men. Further, while the point did offer a good site for batteries to attack the city, Montcalm believed that the distance was too great for them to do much damage. Finally, while devastating to civilian morale, the destruction of the city would have only limited military significance. As long as his army was safe, Montcalm would not be defeated.[35]

While Montcalm may have been loath to heed the concerns of Quebec's residents, Vaudreuil was not. He attempted to use his theoretical powers as commander of the Canadian forces to launch a raid on the British post at Pointe-aux-Pères. On the night of 30 June, Vaudreuil intended to send a substantial force of *troupes de la Marine*, militia and Indians across to the point to harass the British before they could entrench. However, a British deserter claimed that 'the landing at the Point de Levis was merely a stratagem to veil the real designs of the English who intended that very night making an attack at Beauport'.[36] Vaudreuil hurriedly cancelled the planned raid. Even though the British attack never came, the prisoner continued to insist that this was Wolfe's planned strategy. So convincing was the deserter that the French army spent a second night under arms.[37]

The failure to harass the British forces infuriated the residents of Quebec. On 3 July, a large crowd gathered outside the city's Château St Louis and demanded that Montcalm and Vaudreuil take some action. Both agreed, yet almost every night there was another scare of an impending attack and Montcalm continued to believe that the major attack would come at Beauport. For this reason, he refused to release any troops. It would be nine days until an expedition was finally launched. Throughout that time, the residents watched anxiously as British troops completed the batteries aimed at their city.[38]

While Montcalm expected an attack at Beauport east of Quebec, Wolfe continued to seek an attack west of Quebec.

On 8 July, he convened another council of war to review possible landing places. Unfortunately for Wolfe, Montcalm had ordered a detachment of *troupes de la Marine*, militia and Indians to encamp at Sillery four miles west of the city. While Montcalm felt such an attack above Quebec would be extremely rash and unlikely, he felt so unsure of Wolfe's plans that he decided he could spare a small detachment to help protect the shore west of Quebec. This detachment by itself could not have prevented a British landing, but French gun-boats above Quebec continued to harass the British fleet. The failure of the Royal Navy to gain complete control of the river frustrated Wolfe. He recorded in his journal: 'Amazing backwardness in these matters on the side of the Fleet.'[39] However, there was little he or the navy could do. When Wolfe and his commanders met to consider an attack above Quebec, they concluded that the dangers of his army crossing the river on rafts, without the support of warships and in the face of French opposition, made a landing unfeasible. In the meantime, Colonel Carleton would continue with a detachment above Quebec to probe at French defences, while the diversionary landing at Montmorency would proceed as planned. If the opportunity offered itself, then the army could still launch an attack above Quebec.[40]

That night, the night of 8–9 July, Wolfe himself led the landing at Montmorency. Late in the evening, Saunders sent two gunboats, the *Porcupine* and the *Boscawen*, to bombard the French camp to the west of the falls. The bombardment was so fierce that the French struck camp and moved further up the river. This allowed Wolfe to land his men at 2 a.m. without any opposition. So far everything had proceeded smoothly. However, when Townshend arrived with the second landing he found no one to give him directions to the new camp, while the baggage of the grenadiers and light infantry lay strewn across the meadows near the shore. According to Townshend, there was 'no officer in charge, no orders, and nowhere more than five men together'. A skirmishing party of Canadians and Indians could easily have captured and plundered the army's baggage. Townshend was horrified and left a guard to protect the baggage while he pressed blindly on up the hill, delaying to allow some of his men to haul up the heavy guns. After a struggle, he finally arrived at the main camp at daybreak, and immediately received a reprimand from Wolfe for his slowness. Relations between the two were beginning to sour.[41]

If Montcalm had launched an attack while the British forces were landing east of the Montmorency river, he might have inflicted a serious defeat on the British forces. However, he was worried that these activities were merely a ploy to draw his force east to the river, while the main British attack would come at daybreak near the Beauport or St Charles rivers. He confided in his journal that Saunders's bombardment of the French positions 'made in broad daylight and with great show persuades me that it is a diversionary attack in this place and that he would like us to weaken our defences here'.[42] Beyond sending a large skirmishing party of Canadians and Indians to attack the workmen, he would not attack the British camp. With comparatively little opposition, Wolfe had established his camp at Montmorency. Over the next few days and weeks he continued to try to draw Montcalm's army into a decisive battle.

While Wolfe sought to find a means of drawing Montcalm into a decisive battle, the residents of Quebec continued to murmur about the inactivity of their army. In growing dismay they watched the British batteries at Pointe-aux-Pères near completion. Occasionally the French batteries fired at the workmen, but their success was limited and work did not stop. Then, fearing the waste of valuable powder, Montcalm intervened to stop the salvos. This was too much for the Quebecers. On 11 July, two of Quebec's leading citizens presented Montcalm with a petition demanding that he take action against the British batteries before they were completed. Montcalm was still reluctant to commit his regulars to such an attack and complained bitterly of the 'Commotion in the minds of the inhabitants of Quebec who want to make policy and decide strategy'.[43] Eventually, he was compelled to consent to a night-time raid. However, he would provide only one company of *troupes de terre* and 100 *troupes de la Marine* accompanied by 200 Indians. The rest of the expedition would have to be composed of volunteers from the city.[44]

Quebec's residents had so much enthusiasm for the expedition that over 1,000 men volunteered. The expedition, described in one French account as 'only a mob of Militia, without discipline', stood little hope of success. Montcalm seems to have acquiesced in it principally to silence the city's burghers. However, if the British forces were caught off guard, there was a slim chance that the Quebec militia could use the cover of the woods to inflict some damage on the British camp. Unfortunately, as Montcalm feared, the lack of order and discipline proved decisive. The expedition crossed the St Lawrence on the night of 12 July. As soon as the men landed on the south shore, panic spread through the ranks. They began to shoot blindly into the woods and soon engaged in a brisk fire-fight with one another. At this point, 'terror... seized the Canadians, and neither the Entreaties, the prayers, or the threats of the officers had the slightest effect in reanimating their courage; several of them flung down their arms and their hatchets, took to their heels, and ran off to the Boats; all took to flight, and by six o'Clock in the morning the whole detachment (with the exception of the Men who were killed by mistake) had recrossed the River and returned to Quebec'.[45]

In Quebec, 'this disgraceful, and voluntary overthrow, flung all who remained in the Town into the greatest consternation and almost into despair'.[46] Their dismay grew greater when, that night, the British batteries at Pointe-aux-Pères finally opened fire on the city. Montcalm and the chief engineer had presumed that the distance from the batteries to the city was too great for a bombardment to have any serious effect, certainly on the upper town. Indeed, the first few rounds fell short, but then the British artillerymen found their aim. A French eyewitness reported that:

> The Bombs were directed against the Upper Town, & towards those parts of it where there were the largest Buildings, & the greatest assemblage of Houses; changing their aim at every volley – The same Manoeuvre continued after the day had dawned; which showed that it was not so much their object to dismount the Batteries, as it was to frighten the people, and make them abandon the Town, by the bursting of the Bombs, and falling down of the Houses; not any quarter of Quebec afforded shelter against so tremendous a fire – the people all fled from their Houses and sought for refuge upon the Ramparts, on the side next to the Country – When Day appeared, and the Gate was opened, Women & Children were seen flying in crowds along the fields; and the damage done to the town during the first night was very considerable.[47]

The military impact of the bombardment was limited, as Montcalm had predicted. The batteries were not seriously damaged, nor was anyone killed. Civilian morale, however, suffered serious damage. In addition, the bombardment caused Montcalm to make one seemingly unimportant change to the disposition of his forces. Because the British seemed to be able to shell every part of the city, he ordered the main magazine to be moved out of the city to Ste-Foy six miles away. This would prove a costly mistake on 13 September.[48]

The bombardment of Quebec did nothing to bring the British conquest of Canada any nearer. Wolfe needed to engage Montcalm's army, not destroy the city. Ultimately, there were three possible ways he could do this. He could assault the Beauport lines or Quebec directly; he could land his forces above Quebec and entrench above the city, breaking Montcalm's supply lines; he could try to turn Montcalm's left flank by attacking at Montmorency. Wolfe has often been accused of being prepared to risk the lives of his men to gain a decisive victory at Quebec, but it is apparent that in July he was most concerned about the safety of his men and his army. He briefly considered a direct assault on the city, but did not deem it a viable option, as it would certainly have been very bloody. He continued to consider a landing above Quebec, and has been criticised for not committing himself to this strategy earlier. However, this was also a high-risk option. Not only did Wolfe's troops face the difficulty of landing on a steep and thickly wooded shoreline but, as Montcalm had increased the defences above Quebec, they faced the possibility of meeting determined opposition. In addition, British supply lines would be stretched to the limit above Quebec. The French gunboats had already proved themselves a serious opposition to the Royal Navy. Until Wolfe had a large squadron of warships above Quebec, troops landed above the city might become isolated and any attempt to relieve them had to pass by the guns of the city. The third option, to attack at Montmorency, was certainly the safest. Wolfe's attack could be supported and supplied with relative ease. Yet this option was also the least likely to result in the decisive battle that Wolfe sought.

On 16 July, at a meeting with Admiral Holmes, Wolfe made the decision to launch the attack at Montmorency. He had noted that there was a redoubt close to the beach at Montmorency beyond the protection of musket fire from the French lines. His hope was that, if that redoubt could be stormed, Montcalm would be forced to send his army to protect the post. Later that day he wrote to Monckton ordering him to prepare for an attack, but the attack was delayed. The delay was occasioned by the passage on the night of 18-19 July of the British warships the *Sutherland* and *Squirrel* above Quebec. This opened once more the prospect of a landing above Quebec, for now there would be protection for the landing craft. Over the following days Wolfe returned to the south shore and once more reconnoitred upstream of Quebec. Now he felt that an earlier attack would have succeeded. He confided in his journal, 'if we had ventured the stroke that was first intended we should probably have succeeded'.[49]

On 20 July, Wolfe again met with Holmes and this time ordered Monckton to prepare for an assault above Quebec. He was to board his brigade in sixteen flat-bottomed boats and row under the cover of the night past Quebec. Monckton began preparing his men for the task ahead. But no sooner had he begun preparations than Wolfe countermanded his orders, informing Monckton that 'particular circumstances make it necessary to delay our attempts for a few days, & to keep it secret. In the mean while we shall make all the diversion we possibly can.'[50] Unfortunately for Wolfe, Montcalm had witnessed the preparation of the flat-bottomed boats, and received further confirmation of Wolfe's intentions from one of General Townshend's servants who deserted on 20 July. Fearing an assault above Quebec, Montcalm sent an additional 600 men to reinforce his defences there. Wolfe had witnessed the danger of an assault against fortified positions at Louisbourg the previous summer. He had dismissed the attack at Louisbourg as 'rash and ill-advised', only succeeding 'by the greatest of good fortune imaginable'.[51] He would not risk his men again this year. The attack above Quebec was again postponed.

Despite the postponement of the attack, the presence of warships above Quebec did allow Wolfe to expand his operations above the city. On 21 July, a party landed at Pointe-aux-Trembles, twenty miles to the west of Quebec, capturing many women and children who had taken shelter there. They were rounded up, herded onto the British barges and brought down the river to Wolfe's camp. This action caused some consternation, not only among the French but also among other British officers. Brigadier Townshend, who was renowned as a cartoonist and satirist, produced a number of scathing cartoons of Wolfe and his women. Montcalm recorded in his journal that Wolfe had specifically ordered that only 'the prettiest women be taken on board'.[52] There is no evidence that Wolfe intended to mistreat or abuse any of the women who were taken. Indeed, they were returned to Quebec the day after their capture and specifically spoke of their good treatment. However, from the start of the expedition Wolfe's army had been rounding up women, children, old men and other non-combatants. In most campaigns in Europe, an enemy army would not harass non-combatants. The Swiss writer Emmeric de Vattel in his discussion of the rules of war, *Le Droit des gens ou les principes de la loi naturelle*, published in London in 1758, pointed out that in 'the polished nations of Europe: women and children are suffered to enjoy perfect security, and allowed permission to withdraw wherever they please'.[53]

To French commanders, there was no justification for Wolfe's actions. When the British returned the women and children captured at Pointe-aux-Trembles, Knox reported that 'The Town-Major of Quebec... took upon him to reflect on our conduct in making so many captives among the old men, women, and children of the country.'[54] The relations between the British and French armies were already regulated by a cartel agreed between the British and French Crowns at the beginning of 1759. This specified that all soldiers taken should be returned or ransomed within fifteen days. It said nothing about civilians. Both Wolfe and Montcalm had copies of the cartel, and throughout the early stages of the campaign the war was fought in an 'enlightened' manner reminiscent of campaigns in Europe. The cartel was generally honoured. There were frequent truces when the two armies exchanged prisoners and wounded. The commanders sometimes took advantage of these ceasefires to exchange gifts of wine and spirits. Montcalm even allowed Wolfe to evacuate his wounded from the British base at St-Nicholas above Quebec to the main field hospital on the Île d'Orléans.[55]

When British officers arrived in Canada they had fully expected the campaign to be waged in such a formal fashion. On 27 June, as his men made their first landings, Wolfe issued a 'manifesto' justifying the campaign and outlining what treatment civilians could expect. He promised that if they remained in their homes and on their farms they should not fear 'the least molestation' and guaranteed that they would be able to 'enjoy their property, attend to their religious worship; in a word, enjoy, in the midst of war, all the sweets of peace, provided they will take no part directly or indirectly in the contest between the two crowns'. However, Wolfe concluded 'The laws of war are known; the obstinacy of an enemy justified the means used to bring him to reason.'[56] If the *habitants* resisted the British in any manner, they could expect retribution. As the campaign dragged on, the resistance of the *habitants* would justify much more draconian action than the herding up of a few women and children.

Wolfe's initial commitment was more than mere words. At the beginning of July, when over-enthusiastic troops pillaged civilians' household furniture and clothing at Beaumont, they were ordered to return all these items and leave them in the parish church so that their owners could collect them. During the Pointe-aux-Trembles raid the British took special care to ensure that not only the women but also their property was protected. When sailors began to pilfer their belongings, Wolfe quickly intervened, threatening to punish any miscreants severely and forcing the sailors publicly to return all the possessions they had taken.[57]

The British went even further to make their captives feel at home. The women captured at Pointe-aux-Trembles were wined and dined by the officers. Wolfe even allowed a Catholic priest to celebrate Mass with the women on board the Royal Navy warship in which they were temporarily incarcerated. Many returned to Quebec after their three-day captivity with mementoes of their adventure, including the names and regiments of their captors. Indeed, this interaction between British officers and their former female captives may in part explain the frequent contacts which seem to have taken place between civilians in Quebec and British officers during the frequent ceasefires which took place throughout late July and early August. These visits of British officers and men to an enemy city 'under siege' during the campaign underlines the formality with which the campaign was waged in its early stages.[58]

As the end of July approached, Wolfe's army had failed to draw Montcalm into battle, and Wolfe seemed unusually indecisive. He had divided his already outnumbered army into three, by establishing three widely separated camps, and was beginning to face criticism from some of his officers. Montcalm also faced criticism because he had failed to take advantage of Wolfe's seeming irresolution and had refused to attack the British forces even when he had such numerical superiority. All the raids which the French had attempted seemed to have been miserable failures, while the British bombarded the city at will. Meanwhile, the residents of Quebec sheltered as best they could from the British bombardment and the British troops grew accustomed to life in Canada.

4

Frustration

As the end of July drew near, there was a growing sense of frustration on the St Lawrence. Although it was only mid-summer, Wolfe's army had so far shown no sign of drawing Montcalm's army into a decisive battle. The troops of both armies were irritated at their failure to meet in a decisive battle, yet Montcalm knew that he only had to wait. If Wolfe did not defeat his army, the British would have to leave the St Lawrence before the onset of winter. The citizens of Quebec and the Canadian *habitants* did not share Montcalm's patience, but fumed over the lack of protection that his army gave to the settlements along the St Lawrence and to the city of Quebec. Montcalm, however, remained unmoved and over the following month it was Wolfe and his men who would seemingly begin to lose heart as the British attack ground to a halt and both armies settled into the routine of camp life.

The Pointe-aux-Trembles raid had done little to resolve Wolfe's indecision about where to attempt to bring the French to a decisive battle, above or below Quebec. Wolfe realised that a landing above Quebec might draw the French into a decisive battle; he also saw the dangers if a substantial French force opposed this landing. Such dangers only seemed to grow when, following the raid, Montcalm dispatched Adjutant-General Jean-Daniel Dumas with a corps of *troupes de la Marine* and a party of Indians to patrol the north shore and establish batteries at all possible landing sites. Dumas's force was further reinforced by a detachment of 200 cavalry who could move quickly along the shore to repel any landing.[1] On 23 July, Wolfe again met with Saunders, Monckton, Townshend and Murray. They all agreed that the army had to bring the French to a decisive battle, but they could not agree on the method. Wolfe's journal simply recorded of the meeting: 'Resolution to attack the French Army – Debate about the Method.'[2] Within three days, however, Wolfe decided that an attack above Quebec would risk his entire army and instead sought the safer option of attacking the left flank of the French army at Montmorency.

Wolfe initially hoped that he could outflank Montcalm by crossing the Montmorency river upstream from the French camp. On 26 July, after receiving intelligence from several deserters that there were two fords about five miles upstream from the falls, he set out with a detachment to reconnoitre the Montmorency river. As the detachment marched upstream, French snipers took potshots at Wolfe's column from their posts across the river. When Wolfe finally reached the first ford, he discovered it was heavily defended; the second led to a dense forest where the Canadians could easily better his troops in irregular fighting. An attempt to flank the French army across the Montmorency river would clearly not work. Wolfe would need to find a different plan. The British attack did not come.[3]

Wolfe appears to have been exceptionally indecisive during this period. Yet while it is true that he changed his mind several times about the best way to attack Montcalm, the appearance of indecision was increased by his desire to mislead the French commander. Wolfe was extremely conscious of the need to keep his plans secret. Indeed, we know that he had read the Marshall de Saxe's *Reveries*, published only a few years earlier, since an annotated copy was found amongst his papers. De Saxe stressed the importance of good intelligence and of misleading the enemy whenever possible. Wolfe seems to have taken this advice to heart. When he informed Monckton of the postponement of the Montmorency attack, for instance, he stressed that it was essential 'to keep it secret'. He added that 'in the mean while we shall make all the diversion we possibly can'.[4] Wolfe was so preoccupied with secrecy that he did not always inform Townshend, Monckton and Murray of his plans. Such an obsession may seem like paranoia, but it was not without reason. Indeed, on 20 July one of Townshend's personal servants had deserted to the French and happily divulged all the plans that he knew.[5]

To defeat an enemy superior in number and well entrenched, Wolfe would need the advantage of surprise, and thus he did all he could to spread disinformation amongst the French. Surprise was one of the few advantages that the British held. Able to move his troops by water, Wolfe could strike at many different points. Surprise could be further increased by spreading rumours among his own troops which would eventually reach French ears. Some officers understood this. Indeed, Captain John Knox recorded in his journal that 'many new projects are talked of; but, I believe, from no other motive than to amuse the enemy, in order that false intelligence may be circulated throughout their camps, should any of our soldiers desert'.[6] Such tactics seem to have succeeded. One French officer confided, after one false alarm, that 'this was not the first time that Deserters had given intelligence which proved in the event, directly contrary to their report – it was therefore naturally inferred, that the English Generals, more secret than ours in their deliberations, often spread rumours among their Troops of designs, never seriously intended to be realised, and of which we had more than once been made the dupes'.[7] In addition to spreading rumours of false attacks, Wolfe also sent his troops on diversionary manoeuvres. While sitting in their camps at Montmorency, the Île d'Orléans and Pointe-Lévy, most of Wolfe's troops were not involved in any demanding activities, so they were able to haul cannon and *bateaux* in front of the French, to prepare for attacks that never came. Such actions, often viewed as evidence of his indecision, also left Montcalm and Vaudreuil bemused and befuddled.

In addition to confusing Montcalm and Vaudreuil, these actions may also have served to increase tensions with Wolfe's brigadiers, in particular with Townshend. Townshend was particularly sensitive about his rank, and complained on several occasions that Wolfe did not provide him with adequate orders and failed to keep him informed of his plans. For instance, on 13 July he confided in his journal that he had 'heard that the General had set out for the Point of Orleans... leaving me, the first officer in the camp, not only without orders but also even ignorant of his departure or time of return'.[8] Complaints from his commanders caused Wolfe more than a little concern. On 7 July, he recorded, 'Some difference of opinion upon a military point term'd slight & insignificant & the Commander in Chief is threaten'd with Parliamentary inquiry into his conduct for not consulting an inferior officer & seeming to disregard his sentiments!'[9] Wolfe probably did fail on occasion to inform his brigadiers adequately, but equally he had a conviction that senior officers should be able to conduct their men in day-to-day affairs without direct orders from their commander. Townshend, as the brigadier with the least experience, may have found this more challenging than his fellow brigadiers.

Any indecision of Wolfe's was heightened by his desire for victory and fear of derision if he returned to Britain without taking Quebec. Much of this pressure was of his own making. The plans for the expedition had called for an army of 12,000 regulars; Wolfe had only 8,000. He had been expected to face no more than 8,000 enemy troops; yet he faced over 12,000. In addition, the capture of Quebec had not been the sole goal of the expedition. The expedition had already achieved one of its main goals, as it had forced Montcalm to strip his defences to the south and west, on Lakes Champlain and Ontario, allowing British forces to advance on these fronts. Ultimately, if there was a failure in July it lay not with Wolfe on the St Lawrence, but with Sir Jeffrey Amherst on Lake George, who failed to take advantage of the weakness of the French forces on Lake Champlain.

Amherst's army was larger than Wolfe's. He had 10,000 men under his command, including seven battalions of regulars, accompanied by nine battalions of provincial troops, and assorted rangers and Indians. He faced a much smaller army of only 3,000 French and Canadians commanded by Brigadier-General François-Charles de Bourlamaque. Bourlamaque had orders merely to delay Amherst's advance for as long as possible, and then to fall back on the post at Île-aux-Noix at the northern end of Lake Champlain.[10] He was not to offer a concerted resistance. With the majority of French forces concentrated around Quebec, Amherst faced comparatively light opposition and should have been able to advance quickly towards Montreal. Wolfe, in effect, had succeeded in opening the way for Amherst to advance into the heart of Canada. However, in his usual fashion, rather than hurrying to take advantage of this opportunity, Amherst made meticulous preparations for the expedition. He set his men to work rebuilding the roads to his advanced post at Fort George, which had replaced Fort William Henry. It was not until 22 July that his army was ready to begin its advance. As his men pushed forward and neared Fort Ticonderoga, Bourlamaque blew up the fort and withdrew a few miles to the north to Crown Point. Amherst paused briefly, but then resumed his advance towards Crown Point. Once more, as Amherst's men neared the post, Bourlamaque blew it up and withdrew up Lake Champlain to Île-aux-Noix.[11]

There was now nothing between his army and the Richelieu river, which flows from the northern end of Lake Champlain into the St Lawrence. However, rather than pressing his advantage, Amherst halted. He set his men to work building 'a very respectable Fortress', new roads, and ships with which to challenge the small French fleet on Lake Champlain. By the time he was ready to set out for Île-aux-Noix, the summer had passed and Amherst felt it was now too late to risk a campaign. Although outnumbering his opponent by more than three to one, Amherst had not brought Bourlamaque to battle and pushed forward to Montreal, but had merely advanced a few miles and secured his position. Bourlamaque was astonished. He wrote to Lévis pondering how Amherst could now 'save his head', for he had conducted such 'a stupid campaign'.[12] But Amherst had powerful friends; his expedition would not be viewed as a failure.

Amherst's sluggishness had all but condemned Wolfe's expedition. Had Amherst pressed his advance, Montcalm would have been forced to send troops from Quebec to Île-aux-Noix or face the loss of Montreal. Although operating independently, both Wolfe's and Amherst's expeditions were viewed as part of the overall strategy to reduce Canada. Indeed, on receiving news that he was to command the Quebec expedition, Wolfe had written to Amherst: 'I can't promise you, that we shall take Quebec… but this I will venture to promise, that let the Fleet carry us up, and we will find employment for a good part of the Force of Canada, and make your progress towards Montreal less difficult and dangerous.'[13] By the end of July, Wolfe seems to have forgotten such statements. Greatly ambitious, he feared any slight to his reputation that his army's failure on the St Lawrence might produce. With no news of Amherst's progress, Wolfe was anxious and apprehensive.

While Wolfe fretted about his failure to bring Montcalm to a decisive battle, the residents of Quebec fretted about the failure of their army to repel the British. One French diarist confided in his journal that 'the manoeuvres of the English, convinced us, that the only expectation they entertained of accomplishing their enterprise, was by exhausting the patience of the Canadians; and that by threatening several points at the same time, and being regular Troops, they thought they could not have any thing to fear'. He concluded that 'it cannot be denied that the people, seeing our whole force concentrated at one point, yet remaining stationary and acting solely on the defensive became intimidated; most especially as the English, much inferior in numbers, divided their Troops, and executed several bold enterprises without any molestation'.[14]

Finally, on 28 July Wolfe resolved to launch an attack on the French army. He resorted to a version of the plan he had hatched in mid-July to attack the isolated Johnstone Redoubt on the Montmorency shore and thus draw the French into battle. He planned to beach two armed boats, the *Russell* and the *Three Sisters*, on the shore close to the redoubt while the warship *Centurion* would lie close inshore. These would offer covering fire for 1,000 men drawn from the army's grenadier companies and the three companies of Louisbourg Grenadiers, arguably the best troops in the army, who would seize the redoubt. Based upon inspections made from the British camp at the falls and on the Île d'Orléans, Wolfe and his engineers believed that the Johnstone redoubt was beyond effective range of the main French entrenchments. Once taken, it should have been possible to hold it, unless the French sallied out of their entrenchments to launch a full attack. This was what Wolfe hoped for. At this point, as the French left their entrenchments, Townshend and Murray would cross the Montmorency river from the British camp to attack the left flank of the French army and promote a general engagement. Wolfe confided in his journal: 'it seems better to receive the enemy superior in numbers wth the advantage of a small intrenchment than to attack them behind their lines, wth such a Body of Troops as can be landed at once & by so doing put all to the hazard of one action'.[15] This was a relatively secure plan. If the attack failed it would be easy to withdraw his men back over the river. In contrast, a landing above Quebec would have risked his entire army.

Wolfe ordered Monckton to prepare the troops. The brigadiers, however, were less than enthusiastic about his plan. Wolfe noted the 'dislike of the General officers & others to this Business, but nothing better proposd by them'.[16] From their camp, the French observed the movements in the British camp. Following weeks of dissimulation, however, they were unsure whether an attack was coming or where it would take place. Montcalm expected an attack at Sillery as there were a number of barges in the river Etchemin and the ships at Cap Rouge had edged downstream, nearer to Quebec.[17]

When dawn broke on 30 July, the day of the planned attack, there was not a breath of wind. Without a breeze it would be impossible to run the boats ashore or to position the *Centurion* to provide covering fire. The attack would have to be postponed. The postponement made Wolfe fret even more, for one of the grenadiers in Whitmore's Regiment (the troops destined for the landing) deserted to the French. Wolfe fretted. How much did he know? How much would he tell Montcalm?[18]

On 31 July, Admiral Holmes deemed that there was enough wind for the expedition to proceed. At first light, some light infantry marched from the Montmorency Camp into the woods to the north to make a diversion. There they began making fascines and making their presence well known to the French. At 10 a.m. the two boats with the grenadiers on board were run aground below the Johnstone redoubt. However, immediately it became apparent that the plans were going awry. The boats were supposed to bombard the Johnstone redoubt to provide covering fire for the attack. However, the *Russell* – the western boat – was too far from the redoubt for its fire to be effective, while the *Three Sisters* – the eastern boat – shifted as the tide fell and could not fire effectively at the Johnstone redoubt. In turn, it found itself under fierce fire from the Sault redoubt, a little to the east of the Johnstone redoubt. To make matters still worse, the warship *Centurion* found that it could not get close enough to the shore for its fire to be of any use. The two boats and grenadiers were stranded, exposed to a withering fire from the French redoubts.[19]

At great personal risk, Wolfe boarded the *Russell* to reconnoitre the position himself. He found matters even worse than he had expected. Not only were the boats too poorly positioned to be effective against the Johnstone redoubt, but now Wolfe could also see that the redoubt was within range of the French entrenchments. Wolfe and his engineers had been sure that the redoubt was isolated; now it became clear it was not. If the grenadiers advanced into it, they could not hold it for long. Wolfe now had to decide whether to abandon the attack. Such a decision would have damaged the army's morale. For three weeks his men had been waiting for the decisive attack; any delay would seem like cowardice. Wolfe needed to devise a new plan on the spot. From the deck of the *Russell* he could see that the Montreal militia who were manning the French lines above were in some 'confusion & disorder'.[20] He believed that now might be 'a proper time to make an Attempt upon their Intrenchment'.[21] Rather than waiting for the French to come out to attack the British force, Wolfe now decided to storm the French entrenchments at their weakest point, while the men were disordered and confused.

Wolfe informed Monckton of his revised plan and ordered him to prepare his troops at Pointe-Lévy to cross the North Channel and make a landing on the Beauport shore between the two boats. At the same time, Murray and Townshend at the Montmorency camp were to prepare their men to cross over the ford and storm the French lines. This new plan was more than simply a slight tactical alteration to Wolfe's original plan. As Wolfe himself wrote to Saunders: 'you will please to consider the difference between landing at high water with four companies of Grenadiers to attack a redoubt under the protection of the artillery of a vessel, and landing part of an army to attack the enemy's entrenchments'.[22] Unfortunately, Wolfe had not considered all the implications of such a combined attack. Towards midday, Monckton's troops from Pointe-Lévy boarded their boats and paddled across the North Channel. However, as they neared the shore they received orders to delay; the tide was still too high for Murray and Townshend to cross the ford. For the next four hours, as they waited for the tide to fall, the troops paddled up and down the channel under constant, although largely ineffective, French fire.[23]

From their respective camps on the Beauport shore, Montcalm and Lévis watched the antics of the British boats in some confusion. Initially, Montcalm remained at his headquarters at Beauport, believing that such a direct attack on the redoubts made in broad daylight must be a 'false attack', and fearing the main British attack would come from the men in the boats on the river, somewhere on the right of his line between Beauport and the St Charles river.[24] This left Lévis, whose camp was in the centre of the British attack near the Johnstone redoubt, to command the French forces in action. Wolfe's decision to wait for the tide to fall allowed Lévis to change the disposition of his troops and steady the

Montreal militia. He dispatched a detachment of *troupes de la Marine* and several hundred Indians to the far left of his line. They were to support Repentigny who, having observed the march of the British light infantry in the early morning, feared an attack across the upper reaches of the Montmorency river. To strengthen the defences in the centre of his line, between the Johnstone and Sault redoubts, Lévis ordered the Royal Rousillon Regiment to take up positions alongside the Montreal militia in the entrenchments.[25]

Shortly after midday, the wind began to pick up strongly from the south-west and Montcalm realised that the British boats in the river could not now easily make an attack on the right of his line to the west of Beauport; they could only realistically land near the two redoubts or the falls. At 2 p.m. he went to Lévis's headquarters to discuss tactics. He brought with him the Guyenne Regiment, whom he ordered to take up position alongside the Roussillon and Montreal militia between the two redoubts. Following only a brief discussion, Montcalm returned to Beauport satisfied with his subordinate's preparations, while Lévis went down to the lines between the two redoubts to command the defences there in person.[26]

It was late afternoon before the British boats finally received orders to paddle towards the shore. Now, instead of facing the disorganised militia whom Wolfe had noted in the morning, the attackers also faced two battalions of French regulars. The attackers also met with another unforeseen problem: by the time the tide was low enough for Murray and Townshend to cross the ford, it was too low to let the boats from Pointe-Lévy land easily. As they paddled towards the shore, many of the boats ran aground on a ledge of rocks several hundred yards offshore. Wolfe himself was on one of the boats stranded on the rocks and witnessed first-hand the chaos which resulted. As they struggled to reach the shore, the boats were prime targets for the French artillery and snipers. At last, in much confusion, the grenadiers waded through water waist-deep and then across a wide beach covered with thick mud and potholes.[27]

Once ashore, the grenadiers had orders to form into ranks. However, as soon as the men began to land, according to one of their officers, their enthusiasm to attack the French '[a]nimated our Men so much that we could scarce restrain them'.[28] After six weeks on the St Lawrence, the grenadiers had long waited for a chance to prove their worth against the French. The decision to attack with a detachment assembled from different regiments across the army may well have further intensified competition between the separate companies. As they waited in their boats to land, the men boasted about which company would be first to take the redoubt, which would show the greatest bravery. As soon as they were ashore, rather than waiting to form into ranks, the grenadiers rushed forward. A sergeant-major in Hopson's Grenadiers reported that 'as soon as we landed we fixed our Bayonets and beat our Grenadier's-March, and so advanced on'.[29] In the noise and confusion of the battle their officers could not restrain their men. The result was a near-disaster. Without any order or any support, the grenadiers marched forward into a hail of French bullets and shot. The sergeant-major reported that 'during all this Time their Cannon play'd very briskly on us; but their Small-Arms, in their Trenches lay cool 'till they were sure of their Mark; then they pour'd their Small-Shot like Showers of Hail, which caus'd our brave Grenadiers to fall very fast'.[30] Although, according to another account, 'they soon made themselves masters of the advanc'd redoubts and battery, these lay close under the enemy who were strongly entrenched on a very high and steep precipice from whence they pour'd an incessant fire on the grenadiers, who being in great confusion, many of them kill'd and wounded in the redoubt after a little time abandoned it and retir'd to the waterside'.[31]

At this point the weather intervened. A fearsome thunder-storm swept up the St Lawrence, drenching both armies. With most of their powder wet, it was all but impossible to continue the battle. The storm was a relief to both sides. Some of the French and Canadian troops may well have been running out of ammunition. One French account maintained that 'we were in want of powder, of balls, and for a very long time there had not been any matches for the Cannon'.[32] Other French accounts, however, felt that the storm had saved the British army, for 'we could, without presumption, anticipate the total defeat of the English army, had it persisted in advancing'.[33] Whatever the truth was, Wolfe now had to extract his men from the battle, a problem which was complicated by the quickly rising tide.

Wolfe ordered the grenadiers to take cover behind the remainder of Monckton's troops, who had by this time formed up in good order on the beach and had been joined by the two brigades under Murray and Townshend, who had crossed the Montmorency. Monckton's men and the grenadiers hast-ily boarded their boats and paddled back to Pointe-Lévy. Meanwhile Murray and Townshend withdrew in good order over the Montmorency. Only a party of Frasers' Highlanders remained behind on the beach, refusing to retreat until they had brought off their wounded.[34]

The Highlanders had a good reason for risking their lives to rescue their wounded. As the men left the beach, a horrifying sight lay behind them. John Johnson, a sergeant in Anstruther's Regiment, recorded that his men departed the beach 'leaving behind them, a vast number of killed and wounded to the mercy of the merciless Indians and Canadians; who massacred and scalped them in our own Sight, as not being in our power to help them, nor deliver them out of their cruel and barba-rous hands'.[35] As the Indians rushed onto the beach to take their traditional trophies, some nuns from the General Hospital hurried among the wounded attempting to reach them before the Indians. One nun from the hospital praised the bravery of her fellow nuns, who 'conveyed their [the British] wounded to our hospital, notwithstanding the fury and rage of the indians'.[36]

One incident would become a particular *cause célèbre* for the British, clear proof of the barbarity of the French. One of the men left behind on the beach was Captain David Ochterlony, of the second battalion of the Royal Americans. By his side was his close friend and comrade Lieutenant Peyton. For a while they lay unnoticed by the Indians, although not by their comrades as they boarded their boats and paddled back to Pointe-Lévy. Then two Indians and a French soldier discovered them. Ochterlony and Peyton offered to surrender, believing that as one of their captors was a French soldier they would be safe. The French soldier proceeded to rummage through their pockets but then walked away, leaving the men to be scalped by the Indians. One of the Indians clubbed Ochterlony and the other shot him, but, in an act which would later be celebrated by his comrades, Peyton crawled forward and grabbed a musket, shooting one of the Indians and then stabbing the other. Hearing the shot, a large party of thirty Indians began to advance towards the two men. Rushing over, some of Fraser's Highlanders managed to rescue Peyton, while the French nuns reached Ochterlony and took him to the General Hospital were he died a few days later. The British troops would not quickly forget this 'savagery'.[37]

As dusk fell, both armies retired to nurse their wounds. Wolfe recorded in his journal that his army had suffered 210 men killed and 230 wounded, and '[m]any excellent officers hurt in this foolish business'.[38] The French lost only seventy killed and wounded. Vaudreuil, who had spent the entire battle several miles away at his headquarters near the St Charles River, took great pride in the victory. He boasted that now Quebec was safe, and Wolfe's army was exhausted. The threat now, he believed, lay to the west at Fort Niagara. Montcalm was not so sure that Wolfe was defeated. However, Wolfe's determination to break his line at Montmorency made him predisposed to believe that this would be the site of any future attack. This predisposition would prove important six weeks later.[39]

The British defeat at Montmorency brought much criticism of Wolfe's conduct from both within and without the British ranks. Yet the defeat was due to a combination of circumstances. Wolfe's original plan was not the all-out attack that developed. The initial plan to seize the Johnstone redoubt failed because of bad luck – the placing of the two boats and the *Centurion* – and the failure of Wolfe's engineers to judge accurately the distance of the redoubt from the French lines. Once the morning attack had failed, Wolfe was faced with a quandary. He had already been criticised in many quarters for his indecision, his troops were anxious, and Wolfe was aware that time was passing. Not only did he have to worry about the morale of his army, but he was also greatly concerned about how his expedition would be viewed in Britain. The concept of exploiting what Wolfe perceived as the confusion among the Montreal militia, in order to break the French line, was not itself unsound. Wolfe's principal error was not to consider the problems of simultaneously landing troops and crossing the Montmorency. After the battle had commenced, he was unable to consult with Saunders or Holmes, and consequently delayed the landing by several hours. This was his blunder. It allowed the French to reinforce their line with the two battalions of regulars and increased the adrenalin coursing through the veins of the grenadiers lying offshore in their boats, while the low water made the later landing very difficult. The attack was finally condemned by the impetuous charge of the grenadiers. While Wolfe was not blameless, misfortune and poor reconnaissance had wrecked the attack far more than any failure on his part.

Wolfe, however, did not take the failure well. He remained desperate for a chance to engage the French in an open battle, but after the debacle at Montmorency he seemed unable to regain the initiative. His temper grew increasingly short. He raged at the grenadiers, in particular, and announced that he hoped their slaughter would 'be a lesson to them for the future… The Grenadiers could not suppose that they alone could beat the French Army.'[40] His relationship with Townshend had always been tense, but now he also wrangled with Monckton. On 15 August Wolfe wrote to Monckton, worried that he had 'taken something ill… against me' and begging him 'not to be offended at my papers'.[41] The next day he again wrote, 'I do repeat to you, that I wou'd avoid all occasion of offense to an Officer of your rank… & I heartily beg your forgiveness, for this last, or any former error or mistake of mine.'[42]

For the next few weeks the two armies stared at one another from their camps. For the men of both armies, the campaign began to take on a routine of its own. For the British troops in the camps at Pointe-Lévy, and especially at Montmorency, life became particularly claustrophobic. The army remained in these camps throughout most of the summer, yet, apart from occasional expeditions out of the camp, the Native American and Canadian parties that lurked around the fringes of the camps kept the soldiers confined within their bounds. Any soldier who dared to venture beyond the protected perimeter of the camp was likely to be captured, if not killed and scalped. Even parties that were ordered outside the camp, to gather wood or to scout, were prone to ambush in the dense woodland. Sergeant John Johnson wrote that 'hardly a day passed without our parties being surprised; and often routed by the scouting parties of the Indians and Canadians; nay, very often to the very skirts of our Camp'. Consequently, Wolfe was repeatedly forced to issue orders prohibiting his men from leaving the close confines of the camp.[43]

Not altogether surprisingly, orders alone failed to stop the men slipping past the guards. Men left camp for a wide variety of reasons, but most often in search of food. On 7 August, Captain John Knox reported that 'some sailors and marines strayed... into the country, contrary to repeated orders, to seek for vegetables: they were fired upon by a party of the enemy, and three were killed and scalped'. Another party strayed out 'to gather pease and vegetables' and suffered a similar fate.[44] Soldiers were prepared to risk so much to liven up their diet, because, while the rations provided by the army was relatively plentiful, they were plain and lacking in fresh fruit and vegetables. When in Britain, or encamped in Europe, soldiers would be provided with, at best, very basic rations and would be expected to purchase additional food for themselves from local markets. When they were campaigning in isolated regions and in North America, however, soldiers were provided with regular rations by the army, although 2d a day was stopped from their wages to pay for this. Salted pork and bread formed the principal components of the soldiers' rations in Quebec. This was supplemented by any meat from cattle seized from the *habitants*. However, as Captain John Knox noted, 'notwithstanding the quantity of cattle brought in from time to time by our light troops, we are frequently reduced to eat horse-flesh[;] beef, mutton, &c. being reserved for the hospitals'.[45]

There were several ways in which troops could enrich their diet. On occasion, the men had sufficient time to fish in the St Lawrence or one of the many rivers which flow into it. In addition, although seemingly isolated on the St Lawrence, British troops still had many opportunities to purchase additional supplies. In Europe the army allowed licensed sutlers – vendors regulated by the army – to sell food and vegetables to the troops at fixed prices. The same practice was continued on the St Lawrence. Hundreds of sutlers accompanied the expedition, and others arrived from time to time on provision

ships from New England. Some of these sutlers were the wives
of men serving in the army who sought to support themselves by selling provisions to the men. Most of their provisions
they transported across the Atlantic with the fleet, and these
included a wide range of foodstuffs and other items. John
Knox's journal provides a good insight into the wide range
of goods available:

> Beef, from ninepence to one shilling per pound. Mutton,
> from one shilling to one shilling and three pence per pound.
> Hams, from nine pence to one shilling per pound. Salt butter,
> from eight pence to one shilling and three pence per pound.
> Gloucester or Cheshire cheese, ten pence per pound. Potatoes
> from five to ten shillings per bushel. A reasonable loaf of good
> soft bread, six pence. Bristol Beer, eighteen shillings per dozen,
> bottles… London porter, one shilling per quart. Bad malt drink
> from Halifax at nine pence per quart. Cyder, from New England
> from six to eight pence per quart. Bad spruce beer, two pence
> per quart. West Indian rum from six to ten shillings per gallon.
> Sour claret, eight shillings per gallon. Excellent Florence, two
> shillings and six pence per flask. Madeira, twelve shillings per
> gallon, or eleven pounds per cask. Red Port ten shillings per
> gallon, or eight pounds per quarter cask. Lemons from three
> to six shillings per dozen. Lump sugar from one shilling to one
> shilling and six pence per pound. Ordinary powder sugar, ten
> pence per pound. Hyson tea, one pound ten shillings per pound.
> Chouchon,[tea] one pound per pound. Plain green, and very
> bad[tea], fifteen shillings per pound. Roll tobacco, one shilling
> and ten pence per pound. Leaf ditto ten pence per pound. Snuff,
> from two shillings to three shillings per pound bottle. Hard soap
> from ten pence to one shilling per pound.[46]

Sutlers and troops were also able to buy supplies from the
Canadian *habitants*. Although the majority of *habitants* seem,

especially during the early summer of 1759, to have avoided contact with the British, a few were prepared to trade butter, eggs or vegetables for gold and silver or even the dreaded salted pork. While this might seem like a good bargain for the British sutler or soldier, the salted pork, though hardly appetising, would keep well and provide a much needed staple for a stew in the middle of the bitter Canadian winter.[47] To allow soldiers to buy all these items, formal markets were organised where trading could proceed in relative safety. The largest of these markets was at Pointe-Lévy, where sutlers from the fleet and a few *habitants* from the Côte du Sud went to sell their produce. Not only were these markets relatively secure but they also allowed the army to regulate the prices of goods sold there, and even more importantly to regulate the sale of alcohol. Although thousands of miles from Britain and in the middle of a bitter conflict, these markets provided a sense of normality in day-to-day life.[48]

If the diet of the troops was plain and unappetising, the men's living conditions were equally undesirable. Normally, the men slept six to a tent, two men often sharing the same bedding and sleeping head to toe. Because of the need to protect the camp from raiding parties, the tents were pitched close together with only a few inches at most between them. In such close quarters, army camps became breeding grounds for various infectious diseases, in particular typhus carried by lice, and dysentery and typhoid spread by contaminated water from latrines. To try to combat these problems, Wolfe ordered that there should be no more than four, or at most five, men to a tent, and that the tents should be lined 'in double rows... that they may have more air, and more room in their encampment, and consequently be healthy'.[49] Yet such measures were insufficient to keep the troops healthy. Because the Quebec campaign was so static and the British army did not need to strike a new camp after the beginning of July, the three main camps at Pointe-Lévy, Montmorency and on the Île d'Orléans remained in existence for most of the summer. This increased the problems of maintaining a healthy camp. Latrines needed to be kept fresh and clean and repeatedly be emptied or relocated. Human waste was not the only potential source of disease. On 29 July, Wolfe ordered that 'great care [was] to be taken by the Regiments within their Respective Encampments, and in their Neighbourhood, that all offal and Filth of every kind which might taint the Air be buried deep under Ground and the General recommends in the strongest manner to the Commanders of Corps to have their Camps kept sweet and Clean'.[50] Indeed, so obsessed was Wolfe with ensuring that the waste pits and latrines were adequate that Townshend sketched a scathing cartoon of Wolfe inspecting one of the camp's latrines.

The length of time the troops spent in one camp also caused problems with the cleanliness of the tents themselves. Bedding and flooring soon became fouled and dirty. The floors of the tents were supposed to be covered with hay and straw which was to be regularly replaced, but soon none could be safely obtained around the camps. In addition, the heavy rains of the summer of 1759 left many tent floors damp and waterlogged. Wolfe was therefore compelled to issue special orders for the soldiers to burn their old straw and collect spruce boughs instead. When these did not prove sufficient to stop the water seeping into the men's bedding, Wolfe ordered the men to strip the nearby farms of wood to make floorboards for their tents.[51]

Not only were their tents dirty and soiled, but the soldiers themselves had to be forced to wash and keep clean. The women who accompanied the expedition washed the men's clothing and uniforms. However, the men still needed to be persuaded to change into their clean uniforms. In mid-August, Wolfe was forced to issue orders that 'When the soldiers are

not employed in Working they are to dress & clean themselves, so as to appear under Arms, & upon all occasions, in
the most Soldier like manner'.[52] If soldiers were unconcerned
about their appearance, their personal hygiene was even more
lacking. Wolfe gave orders that 'the Officers are... to give
Directions that the men wash their Legs & Feet as well as
the upper part of their bodys that they may be Continued in
Health'.[53] Perhaps in an effort to keep clean, but more likely
in an effort to keep cool, many troops sought to cool off by
taking a dip in the St Lawrence during the middle of the day.
However, such activity frequently resulted in bad sunburn
and Wolfe was forced to issue orders that 'Soldiers are not
to be permitted to Swim in the heat of the Day but only in
the morning & Evening'.[54] All these entreaties do not seem
to have succeeded in maintaining the health of the men. In
early August, Captain John Knox reported that the troops at
the camp at Pointe-Lévy were growing particularly sickly.
Dysentery in particular was beginning to take its toll.[55]

The army was relatively well prepared to tend to the
many sick. Men who suffered from minor ailments and ill-
nesses would be treated in the camp, but those who grew
more dangerously ill, or suffered wounds in battle, would be
cared for in an army hospital. Although the expedition had
a fully-equipped hospital ship, Wolfe believed that the men
would recuperate faster if they were on land. Consequently,
he converted the church of St Joseph on the Île d'Orléans
into a field hospital. Although fairly well-equipped, the hospital lacked trained nurses and orderlies. The expedition did
include a small hospital staff, but as the number of sick and
wounded increased, the women accompanying the army
were ordered to serve as nurses at the hospital. However, for
women whose sole error had been to marry a soldier, nursing detail – desperately attempting to keep alive men whose
limbs had been blown off – was particularly distasteful.[56]

Consequently, nursing care often remained substandard and many troops died of disease or from their wounds.

Apart from disease, the other cause of soldiers' sickness and disability was alcohol. With their day-to-day lives character-ised by boredom and routine, punctuated by the occasional terrifying combat, many troops sought to relieve the tedium and fear by drinking. Alcohol abuse had reached epidemic proportions in the British army by the mid-eighteenth century, and it is possible that many soldiers were habitual drunkards. Soldiers desperately sought rum when available. There were several means through which they could obtain it. Each soldier received a daily allowance of rum, a ration that was increased if the weather was bad or if the men had been engaged in especially hard duty. Some soldiers would trade their ration with their comrades or to sutlers in return for food, kit or other items. If soldiers sought additional liquor they had plenty of opportunities to find it, particularly from the hundreds of sutlers who accompanied the army. On occa-sion sutlers could sell liquor formally to the troops, but more often they were barred from making such sales. However, many if not most sutlers seem to have ignored this injunc-tion. Indeed, on several occasions Wolfe was forced to launch investigations into how his troops had managed to acquire so much alcohol. Whatever problems may have faced his army, acquiring a supply of alcohol was not one of them.[57]

There were other methods of escape from the tedium and routine apart from drinking. Gambling was even more widespread than drinking, and if not encouraged it was at least tolerated by British officers. After finishing their evening meal and duties, many troops would gather round to wager on cards or dice and smoke a pipe. Debts run up through gambling could become substantial. Because in the field the army lacked the cash to pay soldiers' wages, soldiers were often forced to maintain a record of their debts. Consequently, debts could often become considerable. When a soldier was killed in battle his debts would be settled by his commanding officer from any outstanding pay. If this was insufficient, the soldier's effects would be auctioned in front of the regiment. On 7 August, for instance, the effects of several men killed in the action at the Falls of Montmorency were auctioned in front of their respective regiments.[58]

For the French and Canadian troops, life was a little easier. Strung out along the lines between Quebec and the Montmorency Falls, French and Canadian forces were not located in a single encampment. This allowed many troops, in particular officers, to take quarters in the numerous farmhouses which dotted the Beauport shore. While living conditions may thus have been slightly better, the diet of the French and Canadian troops was surprisingly similar to that of Wolfe's forces. French and Canadian forces suffered from a desperate shortage of rations. From 1756 onwards, the combination of the actions of the Royal Navy, the machinations of Intendant Bigot, the lack of manpower to harvest crops and the demands of supplying the army meant that Canada was desperately short of food, or rather that it was difficult to get supplies for the army. During the Quebec campaign, this shortage was exacerbated by problems of transporting supplies overland, because once British ships had sailed above Quebec the St Lawrence was no longer safe for French supply ships. Consequently, many French and Canadian troops lacked rations as much as their British counterparts.[59]

To obtain more supplies, Vaudreuil sent agents to Trois-Rivières and Montreal to requisition flour and cattle. However, the *habitants* had many years of practice in hiding their possessions and few supplies were found. So dire were the army's straits that one French account maintained that by the end of the summer of 1759 'the soldiers were dying of hunger'.[60] While this may be an overstatement, by the end of the campaign French and Canadian troops were reduced to rations of only a quarter of a pound of bread per day. Whereas Wolfe's men were able to acquire additional supplies from the army's civilian sutlers, Canadian civilians had few supplies they were willing to trade with their army. While there were some informal markets, which operated particularly around the city of Quebec, the lack of specie – gold or silver currency rather than paper notes – in the colony, the lack of faith in the colony's paper money and the fear of corruption meant that few civilians were prepared to sell food to French and Canadian troops. Some militia may have brought a small cache of supplies from their homes, but for the *troupes de la Marine* and *troupes de terre* supplies were meagre and difficult to obtain. However, French and Canadian troops, and especially the Canadian militia, were able to supplement their rations by hunting much more easily than were Wolfe's troops, mainly because they could wander out of camp without fear of being ambushed and scalped. Indeed, so widespread was their hunting that Vaudreuil was forced to issue orders banning shooting around Sillery and Ste-Foy, as hunting parties taking potshots at pigeons spread alarms of British attacks.[61]

If French and Canadian troops endured worse supplies than Wolfe's men, they probably enjoyed better medical care. There were two French hospitals which cared for the wounded and sick: the Ursuline Hospital, which was within the walls of Quebec, and the General Hospital, located about half a mile outside the city walls. While they may have been short of supplies, they possessed a dedicated and skilled staff of nuns. Unfortunately, during the campaign conditions in the hospitals deteriorated. The Ursuline Hospital was damaged by the British bombardment of Quebec, while the General Hospital became a place of refuge as it was beyond the range of the British batteries on Pointe-aux-Pères. The lure of the hospital as a refuge was increased by the formal protection hospitals were given in the cartel negotiated between the British and French Crowns at the beginning of 1759. In addition, the good treatment that Captain Ochterlony had received in the hospital following his capture at Montmorency convinced many British officers of the goodwill of the nurses. Wolfe personally sent a letter to Madame de Ramezay, Director of the General Hospital, promising the hospital his protection if his army should take Quebec. Wolfe's promise soon became more widely known and many townspeople attempted to take refuge in the hospital or sought to store their valuables there. This resulted in desperate overcrowding. One of the nuns in the hospital recorded in her journal that 'as our house was beyond the range of the enemy's artillery, the poor people of the city did not fail to seek refuge there. All the out-houses, stables, barns, garrets, &c. were well filled... upwards of six hundred persons in our building and vicinity, partaking of our small means of subsistence.'[62] Eventually, because of this overcrowding, the French established a mobile hospital, or *hôpital-ambulant*, in the suburb of St Jean.[63]

By mid-August, both sides had settled into a routine of war. For troops in Wolfe's army this was a routine of hard labour and confinement within the bounds of their camps. Day-to-day activities continued as normal, punctuated by the threat of raiding parties skirmishing on the outskirts of the camp. For French and Canadian troops the routine consisted of watching Wolfe's every movement, and launching the occasional raid on his camp. Canadian civilians also bore the brunt of the campaign, withstanding shortages of supplies, raids by British detachments and the bombardment of the town of Quebec. Two months of such campaigning and the failure to lure Montcalm into a decisive battle had brought Wolfe's army close to a crisis. The defeat at Montmorency all but paralysed much of Wolfe's army. While soldiers settled into a regular routine of camp life, increasingly the frustrations of the British troops and of Wolfe himself began to surface. In mid-August they would transform the nature of the war on the St Lawrence.

5

The Distasteful War

As mid-August passed, Wolfe became increasingly despondent and increasingly ill. His army had now been encamped on the St Lawrence for nearly two months, yet he had failed to bring the French army to a decisive encounter. Indeed, in the largest clash between the two armies so far, at Montmorency at the end of July, it had been Wolfe's men who had been bettered by the French. Following the battle, Wolfe had been forced to face the possibility, indeed the probability, that he would not be able to capture Quebec. Wolfe still hoped that his army might be reinforced by the arrival of Amherst's army from the south, and that together the two armies could crush the French. However, the lack of news from Amherst made this scenario increasingly unlikely.

It was not until 4 September that the army finally received confirmation that Amherst had taken Forts Ticonderoga and Crown Point and that in the west Fort Niagara had fallen.[1] By that time it was apparent that Amherst's army would not be joining Wolfe's on the St Lawrence. As hopes of victory faded, Wolfe and his troops became increasingly restless. At the end of August he wrote to his mother informing her of his determination to quit the army once he returned home. He begged her not to worry about him since:

> my writing to you will convince you that no personal evils (worse than defeats & disappointments) have fallen upon me The enemy puts nothing to risk, & I cant in conscience put the whole army to risk. My antagonist has wisely shut himself up in inaccessible entrenchments, so that I cant get at him without spilling a torrent of blood, and that perhaps to little purpose. The Marquiss de Montcalm is at the head of a great number of bad soldiers, and I am at the head of a small number of good ones, that wish for nothing so much as to fight him – but the wary old fellow avoids an action doubtful of the behaviour of his army. People must be of the profession to understand the disadvantages and difficulties we labour under arising from the uncommon natural strength of the country.[2]

Increasingly Wolfe fretted about those people not 'of the profession'. How would the failure of the campaign be viewed by his peers and benefactors in Britain? Wolfe himself had witnessed the fate of those who had failed so dismally in Sir John Mordaunt's expedition to Rochefort on the west coast of France in 1757. Indeed, Wolfe himself had written on his return from the expedition that it had 'been conducted so ill, that I am asham'd to have been of the Party; the Publick cou'd n't do better than to dismiss 6 or 8 of us from their service – no zeal, no ardour, no care or concern for the good & honour of our Country'.[3]

Such sentiments now haunted Wolfe as his expedition threatened to fail as dismally as the Rochefort expedition. Wolfe wondered whether he would return to Britain with anything to show for all the money, men and effort poured into the expedition. As the pressures of command began to tell, his health deteriorated quickly. Wolfe was never the most robust of men, and had suffered from a range of ailments, but there is evidence that he was also prone to what Stuart Reid, one of his biographers, has termed 'psychosomatic' illness. After his first experience of combat at Dettingen in 1743, Wolfe had recorded that he was 'very much out of order, and I was obliged to keep my tent for two days'.[4] Dettingen was a British victory; now Wolfe's army had been badly beaten and his health deteriorated much further than it had sixteen years previously. For nearly ten days at the end of August, Wolfe was unable to appear in public and his fellow officers feared greatly for his health.[5]

This was not lost on the rank and file. Sergeant John Johnson recorded in his journal that:

> General Wolfe, whose Spirit was too big to bear a repulse with any degree of moderation, and fearing he should not be able to return to England, with the Laurel of victory planted on his brow, which was a glory he thirsted after to an insatiable degree… was afraid he should be exposed to the unruliness of an ignorant, unthinking populace; and that his Military talents should be exposed to ridicule, instead of meeting with applause, after exerting every faculty, both of Body and Mind, and done all in his power for the good of the Service, and the Honour of his King and Country. These perturbations of his Mind, affected his Body to that degree, that he was for some days intirely unfit for public business.[6]

As Wolfe's morale declined, so did that of his men. Sitting around the campfire, supping their rum, Wolfe's men listened to gossip and rumours, first that a French force had landed in Nova Scotia and taken Halifax and Louisbourg, and then that a French army had landed in Ireland and taken the kingdom and that Great Britain was now suing for peace. Because Wolfe's army was so isolated from outside sources of news, such reports took on a life of their own and forced officers to issue formal denials and assurances to their men.[7]

The most immediate and obvious effect of the decline in morale and order was an increase in desertion from the army. For Wolfe's army, desertion had been a constant problem which sapped manpower, but it increased steadily in August. The greatest risk from deserters was that they would reveal the army's plans to the French. Indeed, they were the principal source of intelligence for the French commanders. Many, perhaps even a majority, of the troops who deserted were foreign recruits into the British army, in particular Germans who had enlisted in the Royal Americans or even Frenchmen who had been recruited at Louisbourg. However, many others were long-serving soldiers. Throughout the summer a constant stream of British deserters arrived at Montcalm's headquarters. Some reported 'that nothing but the dread of the Savages deterred several others from Deserting'. Consequently, Montcalm issued a proclamation, published in French, English and German, 'in which an assurance was given… that all who would desert from the English Army, should receive the greatest favour and encouragement, and would have nothing to fear from the barbarity of the Savages; – they were directed to observe a particular method of holding their Guns (by the stocks) and that at this signal, the savages would fly to succour them; fire upon their pursuers, and conduct them faithfully and in safety to the French Camp'.[8]

Desertion was not an unusual practice and was common in all eighteenth-century armies. Most frequently troops would desert to return to their homes and families, especially when they had been pressed reluctantly into army service. In Canada, British troops who deserted had little chance of ever seeing their loved ones again. Moreover, they took their very lives into their hands. Not only did they have to fear the scalping parties that lurked round their camps, but if they were captured by their own officers they would suffer at best a fierce flogging, at worst execution. The flogging of deserters and other miscreants was sometimes so frequent that it merged with the routine of day-to-day camp life. Stripped to the waist, the men would be tied to a crossed halberd and flogged by the regimental drummers, a new drummer taking over after every twenty-five strokes. Executions were fewer, but were typically stage-managed in an effort to maximise the impact of the occasion. Captain John Knox reported how two soldiers who had been condemned to death were offered a chance of a reprieve. They would roll dice. The first to roll an eleven would be spared; the other soldier would be immediately executed. In front of their entire regiment the two men literally gambled for their lives.[9]

With nowhere to run to, facing the possibility of execution if they failed and scalping if they succeeded, it is surprising that any British troops attempted to desert. Nevertheless, during the course of the campaign several hundred British troops quit their posts to join the enemy. For many of these troops their primary motivation for leaving their unit was not a positive desire to join the French, but rather a desperate attempt to escape the hard conditions of army service. For some troops, the repeated physical labour of the army may have become too much, particularly as during the Quebec campaign troops were required to perform heavy manual labour in the heat of the Canadian summer without the assistance of auxiliaries or pioneers. For other troops, desertion may have represented an attempt to escape abuse from their officers. Non-commissioned officers had surprising powers to inflict physical punishment on soldiers. A repeated blow with a cane when drill was performed inadequately, or more frequent physical abuse for other misdemeanours, could leave some privates physically and psychologically scarred and desperate for escape. This seems to have been particularly true of men who had been drafted from one regiment to another on the eve of the expedition and who had few ties to their new regiment or company. This was of course particularly true of foreign troops who had recently enlisted into the British army. As morale and discipline declined, officers may have been forced to resort to fierce physical punishment more frequently, in turn increasing the men's propensity to desert.[10]

Discipline was essential to morale, but discipline was not always enforced by the lash. By the mid-eighteenth century, military instruction manuals were beginning to argue that soldiers should be treated with humanity and respect and not raw discipline. Wolfe in particular seems to have realised this and paid special attention to the morale of his men, which may have been one reason why the ranks of the army remained so dedicated to him. Officers attempted to maintain morale by fostering comradeship and a shared pride in the unit, an *esprit de corps*. Indeed, such pride may in part account for the rash attack of the grenadiers at Montmorency. Such feelings of loyalty and duty, rather than patriotism and discipline, bound men to the eighteenth-century army. However, for troops who were new to a regiment such ties were at best weak, and the conditions experienced by the British troops on the St Lawrence strained those that existed to breaking point.[11]

As the British grew more despondent, some French officers began to sense victory. On 18 August, Governor Vaudreuil wrote that Wolfe 'no longer makes a secret of saying that the expedition to take Canada has failed'.[12] However, more experienced officers were less sanguine. Montcalm in particular fretted about the growing shortages of supplies and about the numbers of Canadian troops and militia who were now deserting his army. Some French estimates maintained that in the first two weeks of August the total strength of the

French army encamped around Quebec dropped by over a third. Desertion from the French army, however, was rather different from desertion from Wolfe's army, and did not reflect solely a decline in morale as much as a desperate attempt by the Canadians to harvest their crops. Indeed, Montcalm was forced to tolerate a degree of absence as the harvest was essential if Canada was to survive into 1760. (This was a primary reason why Montcalm was so reluctant to use the militia on extended military operations.) Indeed, the lack of supplies and the lack of aid from France remained the major factor undermining morale in Montcalm's army. Morale dipped even further in early August when news of the fall of Fort Niagara reached the French. Unlike Vaudreuil, Montcalm himself now believed that it would take a miracle to save Canada.[13]

For Canadian troops, and the militia in particular, desertion was most frequently 'absence without leave' rather than a total abandonment of the army, and many men would later return to the army. During the Quebec campaign, while many militiamen disappeared for short periods, most returned to their posts relatively quickly. Such behaviour, however, caused great disgust among the French officers. One confided in his journal that 'an evil was noticed to day which had already existed a considerable time, this was the desertion of the Canadians, arising, either from their timidity, or from their not being accustomed to restraint and regular habits of remaining for a length of time inactive encamped… the measures adopted for putting a stop to this practice, succeeded however in checking its daily recurrence'.[14] Those 'measures' entailed encouraging allied Native Americans to scalp the men they saw deserting. Governor Vaudreuil had initially developed the scheme to halt the trickle of deserters from the regulars. He had written to Paris that 'as nothing is more dangerous than the desertion of the soldiers, I have adopted the arrangement which has appeared the best to prevent it; I saw the necessity of employing

Indians. Two soldiers of Berry having fallen into this category, our Indians went in pursuit, overtook them, cut the head off one and obliged his comrade to carry it himself to the fort; the latter was immediately tried and suffered the punishment due his crime. This example was absolutely necessary; I hope it will have made an impression on the soldiers who might have a similar fancy.'[15]

Fear of scalping may have discouraged many French regulars in particular from deserting. Wolfe himself may also have done more to discourage than to encourage Canadians from joining his ranks. The repeated warnings he issued to Canadians not to take up arms against the British convinced many militia-men and the *troupes de la Marine* that their lives were at risk if they deserted to the British. There was of course a final pressing motivation for the Canadians to fight. For them this was a struggle to save their homeland from the invader, and they fought with an unparalleled degree of dedication and desperation.[16]

The determination of the Canadian troops was heightened by the changes in the nature of the war which began almost immediately following the battle at Montmorency at the end of July. Before the end of July the campaign had been con-ducted in a relatively 'honourable' fashion according to the established 'rules of war' and the cartel between the French and British Crowns. Pillaging was strictly forbidden and attempts were made to respect civilian property. However, in the early days of August this began to change. Frustrated at his failure to bring the French to battle and considering what could be done to prepare for a future campaign, Wolfe authorised the burn-ing of magazines of provisions, the slaughter of cattle and the destruction of crops and orchards. If Canada were robbed of supplies, any British army which returned to the St Lawrence the following spring would have an easier task of reducing the colony than Wolfe had had. By mid-August, as Vaudreuil considered the reports of devastation, he wrote that the 'only resource he has found in his despair is to pillage, ravage and burn the settlements which are near his army'.[17]

The drift towards a campaign of terror and destruction had begun with the bombardment of Quebec. On 15 July, the British had completed their first batteries and opened fire on the city. At first, the bombardment had done more to dishearten the civilians who fled the city in fear than to destroy the city itself. Indeed, as the bombardment continued day after day, the British seemed more intent on destroying civilian morale than the military fortifications. Many of the city's residents began to suspect that the primary intention of the British was to spread fear and panic among the inhabitants rather than to weaken the city's ability to resist a siege. One Quebec resident wrote in his journal that 'it was remarked, that the English, altered the direction of their Bombs; at first they flung them into the heart of the place; but having learnt from the letters they found upon the women whom they had taken Prisoners, (and which contained the news of every thing that was passing in the Town of Quebec,) that almost all the inhabitants had fled from it they brought all their fire to bear upon the suburbs, wither the inhabitants had retired'.[18]

The intensity of the bombardment soon increased as Wolfe ordered the construction of a second battery on the Pointe-aux-Pères. When it opened fire an inferno followed, in which, among other buildings, the Jesuit college was badly damaged. The gunners did all they could to maximise the devastation. Seeing the blaze take hold, the batteries targeted their fire on the burning buildings to hinder attempts by the French to extinguish the flames. Over the following nights the bombardment increased as more British guns were brought to bear on the city, destroying the cathedral and damaging the Hôtel-Dieu. Not only did the bombardment increase, but the gunners learned a new skill. The range of the British guns was

limited, but the gunners discovered that by aiming the guns
at a lower angle, which would normally decrease the range,
the bombs would ricochet off buildings, increasing both their
range and the damage inflicted. Using this technique, the batteries were even able to reach the suburbs and the militia camp
outside the St Jean Gate.[19]

By 5 August, one French official estimated that 400 shells
and 10,000 canon balls had fallen on the city. Worse was yet
to come. On the night of 8-9 August a British shell penetrated
into the cellar of a merchant's warehouse in the Lower Town.
The cellar, whose heavy stone vaults had been presumed to
be bomb-proof, was stacked full of brandy and other spirits.
The fire soon caught hold and spread quickly, engulfing the
entire lower town. One Quebec resident reported that 'it was
reduced to ashes in less than four hours, with the exception of
14 or 15 houses'.[20] Another account maintained that 'near 150
Houses were burnt and the fortunes of many persons hereto-
fore accounted very rich had their whole property reduced at
once to ashes. The fury of the flames was greatly increased by
the English, who redoubled the discharges from their Batteries
and fired without intermission; the conflagration had attained
to such a height that there was no possibility of putting a
stop [to] its progress.' However, 'the courage & intrepidity of
the Sailors prevented any great damage being done to the
Batteries'.[21]

British officers seem to have taken a particular delight in
watching the city burn. On 22 July, Patrick Mackellar recorded
in his journal: 'At night there was a considerable fire in Town
by one of our Carcasses wch burnt the Cathedral & Ten or
Twelve good houses.' An officer in Fraser's Regiment recorded
'the town much bombarded, set on fire, and burnt most of the
night'. On 11 August, another officer was able to report that
the British batteries had had 'great effect on the town, setting
[it] frequently on fire, and the lower town is almost destroy'd'.

By early September, Admiral Charles Saunders was able to boast to William Pitt that 'The Town of Quebec is not habitable, being almost entirely burnt and destroyed.'[22]

The bombardment of Quebec marked a shift in the nature of the campaign. One French diarist recorded that 'measures so very harsh pushed against inanimate objects astonished everybody; till we learnt from a Deserter, that it was the intention of the English General completely to demolish the Town of Quebec; without assigning any reason for acting so contrary to the ordinary usages of war'.[23] The bombardment, however, was just a foretaste of the devastation which was to come.

Over a period of about two weeks, following the exchange of the prisoners from Pointe-aux-Trembles on 25 July, the campaign degenerated into a brutal and irregular war. On 25 July, Wolfe had issued a final proclamation to the civilians of the St Lawrence. He warned them that he was 'indignant at the little regard paid by the inhabitants of Canada to his proclamation of the 29th of [June]', and was 'determined no longer to listen to the sentiments of humanity'. Further, he added, 'The Canadians have, by their conduct, proved themselves unworthy of the advantageous offers he held out to them. Wherefore he has issued orders to the Commanders of his Light Infantry and other officers, to proceed into the country and to seize and bring in the farmers and their cattle, and to destroy and lay waste what they shall judge proper.'[24] The failure of the Canadians to lay down their arms, Wolfe warned, justified the destruction of their homes and property.

It was the failure at Montmorency, however, that seems to have marked the decisive turning point. Soon after the battle Wolfe began to form detachments with specific orders to 'scour the Country'.[25] The men were given strict orders to preserve only the churches and respect only 'the persons of ancient men or women, or helpless children', although they were allowed 'to despoil them of whatever moveables they could find in their possession'. Further, they were 'allowed to kill and destroy by every means they could, all the Cattle they could find, of every kind, and specize. They were allowed to burn and destroy all their Magazines, whether of Corn, Hay, Provisions, or whatsoever kind they might be. They were allowed by every means they could to harm and destroy all the Corn, or any other produce of the Field, Garden, or Orchard, and whatsoever else they found growing in the ground.'[26] This would now be a war of devastation and destruction and it would be the civilian *habitants* of the St Lawrence who would suffer the worst hardships.

The first major raiding party set out on 4 August when Wolfe dispatched Captain Joseph Gorham and his rangers to the north shore of the St Lawrence to destroy the settlements between La Petite Rivière and La Malbaie. Gorham landed first at St-Paul, then continued downstream to La Malbaie, destroying nearly seventy farms. From there Gorham crossed to the Île-aux-Coudres, where he established a temporary base before continuing to the south shore and attacking the settlement at Ste-Anne-de-la-Pocatière, where he took great delight in destroying fifty farms. From there he reported back to Wolfe that the south shore seemed much more prosperous than the north shore. Indeed, 'the Parish of St Anne & St Roch contain the Largest farms & produce the greatest Quantity of grains I have seen'. He continued with a hint to Wolfe, 'in case any further Dutys should be Required on the S. Shore in Collecting the Cattle etc. which are good & Numerous... the knowledge I have gain'd would greatly facilitate that Duty and be attended with Dispatch & advantage'.[27] Such settlements should be destroyed as quickly as possible.

Wolfe needed little encouragement to follow up on Gorham's hint. The Côte du Sud was one of the more prosperous and fertile parts of Canada, and had been relatively untouched by warfare during this war or previous wars. It would not be so lucky now.[28] On 1 September, Wolfe gave Gorham command of an even larger detachment of over 600 troops, rangers, regulars and seamen. They were sent to ravage the entire Côte du Sud as far east as Kamouraska. Gorham kept meticulous details of his party's progress, which he was duly to report back to Wolfe. He landed on 10 September close to Kamouraska, where he immediately destroyed 109 farms; on 11 September the party marched west from Kamouraska to Rivière Ouelle, burning 121 farms en route; on 12 September Gorham's men spent the day burning the remaining fifty-five houses in the parish; on 13 September the party marched up Rivière Ouelle, burning 151 houses; on 14 September the party burned ninety houses, marching through the already ravaged parish of Ste-Anne-de-la-Pocatière; on 15 September the party 'halted at St Roche's to ravage the back parts of it'. Although the party then received an order to return to Quebec, it continued and on 16 September burned 140 farms between St-Roch and Cap St-Ignace and a further fifty-six more, before re-embarking on 17 September. 'Upon the whole,' Gorham commented 'we marched fifty two Miles, and in that distance, burnt nine hundred and ninty eight good Buildings.'[29]

It was not only settlements below Quebec that suffered at the hands of the British. On 5 August, Wolfe dispatched Brigadier-General Murray with 1,200 men to destroy settlements upstream from the city, and to destroy the small French naval presence upstream from Quebec, cutting French supply lines. As Murray's force moved upstream, French troops commanded by Colonel Louis-Antoine de Bougainville shadowed his force along the northern shore. Murray made several abortive attempts to land. On 8 August he attempted to land at Pointe-aux-Trembles, but was repulsed by Bougainville with some losses. The next day Murray abandoned his attempt to land on the northern shore and instead established a base of operations in the village of Ste-Croix on the south shore.

From there parties fanned out across the southern shore of the St Lawrence, burning settlements and seizing all the cattle and corn they could find. Under cover of night on 18 August, Murray's men finally descended on the northern shore, raiding the settlement at Deschambault, burning the village and the French magazines of stores and ammunition there. The other major raid took place at the end of August when, preparing to withdraw his troops from Montmorency, Wolfe sent out parties along the Côte de Beaupré, destroying the villages of L'Ange-Gardien, Château Richer, Ste-Anne-de-Beaupré and St-Joachim. By 1 September, one officer was able to report 'All the houses below Montmorency Falls, or to the eastward, sett on fire by our army.'[30]

The scope of these raids was quite remarkable. In a month, British troops destroyed most of the settlements from Kamouraska to Deschambault, a distance of nearly 100 miles. Hundreds of farms were burned, and thousands of acres of crops destroyed. These raids left the civilian population in dire straits. Bishop de Pontbriand of Quebec reported that on both sides of the river 'about 36 leagues of settlement country have been almost equally devastated; it contained 19 parishes, the greater number of which have been destroyed. All those places... will suffer seriously, and are incapable of assisting any person; have no provisions to sell, and will not be restored to their ancient state for more than 20 years.'[31] With no grain, no cattle, and often no shelter, thousands of civilians faced starvation and exposure as winter approached.

The progress of these raids can to some extent be explained by military necessity. With the prospect of capturing Quebec receding, Wolfe believed that he needed to reduce the French ability to continue the campaign in 1760 by destroying French food stores and supplies. Vattel, in his *Law of Nations*, provided a detailed discussion of how enemy civilians should be treated in time of war. He maintained that 'the people... have nothing to fear from the sword of the enemy. Provided the inhabitants submit to him who is master of the country.'[32] Wolfe's justification for these raids was specifically that the Canadians had not fully submitted to him. Yet the Canadian *habitants* were in a dangerous situation. Wolfe's army did not control their villages, he merely sent raiding parties through them. From Quebec, Montcalm and Vaudreuil sent out repeated invectives instructing the Canadians to take every opportunity to harass the British. What were they to do? Who were they to obey? Vattel went even further. He argued that 'the pillage and destruction of towns, the devastation of open country, ravaging, setting fire to houses, are measures no less odious and detestable on every occasion when they are evidently put in practice without absolute necessity, or at least very cogent reasons. But as the perpetrators of such outrageous deeds might attempt to palliate them under pretext of deservedly punishing the enemy,' (as did Wolfe) 'be it here observed, that the natural and voluntary law of nations does not allow us to inflict such punishments, except for enormous offences against the law of nations: and even then, it is glorious to listen to the voice of humanity and clemency, when rigour is not absolutely necessary.'[33] While the destruction of military supplies and provisions might have been an acceptable aspect of eighteenth-century warfare, the wholesale destruction of civilian settlements was not an established practice of warfare.

The raids Wolfe authorised went much further than the destruction of stores and supplies, and military necessity alone cannot explain or justify the ways in which these raids were conducted. Colonel Malcolm Fraser recorded in his journal that on 25 August his men set about cutting down the orchards near L'Ange Gardien. Indeed, one French diarist who later ventured into the region was astonished to discover that Wolfe's men had ensured 'the burning of every house to the ground and cutting down all the Fruit Trees – The Church was spared, and the cornfields were untouched – They found in the Camp and around it, about fifty horses feeding quietly.'[34] The raiding party had not touched the crops, or killed the horses – the two items which would seemingly be of most military significance in depriving the French of supplies – but instead had sought to inflict long-term losses on the civilian population by destroying all the buildings and orchards. This was not military necessity, it was vengeance. Indeed, Vattel had concluded that 'those who tear up the vines and cut down the fruit-trees are looked upon as savage barbarians, unless when they do it with a view to punish the enemy for some gross violation of the law of nations. They desolate a country for many years to come, and beyond what their own safety requires. Such conduct is not dictated by prudence, but by hatred and fury.'[35]

Wolfe had his own particular rationale for such a degeneration in the nature of the campaign – the 'enormous offences against the law of nations', the activities of the French, and in particular the Canadian troops and militia, and their Native American allies. British officers complained repeatedly about the maltreatment of their men if they fell into the hands of Canadians or Native Americans. From the start of the campaign British troops who strayed too far from their camp, in particular into the notorious 'woods' which covered most of the St Lawrence Valley, were prone to capture by small 'skulking' parties of Canadians and Native Americans. Wolfe himself complained to the Earl of Holderness that his men 'have continued skirmishes; old people seventy years of age, and boys of fifteen fire on our detachments, and kill or wound our men from the edges of the woods'.[36]

In particular, Wolfe and his officers were outraged by the rumoured treatment of several grenadiers who were captured by the French on 22 July. Upon hearing reports that the grenadiers were to be burned alive in the middle of the French

Right: 1 William Pitt
the elder. As leading
minister of the Crown
and Secretary of State
for the Southern
Department, Pitt was
not only a senior
government minister
but specifically
responsible for affairs in
North America.

Below: 2 View of
Louisbourg. This view
of Louisbourg during
the siege of 1758 was
published in Britain
in the 1760s as pride
in Britain's wartime
achievements reached
its peak.

3 'A View of Miramichi'. Miramichi Bay was one of the French Acadian settlements destroyed by raiding parties sent out from Louisbourg.

4 'A Perspective View of Quebec drawn on the spot'. This engraving from the mid-eighteenth century reflects the importance of Quebec's public buildings.

5 'A Perspective View of the City of Quebec'. This print is derived from a sketch by Hervey Smyth which was published in London in 1760.

6 'A View of Quebec from the Southeast', drawn in the second half of the 1760s and first published in London. This view emphasises the steepness of the cliff, and the cliffs stretching towards L'Anse au Foulon are clearly visible to the left of the picture.

7 'The Thunder Bolt'. A contemporary engraving reflecting the perilous navigation of the St Lawrence River.

Above left: 8 The church of Notre-Dame des Victoires in the lower town of Quebec as it appears today. Built to commemorate and give thanks for the defeat of the British attempts to take Quebec in 1690 and 1711.

Above right: 9 Eighteenth-century merchant's house in the lower town of Quebec as it appears today. Typical of many of the buildings clustered along the St Lawrence and destroyed by the bombardment.

Clockwise from above: 10 The city walls of Quebec as they appear today. While these walls represent the image of a fortified city, they are a nineteenth-century construction and the walls of the eighteenth century were much less substantial.

11 A twentieth-century depiction of the Régiment de Languedoc, 1755. Dispatched to Canada in 1755, the Régiment de Languedoc fought at the battle of Montmorency and the battle of the Plains of Abraham and participated in the defence of Montreal. The uniform consisted of a grey-white coat, lining and breeches, blue cuffs, collar and waistcoat.

12 A twentieth-century depiction of the Régiment de Guyenne, 1755. Dispatched to Canada in 1755, some of the Régiment de Guyenne had been sent to Niagara and to Île-aux-Noix but the remainder fought at Montmorency and at the Plains of Abraham. Some of the men surrendered in Quebec in September 1759; the remainder of the regiment continued fighting until September 1760. The Régiment de Guyenne could be distinguished by their red cuffs, collar and waistcoat.

13 A modern company of re-enactors at Fort Ligonier, Pennsylvania. The uniform of the *compagnies franches de la Marine* was very similar to the *troupes de terre*, but they were distinguished by the blue breeches and blue lining of the coat and waistcoat.

14 Twentieth-century depiction of a Canadian militiaman. The militia had no formal uniform but dressed themselves for irregular warfare. This also enabled the militia to return quickly to civilian life.

15 Canadian militia officer. While the militiamen had no formal uniform, many of the officers wore a uniform imitative of the regular officers.

16 'Guerrier Iroquois'. A rather stylised view of an Iroquois warrior from the late eighteenth century. The majority of the Iroquois were British allies and were not present at Quebec. However, some of the Iroquois, particularly those from the French mission villages, fought alongside the French in the defence of Quebec.

17 'Iroquois allant à la Découverte'. Another depiction of an Iroquois warrior from the late eighteenth century, typically equipped for war with a musket sling over his shoulder, a tomahawk in his belt and a war-club in his hand, wearing snow-shoes which were a Native American invention.

18 Fraser's Highlanders. An early-twentieth-century watercolour of an officer and private of the 78th Regiment, Fraser's Highlanders. Raised in the Highlands of Scotland in early 1757, the regiment had served at Louisbourg before joining Wolfe's expedition.

19 Re-enactors of Montgomery's 77th Regiment. The uniform of the 77th was very similar to that of the 78th. The exact tartan worn by the troops is unknown.

20 58th Regiment. An early-twentieth-century watercolour of grenadier and private of the 58th Regiment or Anstruther's. Raised in 1756 in the west of England, the regiment had fought at Louisbourg before joining Wolfe's expedition.

21 Major-General James Wolfe. The popular image of the hero of Quebec, as published in a print by James Bowles in London in the early 1760s. Such images graced the homes of many of the British gentry and served to popularise Wolfe as a national hero.

22 Major-General James Wolfe. This contemporary sketch by George Townshend is probably one of the most accurate surviving images of Wolfe. The image was a gift from Townshend to Wolfe's aide-de-camp Isaac Barré.

Right: 23 Brigadier-General Robert Monckton. A near-contemporary mezzotint of Wolfe's senior brigadier from a painting by Thomas Hudson.

Below left: 24 Brigadier-General George Townshend. Possibly the most critical of Wolfe's brigadiers and creator of a series of brutal caricatures and sketches depicting the campaign. Print after Muller.

Below right: 25 Brigadier-General James Murray. Wolfe's junior brigadier who later served as governor of Canada.

GENERAL TOWNSHEND.

26 Vice-Admiral Charles Saunders. Commander of the British fleet in the St Lawrence.

27 Sir Jeffery Amherst, Commander-in-Chief of British forces in North America. In this almost ludicrous painting, Amherst is portrayed at the Siege of Louisbourg in full armour. This was Amherst as he liked to see himself.

28 Sir Jeffery Amherst. A caricature from later in his life captures much more of the essence of Amherst the martinet, whose obsession with detail was largely responsible for the organisation of the forces and fleet in North America for the Quebec campaign.

29 Governor Pierre de Rigaud de Vaudreuil, the civilian governor of Canada. Vaudreuil is wearing the eight-pointed gold Cross of St Louis which he received in 1730. It was the highest honour that could be bestowed on officers stationed in New France.

L.^{is} A.^{ne} DE BOUGAINVILLE

Clockwise from above left:
30 General Louis-Joseph, Marquis de Montcalm-Gozon de Saint-Véran, Commander-in-Chief of French forces in Canada.

31 François Gaston, Duc de Lévis. A nineteenth-century image of Montcalm's second-in-command.

32 Colonel Louis-Antoine de Bougainville. Bougainville commanded a detachment of French troops and Canadians who opposed any landing of the British above Quebec.

33 'The Defeat of the French Fireships attacking the British Fleet at Anchor before Quebec, 28 June 1759'. An eighteenth-century copy of a painting completed in 1760 depicting the effect of the French fire-ships launched shortly after the arrival of the British fleet.

34 'A View of the Fall of Montmorenci and the Attack made by General Wolfe, on the French Intrenchments near Beauport'. This detailed engraving shows the British troops drawing up on the beach at Montmorency supported by the armed boats the *Russell* and the *Three Sisters*, with the warship *Centurion* closer to the falls.

MONTCALM'S HEAD-QUARTERS BEAUPORT.

35 Montcalm's headquarters at Beauport. From this house in the centre of the French lines, Montcalm commanded the defence of the French lines.

36 Wolfe inspects the latrines. One of Townshend's scathing caricatures drawn during the campaign shows Wolfe's obsession with camp cleanliness.

37 Modern re-enactors depict Highland officers in camp. For officers, camp life was moderated by the presence of servants and a plentiful supply of wine and spirits.

38 Modern re-enactors depict the camp life of ordinary troops. While officers dined in splendour, ordinary troops would cook their own food round a campfire and share a pipe. Often this was the time when rumours of French victories or atrocities would spread through camp.

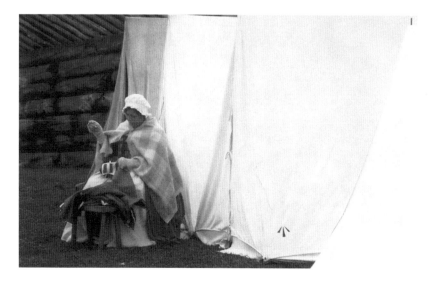

39 A modern re-enactor depicts the life of camp followers. While the men were on duty, women were responsible for repairing and cleaning clothes. Note also how close tents were pitched together. This was to facilitate the protection of the camp, but when the camps did not move for months this could create problems of hygiene.

40 'Indian with tomahawk'. A sketch by Townshend, made while he was on campaign in Quebec, captures the fear of British troops, as a Native American warrior strides confidently along the banks of the St Lawrence, musket in one hand, raised tomahawk in the other.

An Indian war chief compleatly equipped with a scalp in his hand

Ah, Monsieur le General si Quebec tombe – Votre Altesse épargner les femmes? Cela depend. mes bonnes – plus des Petitions écrites. Depechez 50 belles vierges toute de suite à Moi – et nous verrons

Above: 41 'An Indian of ye Outawas Tribe & his Family going to War.' In this sketch by Townshend even the child has a tomahawk and is smoking a pipe. These sketches reflect the British troops' fear of Native Americans.

Left: 42 Townshend cartoon depicting Wolfe and two French women. The women are asking Wolfe whether, if Quebec falls he will spare the women. His response is 'That depends, my beauties. More Petitions! Send me fifty beautiful virgins immediately and we will see!' This reflects the unease of some of Wolfe's brigadiers at the conduct of the campaign.

43 Townshend cartoon depicting Wolfe discussing tactics with Isaac Barré, his aide-de-camp. Holding a copy of one of his proclamations, Wolfe assures Barré 'We will not let any of them escape my dear Isaac, the pretty ones will be furnished at Headquarters.' Barré replied 'I understand you completely General. Strike 'em in their weakest part Egad!' Meanwhile, the servant who is listening to the conversation ponders 'I wonder if I shall have my share.'

44 Townshend cartoon depicting Canadian civilians begging Wolfe for mercy. Wolfe replies, 'My orders are strict. For each captured man one bullet, for each woman two.' This bitter satire depicts Townshend's horror at what he saw as a campaign against civilians.

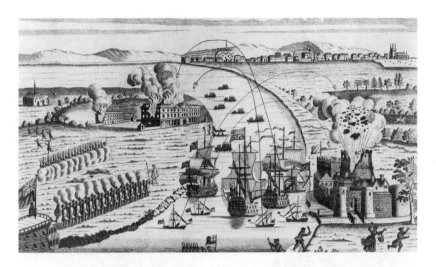

45 'The Siege and Taking of Quebec'. A stylised view of the bombardment of Quebec published in the *London Gazette* on 17 October 1759 when first news of the fall of the city arrived in London.

46 Modern reproduction of a British Army Howitzer of the Seven Years' War at Fort Ligonier, Pennsylvania. Such howitzers were capable of discharging an eight-inch shell and were responsible for much of the bombardment of Quebec.

47 'A General View of Quebec' from Pointe-Lévy as it would have appeared during the Quebec campaign. This was the view of the city as seen by the men in Monckton's camp. A contemporary engraving published in London in 1761.

48 'A View of the Bishop's House with the Ruins, as they appear up the Hill from the Lower to the Upper Town'. This contemporary engraving, the first of a series, shows the ruins of Quebec when the British army occupied the city.

49 'A View of the Bishop's House with the Ruins as they appear in going down the Hill from the Upper to the Lower Town'. Another view of the Bishop's Palace shows Quebec as little more than a ruin.

50 'A View of the Treasury and Jesuits' College'. Civilians and soldiers pick through the rubble of the devastated city.

51 'A View of the Inside of the Jesuits' Church'. One of the most substantial and least damaged of the buildings in Quebec, the Jesuits' church was still badly damaged, although some the engraving still provides a sense of its former grandeur.

52 A view of the church of Notre-Dame des Victoires. The total devastation of the Lower Town is clearly visible in this engraving. Not a building is habitable.

53 'A View of the Intendant's Palace'. Richard Short, who produced these images, was purser on the *Prince of Orange* and witnessed first-hand the devastation of the city.

54 'A View of Cape Rouge'. Cap Rouge above Quebec was the focus of early plans for a landing above Quebec.

55 'A View of the Landing Place above Quebec'. An etching dating from 1761 provides a montage of all aspects of the landing at L'Anse au Foulon. The landing craft approach the cove from upstream, while the light infantry scale the cliff further downstream. Other craft ferry the troops across the St Lawrence from Pointe-Lévy. Meanwhile, on the Plains of Abraham smoke rises from the battle.

56 The cliffs near L'Anse au Foulon as they appeared in the late nineteenth century. With no vegetation then growing on the cliffs, the task of the British light infantry is quite apparent. Fortunately, in 1759 there was brush and undergrowth to assist them in their ascent.

57 Modern view of the Plains of Abraham from the Buttes-à-Neveu looking west. This would have been the first view that most French and Canadian troops had of the battlefield.

58 'The Death of General Wolfe'. West's famous portrayal of Wolfe's death, first exhibited in 1771, contains great detail. The city of Quebec can be seen through the smoke of the battle, while a soldier, with cap raised, runs to the dying general with news of the rout of the French. West went to great pains to provide the correct detail of the uniforms and people depicted, and even acquired Native American artefacts to paint the Iroquois warrior at Wolfe's feet. Unfortunately there were no Iroquois accompanying the British and much of the painting is pure invention. Indeed, C.P. Stacey maintained that 'as a representation of an historical event it is among the worst ever produced'. It serves, however, to capture the spirit which emerged in Britain after the battle.

Above: 59 'The Death of General Montcalm'. If West's portrayal of the death of Wolfe is inaccurate, this painting is pure fantasy. Montcalm on the field of battle dies under a palm tree, while the Native American warriors at his feet look more like exotic Polynesians. The work was produced in the 1780s as a conscious French attempt to combat West's idealised view of the battle.

Left: 60 The Ursuline Convent in Quebec as it appears today, where Montcalm was taken before his death.

61 Montreal in 1760. A contemporary engraving of the city of Montreal. Unlike Quebec, Montreal had few defences with which to resist a British assault.

62 'Passage of Amherst's Army down the Rapids of the St Lawrence toward Montreal'. In this contemporary engraving, the dangers of the passage are quite apparent as the boats bob perilously in the rapids.

63 Fort Chambly. Although heavily repaired, Fort Chambly still retains much of its mid-eighteenth-century appearance. Built in stone by the French to protect the rapids of the Richelieu river to the south-east of Montreal, the British never had to besiege the post.

64 'England's Triumph Over France'. This engraving from *c*.1760 celebrates the British conquest of Canada. The main image depicts France kneeling in homage to Britannia handing over the keys of Quebec. A circular medallion portrays George II as a Roman general, while the capture of Louisbourg is also commemorated in a small cartouche. Such engravings served to stir up British patriotism in the wake of the campaign.

camp, Wolfe's aide-de-camp, Isaac Barré, wrote a heated letter to Governor Vaudreuil demanding to know whether there was any truth in the rumours and warning that 'the British troops are only too much exasperated; the enormous cruelties already committed, and especially the base infraction of the capitulation of Fort William Henry are yet fresh in their minds. Such acts deserve and if repeated will certain meet, in future, the severest reprisals; all distinction will cease between Frenchmen, Canadians and Indians; all will be treated as a cruel and barbarous mob, thirsting for human blood.'[37] Wolfe himself wrote to Monckton that if he discovered that these reports were true then 'the country shall be but one universal blaze'.[38]

While many such reports may have been little more than campfire stories told to frighten jittery soldiers staring into the shadows, there was some basis for the British fears. Throughout the campaign British troops were regularly captured by Native Americans skulking around the British camps. On many occasions their bodies were later found mutilated lying outside the camp. John Johnson, for instance, reported that on their first landing on the Île d'Orléans three soldiers were 'suprized by one of these Skulking parties of Savage Canadians, and butchered in the most cruel, and barbarous manner; for besides their killing and scalping them, they ripped them open, and took out their hearts, and left them on the spot where they had committed this horrid barbarity'.[39] The greatest insult occurred when British troops withdrew from the failed assault on the French lines at Montmorency. As they paddled away across the St Lawrence, they watched in horror as the Native Americans came down to the beach to scalp the dead and dying.[40]

The scalping of prisoners was certainly routinely carried out by some of the Native American allies who supported the French. Indeed, Governor Vaudreuil was so concerned by reports which reached his ears of the scalping of women and children who accompanied the British army that he ordered

Lévis to investigate such reports and put a stop to such practices immediately. However, Vaudreuil himself had encouraged
such practices where it was convenient. Vaudreuil, a Canadian
by birth, felt that it was essential that the Canadians and their
allies be allowed to wage war in this fashion. The Canadians,
he argued, were masters of the woods, and could fight irregular
skirmishes in the woods to great advantage. Canadians also had
great experience in waging war in such a manner as a result
of the almost continual warfare against the British colonies
which had continued for the past seventy years. Here Native
American and Canadian parties had combined to attack the
colonial frontier from New England to Virginia with amazing
success. The use of irregular warfare in this way concerned
Montcalm, who sought to wage war in a more European fashion. Indeed, such disputes over how to wage war in Canada
drove a deep and irreconcilable wedge between Vaudreuil and
Montcalm.[41]

Montcalm's greatest concern, however, was restraining his
Native American allies from their traditional practices of scalping, mutilating the bodies of their victims and torturing some
of their captives. To Europeans, such as Montcalm, such practices were merely barbaric violence. To many Native American
warriors, however, such practices were not only a central part of
their culture, but more importantly had religious significance.
Particularly amongst the Iroquois, the torturing of captives
represented an attempt to assuage the grief felt at the death of
a relative. Similarly, the taking of a scalp represented not only a
trophy of war, but also an attempt to capture the spirit or soul
of an enemy warrior. Canada's allies expected to be allowed
to continue such traditional practices from time to time but
Montcalm and other French officers sought to restrain them.
On occasion this proved impossible, most infamously after the
surrender of Fort William Henry in 1757, when Montcalm's
Native American allies had butchered a substantial part of the

garrison. This violation of the surrender was seen by the British as manifest proof of French duplicity, and was frequently cited as justification for British barbarities.[42]

Wolfe thus had some justification for viewing France's Native American allies as outside the protection of the European rules of war. Yet even if Native Americans were excluded from the protection of European military conventions, Canadians must surely have been included in them. The issue, however, was complicated by the manner in which Vaudreuil and Montcalm used the Canadian militia to hamper the British war effort by using irregular warfare. The Canadians held a huge advantage in irregular skirmishes in the dense woodland, and the Canadian woods essentially became a no-go area for British forces during the campaign. Wolfe himself wrote to the Earl of Holderness that in 'a woody country, so well known to the enemy, and an enemy so vigilant and hardy as the Indians and Canadians are… scarce a night passes that they are not close in upon our posts, waiting an opportunity to surprise and murder. There is very little quarter given on either side.'[43]

The ways in which the Canadians were used in combat also served to blur irrevocably the distinction between civilians and military in Canada. The militia formed the backbone of the French defence. It was not only employed alongside the French army, but was often used in small numbers to harass British parties, or to act as a local police force. The local militia was instructed to evacuate women and children and ensure that supplies were hidden before any British detachment approached. They were then to do all they could to hinder British operations.[44]

Irregular warfare and the skirmishes around British camps were a fully accepted part of European warfare, and one for which Wolfe and his fellow officers were fully prepared. However, in European 'conventional' warfare such combat should have been conducted by identifiable combatants. What distinguished the campaign on the St Lawrence from campaigns in Europe, however, was the ease and speed with which Canadian farmers could slip between a military and a civilian role. Because the militia was composed of all the adult male population, because they lacked military uniform and insignia, and because most of these operations took place away from the regular army, it was difficult to distinguish between combatants and non-combatants. Wherever they went, British forces found the local militia mobilised to oppose them. It was thus all but impossible for the British to distinguish between combatants and non-combatants, and by early August British officers viewed most Canadian civilians with deep suspicion.

This problem was exacerbated because of the practice of using Canadian militia alongside Native Americans. The two forces had been combined in frontier raids against the British colonies for the previous half-century. The presence of Canadians in Native American raiding parties had seemed to provide some discipline and order, for Native American parties seemed wont to abandon their attacks, or to attack targets which seemed more appealing but which often lacked military importance, yet they showed greater skill in surviving in the forest and locating potential targets. Thus it made sense to use Canadians and Native Americans in this fashion on the St Lawrence. On 3 July, for instance, Montcalm sent out Le Sieur Legris with a raiding party of thirty farmers and thirty Abenakis against British positions near Pointe-Lévy and Pointe-aux-Pères opposite Quebec. Indeed, in mid-August Montcalm specifically created a flying party of Canadians and Native Americans to harass the British camp.[45]

It was not only the militia who organised local defence. The local parish priests traditionally served as a link between local communities and central government. They would transmit government edicts and orders from the governor to the local population. Further, they would encourage their congregations to provide men for the militia whenever needed to resist the British onslaught. It was the parish priests who oversaw the militia in the evacuation of supplies and property into the woods when British troops approached. Thus the lines of division between civilian non-combatant and military combatant were desperately blurred. Even priests could form a part of the Canadians' defence.[46]

The frequent combination of Native Americans with Canadian militia had unfortunate consequences. Practices of scalping and the ritualistic torture of prisoners were an established feature of Native American warfare and a feature recognised by Europeans. Because of their frequent contact with Native Americans, Canadians may also on occasion have treated prisoners with some brutality and perhaps even resorted to scalping. Moreover, in these combined parties of militia and Native Americans it was not unusual for the Canadians to take prisoners, who would then be seized by the Native Americans and subjected to torture. Malcolm Fraser's journal reveals how these ideas could impinge on British soldiers. At the beginning of July a detachment of Highlanders found several men who had been killed by the enemy. 'They were all scalped & mangled in a shocking manner. I dare say no human creature but an Indian cou'd be guilty of such Inhuman cruelty.' As an afterthought Fraser had corrected his journal to read 'no human creature but an Indian or Canadian cou'd be guilty'.[47]

The scalping of prisoners became, if not commonplace, at least not unusual, but British officers were unable to distinguish between Canadian and Native American military practices. When a party of militia and Native Americans scalped some unfortunate victim, British officers would blame both Canadians and Native Americans equally and fume at the French commanders for conniving in such practices. With the Canadian militia viewed as committing outrages on troops, all male civilians viewed as potential militia, and Canadian women viewed as offering succour to their menfolk, it is not entirely incomprehensible that the British should begin to target civilian settlements for attack.

Towards the end of July, Wolfe wrote to Montcalm arguing that the scalping and mistreatment of captives 'were intirely contrary to the Rules of War, highly dishonourable, and disgraceful to a General to suffer, much more so too encourage; and therefore begged the Colonists and Indians might be restrained'. When Montcalm failed to halt such abuses, Wolfe, 'in order if possible, to intimidate these monsters in cruelty, found it absolutely necessary to connive at some irregularities which were committed by our Soldiers in return'.[48] On 25 July he announced that the Canadians had 'by their conduct, proved themselves unworthy of the advantageous offers he held out to them. Wherefore he has issued orders to the Commanders… to destroy and lay waste what they shall judge proper.'[49]

In some ways, therefore, the degeneration of the campaign was a response by the British to the irregular way of waging war which was common in North America. However, the attacks on these settlements were particularly brutal and reflect in many ways what appears to be a breakdown of order and discipline amongst British troops on the St Lawrence. Indeed, from the beginning of August the British units on the St Lawrence seem to have become increasingly disordered. On 18 August, for instance, Wolfe was forced to issue a general order that 'if a soldier pretends to dispute the authority of an Officer of another corps under whose command he is, and if any soldier presumes to use any indecent language to the non-commissioned Officers of his own, or any other corps, such soldier shall be punished in an exemplary manner'.[50] The breakdown of order in the British ranks was even noted by the French. One French diarist commented that during Murray's expedition above Quebec, 'the English lost more than 300 men; whilst on our side the loss was not more than 3 or 4;

which was attributable partly to most of the English soldiers being intoxicated'.[51]

British troops soon began to resort to the practice that they themselves had dismissed as the most barbarous of all: scalping. Initially, the thought that British troops might scalp their victims was anathema to British officers. This did not, however, prevent the practice. On 10 July, Malcolm Fraser recorded in his journal that a party of rangers had taken a man and his two children prisoners. When the screams of the terrified children threatened to alert nearby Native American parties to the rangers' presence, the children 'were in the most inhuman manner murdered by those worse than savage Rangers... I wish this story was not fact, but I'm afraid there is little reason to doubt it, the wretches having boasted of it on their return.'[52] Matters got worse. On 27 July Wolfe relaxed the army's regulations, and issued the order banning 'the Inhuman practice of Scalping, except when the Enemy are Indians, or Canad[ian]s dressed like Indians'.[53] This essentially allowed the British to scalp any Native Americans or Canadian militia they came across. By mid-August British rangers, in particular, routinely displayed the scalps of their victims as trophies of their victories, hanging around their belts or on their muskets. Wolfe himself seems to have been overtaken by some of this bravado, when he boasted to Townshend after a skirmish near the Falls of Montmorency on 15 August that 'our little Detachment brought off one Scalp & a number of Trophies'.[54] The most notorious incident occurred on 23 August, when a party of light infantry commanded by Captain Alexander Montgomery of the 43rd Regiment were posted west of St-Joachim on the Côte de Beaupré. The party captured the Abbé de Portneuf, the local parish priest, and nine militiamen who had been protecting him and had surrendered to Montgomery's troops. Not content with capturing this party, according to one of the British eyewitnesses, 'the barbarous Capt. Montgomery who

commanded us ordered [them] to be butchered in a most
inhuman and cruel manner'.[55] Montcalm was horrified by the
new-found savagery of the British. He confided in his journal:
'The English, good imitators of the savagery of our Indians,
scalped several inhabitants of the south shore. Would you think
that a civilised nation, persecuted for their composure, would
mutilate the bodies of the dead?'[56] Some British troops also
seem to have been horrified by the increasing savagery of the
campaign. Captain John Knox recorded in his journal that
'Though these acts of hostility may be warrantable by the
laws of nations and rules of war, yet, as humanity is far from
being incompatible with the character of a soldier, any man,
who is possessed of the least share of it, cannot help sympathising with, and being sincerely affected at, the miseries of his
fellow-creatures.'[57]

   The troops most likely to commit atrocities or looting were
rangers. Rangers were different from other regular troops in
several ways. The three ranger companies which joined Wolfe
at the start of the campaign were not raised in Britain but
originally raised in New England and had served on the
Louisbourg campaign. Many of the men had already served in
provincial forces before volunteering for service amongst the
regular forces. They brought with them a deep-seated hatred
both of Native Americans and of the 'Popish French', who had
subjected the American colonial frontier to years of violence.
They also brought an extensive experience of frontier and
irregular warfare of the type practised in North America, of
which British regulars had only limited knowledge. Indeed,
their experience of frontier warfare was the principal reason
why their presence was valued by British officers. This experience had often been learned, or adapted, from Britain's own
Native American allies, such as the Iroquois, and included a
propensity, like their Canadian opponents, to resort to practices
such as scalping. Indeed, one officer recorded in his journal

an incident in Nova Scotia in the spring of 1759, when a party of rangers commanded by Lieutenant Moses Hazzen 'brought in 6 prisoners and after the cruel custom of the savages from whom the Americans copy, scalp'd two women and two children'.[58]

Another group who were predisposed to the other major disorder of the British forces – looting rather than scalping – were British seamen. Once ashore, British sailors seem to have been quite happy to go on a rampage. Captain Thomas Bell lamented during an expedition along the Gaspée coast the previous summer that 'the Seamen... shewed their accustomed rage for plundering in a very shamefull manner'.[59] Once on the St Lawrence, the seamen, who were usually the first to land, would often ensure that they got first pickings of any plunder which was available. When British forces landed on the south side of the Île d'Orléans at the end of June they 'found the Churches... plundered by the Seamen'.[60] Indeed, at the end of 1759 one group of seamen were so desirous of plunder when several French ships ran aground outside Quebec that they rushed on board just before one of the ships blew up. For seamen such activity may not have been particularly unusual. One of the few lures of a life at sea in the eighteenth century was the distribution of prize money after an enemy ship had been captured. Consequently, many seamen may have seen looting Canadian property as merely their share of the prize. Rangers and seamen shared a number of experiences. Many seamen were also natives of Britain's North American colonies who had been pressed into naval service. In addition, many had been involved in the bitter deportation of French settlers in Nova Scotia and Acadia. In particular, in the months following the fall of Louisbourg in July 1758, many seamen had accompanied the rangers in their expeditions to deport the Acadians. This may have accustomed them to plundering the civilian population.[61]

By the end of August, the nature of war on the St Lawrence had been transformed from the restricted and restrained campaign that had initially been envisaged by British officers. The British army seemed preoccupied with burning and ravaging the Quebec countryside, and blowing apart Quebec City. Victory seemed no nearer. Wolfe's senior officers, Monckton, Murray and Townshend, all felt uneasy at the destruction which was being meted out against Canadian non-combatants. General Townshend wrote at the beginning of September to his wife, that 'I am now in Sceene[sic] of Ambition, Confusion, & Misery... One month more will put an End to our Troubles. I never served so disagreeable a Campaign as this. Our unequal Force has reduced our Operations to a Sceene of Skirmishing Cruelty & Devastation. It is War of the Worst Shape... Genl Wolf's Health is but very bad. His Generalship in my poor opinion – is not a bit better.'[62] Townshend and Monckton voiced their concerns to Wolfe and soon a deep split developed. So deep was the split that the two brigadiers had even prepared a case against Wolfe to be heard upon their return to Britain.[63]

For the French *habitants* of the St Lawrence, these raids and the destruction of their property proved a calamitous misfortune. However, not everything was destroyed. Many *habitants* managed to hide much of their valuable property and foodstuffs in stashes deep in the woods. Indeed, perhaps the failure to find more of the food stores was one of the causes of frustration amongst British troops. Ironically, the raids may also have done as much to undermine the *habitants*' attachment to the French regime as they did to spread fear of the British. For Montcalm and his army sat outside Quebec and made no attempt to prevent the destruction of the heart of Canada – or so it must have seemed to many Canadian settlers as they watched their homesteads disappearing in flames.[64]

Many of the *habitants* found themselves in a desperate situation. Wolfe had now demanded that they lay down their arms and remain neutral. Indeed, one French deserter maintained that the *habitants* were quite willing to 'return to their respective habitations, and remain neuter; but when there is the least murmur or discontent among them, M. Montcalm and the Governor General threaten with the savages'.[65] Such claims were not without foundation, for Montcalm wrote to Lévis at the end of July that 'the people of l'Ange Gardien and of the côte de Beaupré should not make their own peace… We shall need a large detachment of Indians and Canadians to correct them.'[66] Pillaged and plundered by British troops if they laid down their arms, pillaged and plundered by Native Americans if they did not, the residents of the lower St Lawrence faced a dismal fate.

If life was desperate for the *habitants* of the lower St Lawrence, it was little better for the residents of Quebec City. As the townspeople fled for safety, the city itself became the haunt of looters. One French diarist recorded that 'during these disasters the persons who were left in the Town for its defence, became, for the most part, Robbers. No sooner had the bursting of a Bomb shattered the Doors or Windows of a house during the Night, than it was pillaged and stripped.' Food supplies were desperately short, and the bombardment destroyed all the ovens in Quebec so the residents had to rely for some time on supplies of dry biscuits before a new network of ovens outside the city could be constructed.[67]

For British troops, as the campaign dragged on weariness increased and morale dropped. For Wolfe himself the slow degeneration of his army must have been difficult to witness. However, for much of late August Wolfe probably witnessed little. Too ill to attend to business himself, he frequently left command in the hands of his subordinates. This begs the question of how far Wolfe himself can be held responsible for the breakdown of the campaign into a war of burning and plundering. Two pieces of evidence suggest that Wolfe played a role. The first is that the senior officers, Monckton, Murray and Townshend, all seem to have felt uneasy at the destruction which was being meted out against Canadian non-combatants. Townshend and Monckton in particular voiced their concerns to Wolfe. However, Wolfe's untimely death on the Plains of Abraham on 13 September sanctified his memory and ensured that these complaints and concerns were never given a full public airing, although reverberations and recriminations from the case continued to be printed in the London press through the winter and spring of 1759–1760. The second piece of evidence is that Wolfe himself felt compelled to destroy the pages of his journal dealing with the period from 12 August to 12 September. This certainly suggests that there were some aspects of the campaign which Wolfe did not wish to be widely known in Britain. Had Wolfe been fitter and more capable of providing energetic leadership during August, it is possible that the British Army would have made another attempt to dislodge the French, rather than resorting to a campaign of pillage and plunder. However, it also seems likely that Wolfe was himself frustrated at his inability to defeat the French and was more than content to allow the war of plunder to develop. Indeed, it was Wolfe who gave specific orders to Gorham for his devastating expedition to the Côte du Sûd in September, at the time when he knew the men would be needed for an attack on Quebec.[68]

During the second half of August, the British army had focused its attention on the destruction of the St Lawrence rather than the destruction of the French army. By the end of the month both British and French troops were growing weary of the campaign, and it was apparent that the British army would have to withdraw before too long, if they were to escape spending the bitter Canadian winter encamped along the St Lawrence. The issue was whether they would be able to launch another attack before they had to depart.

6

The Plains of Abraham

At the beginning of September, Montcalm's army had every reason to feel satisfied at its performance and confident of the prospect of a dramatic victory within a few weeks. News from the west and south, which had been bleak in August following the fall of Forts Ticonderoga, Crown Point and Niagara, now suggested that the British did not intend to advance any further on these fronts. Outside Quebec, Wolfe had failed to dislodge Montcalm's army from its entrenchments and all intelligence suggested that he was preparing to leave. The Chevalier de Lévis, in particular, believed that the British fleet would leave in early September.[1] Indeed, Wolfe himself was considering establishing a fortified outpost on the Île-aux-Coudres, where some of his men could spend the winter, while the remainder withdrew to Halifax and other North American ports. He wrote mournfully to William Pitt that 'the army is much weakened. By the Nature of the River, The most formidable part of this Armament is deprived of the power of acting; Yet we have almost the whole Force of

Canada to oppose. – In this Situation, there is such a Choice of Difficultys, that I own myself at a Loss how to determine. The Affairs of Great Britain I know, require the most vigorous Measure; But then the Courage of a Handfull of brave Men should be exerted only where there is some Hope of a favourable Event.'[2] Wolfe's despondency was echoed by Admiral Saunders, who wrote that 'the Enemy appear Numerous & seem to be strongly posted, but let the Event be what it will, we shall remain here as long as the Season of the year will permit, to prevent their detaching Troops from hence against General Amherst, and I shall leave Cruizers at the Mouth of the River to cut off any Supplies that may be sent them, and with strict orders to keep that station as long as possible'.[3] However, while Montcalm's army had every reason to feel confident, in reality the army's spirits were not so high. It had supplies only until 20 September. If the British army had not left by that time, it was unclear how long they could continue to fight. The British army had only a few weeks to determine the fate of Canada. In those few weeks, a combination of planning, leadership, skill and luck would change Canada for ever.[4]

Wolfe himself had grown increasingly impatient to launch another attack on the French, but he was held back by two obstacles. The first was the absence of Brigadier Murray, whom he had sent above Quebec with 1,200 of the army's best troops; the second was Wolfe's own ill health, which showed little sign of improving. Wolfe had dispatched Murray upstream following the debacle at Montmorency in the hope of disrupting French supplies and communications and spreading the war of terror and destruction above the town. However, from his base at Ste-Croix, twenty-five miles above Quebec, Murray could not remain in regular communication with Wolfe. He did not receive Wolfe's orders to return to the main army for some days. Further, the orders he had been given on departure were imprecise about when he should return and as the days turned into weeks Wolfe began to fret. On 22 August he wrote to Monckton that 'Murray by his long stay above & by detaining all our Boats, is actually master of the operations or rather puts an entire stop to them. I have writ twice to recall him.'[5] When Murray finally returned to Pointe-Lévy on 25 August, Wolfe now had the troops he needed to consider another attack.

Wolfe's illness posed a different problem. On 19 August his health, which had not been good for some time, deteriorated further. He developed a severe liver complaint which his doctors could only attempt to mollify through constant bleeding. Throughout the army there were fears that Wolfe might die, and indeed Wolfe himself believed that he was at death's door. He wrote to his brigadiers to ensure that 'the Publick service may not suffer by the General's indisposition, he begs the Brigadiers will be so good to meet & concert together for the publick utility & advantage, & to consider of the best method of attacking the Enemy'.[6] On 28 August, the three brigadiers met with Admiral Saunders to discuss possible plans for an attack. They met again on the following two days. Then on 31 August they were joined by Wolfe, who had recovered sufficiently to rise from his bed. Wolfe proposed another attack across the Montmorency, this time marching nine miles upstream in an attempt to flank the French entrenchments. The brigadiers opposed this, and recommended strongly to Wolfe that instead of seeking to attack Montcalm's army at Montmorency, the army should instead try to attack above Quebec. They argued that 'if we can establish ourselves on the north shore, the Marquis de Montcalm must fight us on our own terms[as] we are between him and his provisions and between him and the army opposing Genl Amherst'.[7]

The brigadiers proposed abandoning the post at Montmorency, leaving a skeleton guard of about 600 men at the posts on the Île d'Orléans and at Pointe-Lévy, and marching the remainder of the army overland to the mouth of the river

Etchemin. From there they could cross the St Lawrence river, using the many barges and transports which were by this time upstream of Quebec, and land somewhere near Pointe-aux-Trembles. They hoped that a landing this far above Quebec would be met without opposition. A landing closer to Quebec would be difficult, since most of the possible landing sites closer to the city were defended and garrisoned. Murray's raiding parties, which had been operating in this part of the St Lawrence for most of August, had been able to land without too much difficulty. Wolfe was not entirely happy at this plan. The landing place was twenty miles above Quebec. It would take his army at least a day to march to Quebec. This would give Montcalm plenty of time to move his troops from the Beauport shore to the Plains of Abraham, where they could entrench themselves. However, for the moment there was no better plan. Wolfe wrote despondently to Admiral Saunders that 'the Generals seem to think alike as to the operations, I, therefore, join with them, and perhaps we may find some opportunity to strike a blow'.[8]

For the attack above Quebec to take place in force, the camp at Montmorency had to be abandoned, since it could not be held against the French with a garrison of only a few hundred men. The evacuation of the camp was one of the more dangerous parts of the plan, for as the troops were withdrawing they would be vulnerable to attack from French forces across the river Montmorency. However, rather than seeing the withdrawal as potentially dangerous, Wolfe saw it as an opportunity to draw Montcalm out of his entrenchments. Consequently, before the men prepared to evacuate the camp on the morning of 3 September, he ordered several companies to hide themselves in the woods skirting the camp to create the impression that the camp had already been abandoned. Unfortunately there was some confusion during the evacuation, when troops mistook the burning of the barn in front of Monckton's headquarters, which was the sign for the start of the evacuation, as a French attack, and the chance to draw Montcalm into battle passed by. However, Wolfe had successfully extricated his men from the camp, a task which in itself was not easy.[9]

Wolfe now collected the main strength of his army at Pointe-Lévy and prepared his men to move above Quebec. One possible sign of Wolfe's lack of confidence in the expedition was his decision to dispatch Gorham with 1,500 men to raid the St Lawrence – a decision which seems strange at a time when he knew he needed all the manpower possible to attack Quebec, unless he secretly believed that such an attack was bound to fail. By 4 September, Wolfe's health seems to have recovered enough for him personally to supervise preparations for the expedition. With his usual concern for secrecy, he organised the marching orders of the men from Pointe-Lévy to the Etchemin river without consulting his brigadiers, who grew increasingly exasperated that he had taken over the direction of their grand enterprise. With just '1 Shirt, 1 pr Shoes, 1 pr of Stockings & a Blanket', crowded eight men to one tent, the men would have to endure cramped conditions. The rank and file of the army knew that some grand plan was afoot, but they were not sure what. Some believed that a grand attack was planned on Quebec City; others that the army was about to depart. With his concern for secrecy, Wolfe did nothing to dispel these contradictory rumours.[10]

The French army watched the movements of the British with some concern. Vaudreuil was hopeful that the British were preparing to withdraw. Their determination to burn the country seemed to support this conclusion, and news from deserters also suggested that they believed the army was withdrawing. Vaudreuil breathed a sigh of relief. Montcalm supposed that another attack was imminent and wavered between a belief that Wolfe was preparing to attack upstream from Quebec and a fear that this was just a ruse to force him to weaken his defences along the Beauport shore, whence the real attack would come. Wolfe's constant preoccupation with the Beauport shore during July and August finally convinced Montcalm that this was where he still intended to attack. He would not move his army, but he did send reinforcements to Bougainville, who was stationed above Quebec. The civilians who remained in Quebec and the surrounding countryside followed the movements of Wolfe's army and braced themselves for an attack. Having seen the smoke rising from the settlements along the St Lawrence, they feared for their safety. However, when no attack came, despair quickly turned to relief, and most also believed that the British were finally leaving.[11]

On 5 September, the British troops began their march from Pointe-Lévy. They proceeded overland to Gorham's Post on the Etchemin river, where they boarded the flat-bottomed boats and transports which were to take them upstream. By 6 September the bulk of the British army was above Quebec. The whole nature of the campaign had changed. The following day, 7 September, the men were given their final orders and prepared to make their landing. However, the weather deteriorated, with heavy rain and a choppy wind. The attack was delayed. Over the next two days the weather remained dismal, and Wolfe decided that he still could not order the landings.[12]

This delay was fortuitous. On 8 September, Wolfe travelled upstream, reconnoitring the north shore looking for a possible landing site. He returned the following day and spotted a potential landing site much closer to Quebec, at L'Anse au Foulon. On 10 September ,Wolfe took Holmes, Monckton and Townshend to look closely at this possible landing site, while Murray remained in command of the army. From their vantage point on the south shore the officers could see the spot clearly, and the open ground between it and the city. It was a mile and a half below Quebec, close enough to the city that the army could land and be upon the city without warning. The banks were steep and rocky, so steep that the French had stationed only a small number of troops there. Wolfe, however, thought that a landing there was possible, and there was a cart track from the river that wound up to the Plains of Abraham above. This could provide access for his army.[13]

Wolfe had now abandoned the brigadier's scheme of attack for one of his own, one that Townshend and Murray thought was particularly dangerous. While Wolfe met with his brigadiers he does not seem to have briefed them over these changes to the attack, and not surprisingly they resented this. Indeed, Murray would later write to Townshend that he had no record of Wolfe's 'concerning his scheme of landing betwixt point au Tremble, and St Augustin, but the publick orders are a sufficient proof of his intention to do it, and likewise of the suddenness of the thought of landing where we did. Indeed his orders throughout the Campaign shews little stability, stratagem or fixt resolution.'[14] Even the otherwise placid Holmes showed his frustration, writing that 'the alteration of the Plan of Operations was not, I believe approved of by many, beside himself. It had been proposed to him a Month before, when the first Ships passed the Town, and when it was entirely defenceless and unguarded: but Montmorency was then his favourite Scheme, and he rejected it. He now laid hold of it when it was highly improbable he should succeed, from every Circumstance that had happened since.'[15]

The brigadiers felt so strongly at their exclusion from Wolfe's deliberations that they considered themselves compelled to write a haughty letter to him on 12 September. They informed him that:

As we do not think ourselves sufficient inform'd of the several parts which may fall to our share in the execution of the

Descent you intend to morrow, We must beg leave to request from you as distinct orders as the nature of the thing will admit of, particularly to the place or places we are to attack. This circumstance, perhaps very decisive, we cannot learn from the publick orders, neither may it be in the power of the Naval Officer who lands the Troops to instruct us – As we should be very sorry no less for the publick than our own sakes, to commit any mistakes, We are persuaded you will see the necessity of this application which can proceed from nothing but a desire to execute your orders.[16]

Despite the misgivings of his brigadiers, Wolfe was determined to press ahead. Now that they knew they were to attack the French once more, the morale of the troops had risen sharply. An officer in Fraser's Regiment, for instance, reported that 'The army is in great spirits.'[17] However, crowded on board the small flat-bottomed boats, tossing about in the stormy St Lawrence, drifting downriver with the ebb tide then back upstream with the flood tide, many of the men grew sick and weak. On 9 September, Wolfe decided that the men would have to land at St-Nicholas and wait for better weather.[18]

The delay may also have given Wolfe the chance to confer with Holmes and Saunders about making the best use of the current and tide, for Wolfe made full use of tide and moonlight to time the assault perfectly. On 11, September the troops received orders to prepare to re-embark on the following afternoon. As they prepared to board, the men debated where they would attack. Some even feared that a direct assault on the town was intended. One British officer confided in his journal, 'By this day's orders it appears the general intends a most vigorous attack, supposed behind the town, where to appearance a landing is impracticable.'[19]

The vessels cast off from their anchorage at St-Nicholas around 2 a.m. They were to drop down with the tide at night to reach the landing place at L'Anse au Foulon just before dawn. Over the next two hours the ebb tide hurried the fleet down the river at a speed of up to six knots. By 4 a.m. the fleet had silently dropped nearly nine miles to the landing site. Not only was the tide perfect for the descent but so was the moon. The moon, which was in its last quarter, cast enough light to enable Wolfe's men to distinguish the vague outlines of the northern shore, but the direction of the moonlight meant that French sentries on the shore had little chance of identifying the fleet as it drifted downstream. It is not clear how far Wolfe was simply fortunate in his choice of night, or how far it was on the advice of his naval officers that he delayed the expedition until the night of 12–13 September. Almost certainly the skills honed by the captains of navy vessels operating on the St Lawrence during the previous eleven weeks influenced the fleet to choose the best time and tide for their purpose. The importance of the successful navigation to L'Anse au Foulon cannot be overstated. At Montmorency at the end of July, failures in navigation – to position the supporting gunboats and bring the landing vessels close to shore – accounted to a large extent for the British failure. On 13 September, the fleet performed its manoeuvres like clockwork. Indeed, Saunders himself wrote to Pitt that 'considering the Darkness of the Night & the Rapidity of the Current, this was a very critical operation; & very properly and successfully conducted'.[20]

If the tide and moon favoured the British, they may also have been fortunate in the state of the French defences at L'Anse au Foulon. There have been some suggestions that the landing was made possible by the treachery of Bigot and his officers, who sought to hide their mass of corruption by betraying Canada to the British, and who had been in secret correspondence with Wolfe. The evidence for this is entirely circumstantial, and instead it appears that the British were simply very lucky. The force guarding L'Anse au Foulon was reduced to a tiny garrison when the Guyenne Regiment, which had been stationed nearby, was recalled to the Beauport shore.[21] This was not treachery, but an indication of Montcalm's conviction that the British intended merely to force him to weaken the Beauport shore while still planning the major assault there, a belief which was encouraged by Saunders, who employed his warships below Quebec in making feints on the Beauport shore, and by deserters who still reported that this was the target for the attack. Montcalm believed that the cove at L'Anse au Foulon would not make a suitable landing place, and when Vaudreuil had suggested it should be guarded more securely he had written in reply that 'Only God, sir, can do the impossible... and we cannot believe the enemy have wings that would allow them in one night to cross water, land, climb rugged slopes and scale walls.'[22]

The British fleet was to land the troops in three waves. The first wave was to consist of Bragg's 28th Regiment, Kennedy's 43rd, Lascelles's 47th and Anstruther's 58th. The second wave consisted of part of Fraser's 78th, Amherst's 15th, Otway's 35th, the Louisbourg Grenadiers, and part of the second and third battalions of the 60th Royal American Regiment. The third and final wave to be landed would consist of the remainder of the Royal Americans and the troops who had remained at Pointe-Lévy, in particular Webb's 48th, who would be ferried directly across the St Lawrence.[23]

At about 4 a.m. the British flotilla approached L'Anse au Foulon. According to Major MacKellar, the British had discovered from a deserter that the French were expecting supply ships from Montreal to arrive in the early morning of 13 September. According to popular legend, when French-speaking Captain Donald MacDonald of Fraser's Highlanders was challenged by the French guards he replied that the boats were a supply convoy from Montreal and that if the guards did not keep quiet the British would hear them. If throughout their history providence had protected the Canadians against British attacks, on the morning of 13 September it deserted them. For once, good luck was with the British. MacDonald's replies were believed, and the flotilla remained undiscovered.[24]

There was more good fortune for the British when the tide carried the first boats a little further downstream. These boats contained the light infantry, commanded by Colonel William Howe, who now faced the task of climbing the steep cliffs nearly 200 feet high from the shore. However, they had landed just downstream from the French post, and were able to scramble up the cliff to the plain above undetected. Had any other troops landed at this point they might have been stranded, but with their training and light equipment Howe's men were able to scale the precipice. By the time the main body was landing at L'Anse au Foulon, the light infantry had appeared on the Plains of Abraham and were already engaging the French picket on the cliff top. The commander of the French post at L'Anse au Foulon was Captain Louis de Vergor. His detachment of around 100 men was clearly unprepared for the landing – but then the men had little reason to be particularly alert. In the first moments of the landing, Vergor's men were confused and disordered, as shots rang out in the darkness. Rather than being concentrated in one place they were scattered along the cliff top, and in the darkness disorder grew. Vergor did manage to send a messenger off to Quebec City raising the alarm, and there was sufficient skirmishing that the neighbouring pickets were alerted. However, according to MacKellar, 'after a little firing, that picket was dispersed by... three companies only, the captain was wounded, and with about half his picket taken prisoners; the remainder made their escape along the edge of the bank towards the town'.[25]

By 5 a.m., as the first light was beginning to appear over the horizon, the light infantry had scattered the French picket at the cove. The first landing, which included Wolfe himself, was safely ashore and the track up to the Plains of Abraham was secure. Wolfe hurried his men up to the Plains and gave orders to the light infantry to clear the few snipers who remained on the cliff top. At this point the battery at Samos, above L'Anse au Foulon, began to open fire on the second wave of landing craft as they approached the shore in the early morning twilight. Wolfe dispatched Murray with the 58th Regiment and some light infantry to take the battery and soon its guns were silenced.[26]

For Montcalm and Vaudreuil, all was confusion. When the first shots were heard in Quebec, it was presumed that a British ship had discovered the supply convoy from Montreal and was challenging it. When the alarm was rung in Quebec, most people presumed that it was yet another false alarm of a British attack and took no notice. At the main French camp on the Beauport shore the men, who had spent the night in their entrenchments waiting for a British assault, were preparing to go to sleep. Suddenly a messenger arrived. He brought a wild story about a British army landing at L'Anse au Foulon and reaching the Plains of Abraham above Quebec. It was clearly just another scare and another Canadian panic. One officer commented: 'We knew so well how difficult it would be to penetrate our lines at the point – if it was defended – that we did not believe a word of the mans story; we thought he had been driven out of his senses by fear.'[27] Slowly it became all too clear that the man was not out of his senses: the British had landed, but with how many men? Montcalm prepared to march his men to the Plains of Abraham, but without informing Vaudreuil of this. No one thought about recalling Bougainville, who was near Cap Rouge with 2,300 crack troops.

At 6 a.m. Wolfe began forming the main body of his troops on the Plains. The Plains of Abraham were an area of open ground to the west of the city of Quebec. The south side of the Plains was bordered by the steep cliffs dropping down nearly 200 feet to the St Lawrence. The north side was marked by the Ste-Foy road, which was lined with a scattering of houses and farm outbuildings and some rough scrubland. To the west were the Sillery Woods and to the east the land rose in the Buttes-à-Neveu which hid the city of Quebec. On the Plains the ground was generally open, with just a few defiles and rises offering cover. In addition, there may also have been a few acres of corn, and MacKellar also reported that there were 'some clumps of high brush' which all gave cover to French skirmishers in the centre. As his men first reached the plain, Wolfe drew them up in a line with their backs to the St Lawrence, but when the French army failed to materialise, and as his own numbers grew, Wolfe deployed his men in battle order across the Plains.[28]

On the right of his line Wolfe deployed Otway's 35th, who had to deal with French snipers in the uneven ground along the top of the cliff. To their left were the Louisbourg Grenadiers and then Bragg's 28th, Kennedy's 43rd, Lascelles's 47th, Fraser's Highlanders the 78th, and Anstruther's 58th. At 8 a.m. the third wave of troops, with Webb's 48th and the remainder of the 60th Royal Americans, landed from Pointe-Lévy. Wolfe immediately deployed the 48th as his main reserve while posting the Royal Americans on his left flank, with Amherst's 15th facing the growing menace of Canadian and Native American snipers in the houses and scrub along the Ste-Foy road.[29]

Among the French there was still some confusion. By now Montcalm and Vaudreuil knew for certain that the British had landed at L'Anse au Foulon, but it was not clear whether this was simply a diversionary attack to force Montcalm to pull his troops away from the Beauport shore, or an attack in force. Consequently, no order was yet sent to Bougainville to march to Quebec. One French officer wrote in his journal that so ill prepared were the French that the British:

were already in order of battle on the heights of Quebec where they even had some field pieces of small calibre, ere anyone in our camps was as yet aware that the enemy wished to attack us in that quarter. M. de Bougainville, who was only two leagues off, did not learn the fact, as he says, until eight o'clock in the morning, and M. de Vaudreuil, who was at much less than half that distance, was not exactly informed of it until about half-past six. The army, which had passed the night in bivouac in consequence of a movement perceptible among the enemy's barges at Point Levy, had returned into its tents.[30]

Sometime before 7 a.m., however, Montcalm and Vaudreuil seem to have realised that this was indeed the main attack; Saunders' movements near the Beauport shore had been just a feint. Montcalm now ordered the Chevalier Johnstone to the Beauport line to order the troops encamped there to march immediately for Quebec, while he set out for Quebec himself. Johnstone's task proved more difficult than anticipated, for, on first hearing the firing, Vaudreuil had sent orders to the line that the troops were to remain there and not on any account leave their posts. Johnstone now had to convince them to diso-bey their earlier orders and march with all haste to the defence of Quebec. It was not until 8 a.m. that French troops were crossing the St Charles River. Montcalm now withdrew all the *troupes de terre* from the camp at Beauport, leaving behind only a few *troupes de la Marine* and a more substantial number of militia totalling perhaps 1,500 men.[31]

The first French troops to arrive on the battlefield, not long after first light, were Canadian militia and a few Native American warriors who began to appear on the British flanks, particularly along the Ste-Foy Road. From here they skir-mished with the left flank of Wolfe's army. They were soon followed by the Guyenne Regiment and some of the garrison troops from Quebec City, who formed themselves on top of the Buttes-à-Neveu between Wolfe's army and the city walls. These troops were sufficient to prevent Quebec from being taken by a *coup de main*, but would hardly prevent Wolfe's army from taking the city by storm.[32]

Montcalm now began to assemble his army between the Buttes-à-Neveu and Quebec, just out of sight of Wolfe's men. By about 9.30 a.m. he had completed assembling his force. He had perhaps 4,500 men under his command. It is difficult to determine the exact composition of his army, but the force probably contained around 2,000 *troupes de terre*, and 600 *troupes de la Marine*, the remainder consisting of militia. This was a number very similar to Wolfe's army, but the large proportion of militia meant that Montcalm's army was inferior in quality to Wolfe's, which was composed entirely of seasoned regulars. Even the French regular regiments contained a number of militia men who had been incorporated into the units at the start of the campaign. There was little artillery on either side. The British had dragged two field guns onto the battlefield. The French had more, but how many is unclear. It seems most likely that there were only five French artillery pieces on the field of battle, but they do not seem to have been particularly well used.[33]

Montcalm now began forming his line of battle. On his right were the La Sarre and Languedoc Regiments under the command of Colonel Senezergues. In the centre, Montcalm himself commanded the Béarn and Guyenne Regiments, and on the left under Colonel Fontbrune was the Royal Roussillon Regiment. The militia and the *troupes de la Marine* were deployed on the flanks, particularly on the right flank where they occupied the scrub and houses along the Ste-Foy road and skirmished with Wolfe's left flank. Montcalm also deployed some militia and *troupes de la Marine* in front of his line as skirmishers to harass Wolfe's main line. Indeed, Townshend commented that 'the Enemy lined the Bushes in their Front with 1500 Indians & Canadians & I dare say had placed most of their best marksmen there who kept up a very galling tho' irregular fire upon our whole line'.[34] By now it was nearly 10 a.m. Why Montcalm made his next move will always be hotly debated. He knew that by this time Bougainville must be marching from Cap Rouge and would join him with some of the army's best troops before too long. Indeed, Bougainville could threaten Wolfe's men from the rear. With more time, he would also have been able to bring up more artillery from Quebec. Prudence should have dictated that he now wait and rest his men, many of whom had just rushed to the Plains from the Beauport camp. Instead, he gave the order for his men to advance and attack the British ranks. His opponents blamed the impetuosity on his jealousy of Vaudreuil, who was not yet on the field. If the battle was won before Vaudreuil arrived, he would have no share of the victory. Indeed, one French observer wrote:

> The rash haste with which M. de Montcalm had made his attack originated in jealousy. M. de Vaudreuil had, in a note requesting him to postpone the attack until he had reunited all his forces, previously advised him that he was marching in person with the Montreal battalions. Nothing more was required to determine a General who would have readily been jealous of the part the simple soldier would have taken in his successes. This ambition was that no person but himself should ever be named, and this turn of mind contributed not a little to make him thwart the different enterprises in which he could not appear.[35]

It seems more probable, however, that Montcalm was worried either that Wolfe would receive further reinforcements if he delayed an attack or, most likely, that he believed Wolfe's men were entrenching on the plain. Indeed, Wolfe had ordered his men to lie down to get some cover from the fire of the French skirmishers and this may have confused Montcalm. It may also have made him think that the British forces on the plain had been thrown into some confusion by the French artillery. At about 10 a.m. Montcalm gave the signal for his men to advance.[36]

Montcalm now ordered his regular units in the centre to attack the British line in column formation. That is, rather than all the men drawn up two or three deep facing the enemy, they were in column as if marching, with the front of the column facing the British. Townshend recorded in his journal: 'Their center was a column and formed by the battalions of *Bearn* and *Guienne*.'[37] This was not confusion, but reflected a traditional French offensive movement where the units advanced rapidly in columns, attempting to break the enemy formation not by their firepower but by close combat with the bayonet.[38] (It was also a formation which would be used successfully at the battle of Ste-Foy in April 1760.) Montcalm appears to have decided that he could not rely on the *troupes de la Marine* and the militia on the flanks to hold their ground against the British regulars, and instead sought to break the centre of the British line with his best regular troops. As the French advanced, the two pieces of British artillery played on them with grapeshot. This grapeshot, a collection of small iron balls put into a thick canvas bag and fired from a cannon, tore into the flesh of the advancing French units. One British officer reported that quickly 'the smell of gunpowder became nautious'.[39] At this point, Montcalm's earlier decision to combine militia with regular units proved a critical weakness. The Canadian militia among the regulars began to waver, but the main French body continued to advance, although by now in a little disorder and drifting to their right, towards the Ste-Foy road. One officer in Fraser's Regiment recorded the advance in some detail.

When they came within a reconoitring view they halted,
advancing a few of their Irregulars, who kept piquering with
one or two platoons, who were advanced for that purpose, at
the same time playing with three field pieces on our line. On
which the General [Wolfe] ordered the line to lay down till
the enemy came close, when they were to rise up and give
their fire. The enemy, thinking by our disappearing, that their
cannon disconcerted us, they thought proper to embrace the
opportunity; wheeling back from the centre, and formed three
powerful columns, advanced very regular with their cannon
playing on us. By this time we had one field piece on the right,
and two howats [howitzers] on the left who began to give fire;
the enemy huzza'd, advancing with a short trott (which was
effectually shortened to a number of them) they began their
fire on the left, the whole of them reclining that way.[40]

In the meantime, Wolfe was hurrying across the British line
directing his men and leading the defence. Here, more than
at any other time during the campaign, he showed his true
strength as a leader of his men. The French drew nearer and
nearer to the British line, literally until they could see the
whites of the British soldiers' eyes. The Canadian and French
troops were accustomed to wilderness fighting. Across North
America they had repeatedly bettered the British redcoats in
bush-fighting, but now on the Plains of Abraham this was the
style of fighting that the British troops had been trained for;
this was what the parade ground discipline had been intended
for. The British held their fire. The French closed to forty yards,
just one and a half times the length of a tennis court. Then the
British line opened fire. Townshend recorded that 'our Troops
reserved their fire till within 40 yards which was so well continued that the Enemy everywhere gave way'.[41]

The Canadians threw themselves to the ground. This was
interpreted by the regulars as fear and cowardice, yet it was

simply their traditional manner of fighting – when the enemy fired they lay down. In the heat of battle, the militia incorporated into the regulars simply fought as they had always fought. For the French regulars, their ranks already battered by grapeshot, the sudden apparent panic of the Canadians threw them into confusion and within moments they were broken and routed. They turned and ran. MacKellar reported that they were pursued 'within musket shot of their walls, and scarce looked behind till they had got within them'.[42]

On the British left, the battle had not been so decisive. Here the two battalions of the Royal Americans and Amherst's 15th faced the Canadian militia and *troupes de la Marine* who had formed in the scrub along the Ste-Foy road. Seeing the regulars routed, these Canadians did not give way. Indeed, one French officer reported that 'The rout was total only among the Regulars; the Canadians accustomed to fall back Indian fashion (*and like the ancient Parthians*) and to turn afterwards on the enemy with more confidence than before, rallied in some places, and under cover of the brushwood, by which they were surrounded, forced divers corps to give way, but at last were obliged to yield to the superiority of numbers.'[43]

The British troops should have been celebrating their victory. But then news spread among the army that their commander was mortally wounded. Captain John Knox recorded that 'our joy at this success is inexpressibly damped by the loss we sustained of one of the greatest heroes which this or any other age can boast of, – GENERAL JAMES WOLFE, who received his mortal wound, as he was exerting himself at the head of the grenadiers of Louisbourg'.[44] Wolfe's death was surrounded by pathos and symbolism: the great hero sacrificing himself for his country. Expiring at the moment of victory, the tragedy of Wolfe's last moments was later immortalised in Benjamin West's famous and inspiring, but grossly inaccurate, painting of the death of Wolfe. Wolfe had tirelessly paced the lines and with his familiar lean figure and bright scarlet coat he was probably a prime, if not easy, target for French snipers. He had received his first wound before the battle had even commenced. Shortly after 9 a.m., while on the left flank, he was struck by a bullet from a French sniper along the Ste-Foy road. The wound was not serious. As the French began to advance at 10 a.m. Wolfe was in the centre of the British ranks when he was again hit, this time in the groin, but he continued his duty without hesitation. He received his third and fatal wound when on the right wing with the Louisbourg Grenadiers, shortly after the Redcoats had fired their first volley. A musket ball entered his chest, and he collapsed to the ground. His final moments are enshrouded in as much myth as reality, as befits a hero who would come to embody the 'British spirit'. Wolfe seems to have been concerned that his men did not see how badly he was wounded and he was carried away from the front line.[45] James Henderson, a volunteer in the Louisbourg Grenadiers, recounted that:

When the Genrl Received the Shot I Caut Hold of him And Carried him off the Field, he Walked About one Hundred yards And then Beged I would Let Sit Down, Which I Did. Then I Opened his Breast, And found his Shirt full of Blood At Which he Smiled And When he Seen the Distress I Was In, My Dear, Said he, Dont Grive for me, I Shall Be Happy In a Few Minutes. take Care of your Self As I see your Wounded. But Tell me O tell me How Goes the Battle their, Just then Came some Officers Who told him that the Freinch had civen Ground & Our trooups Was pursuing Them to the Walls of the town, he Was then Lying in my Arms Just Expirin That Great Man Whos Sole Ambition Was his Country Glory Raised himself up on this News And Smile in my Face. Now, Said he, I Die Contented.[46]

With Wolfe's death, command devolved onto Monckton, but he was also too badly wounded to command the army, as were many other officers. Townshend thus found himself in command of the army. However, with so many officers wounded it was some time before he realised that the command was now his. This gave the French a chance to extricate themselves and allowed the British pursuit to degenerate. On the British left, Murray led the Highlanders in an attempt to take the bridge over the St Charles River. Wielding their broadswords, they rushed into action and drove the French back. However, despite the rout of the main French army, the Canadian militia and *troupes de la Marine* in the scrub still continued to fight and peppered Murray's troops with gunshot from their left, while Quebec's cannon poured grapeshot at them from their right. The Highlanders suffered considerable losses. Indeed, MacKellar commented that 'We had more killed and wounded in the skirmishing than in the general action.'[47] Townshend's first order was therefore to call off the pursuit. This allowed the French to regroup their forces. However, Townshend had little choice for he needed to prepare his own forces to meet the expected counter-attack from Bougainville, advancing from Cap Rouge. During the course of the battle, the British had lost about sixty men killed and 600 wounded. French casualties are more difficult to ascertain but were probably slightly higher, around 900 men killed and wounded.[48]

For the French, the situation was now desperate. Following the rout of the main attack, it should have been possible for the French army to reform, and to wait for the arrival of Bougainville and his fresh troops before counter-attacking. French losses had been considerable but not overwhelming, and the militia and *troupes de la Marine* were still fighting. The battle could have been continued into the afternoon. Shortly before noon, the main body of the army began to muster in the entrenchments at the western end of the St Charles bridge. Some of the officers, however, seem to have lost their nerve. One French account maintained that 'Divers officers of the Regular troops hesitated not to say openly, in presence of the soldier, that no other course remained for us than to capitulate promptly for the entire Colony.'[49] The collapse of French morale was in part due to Montcalm's own injury, for he too had been seriously wounded towards the end of the battle in the stomach and thigh, as had his junior officers. Montcalm was carried into Quebec, to the Ursuline Hospital, where he died early the next day. Vaudreuil, who only seems to have arrived on the battlefield after the French columns had been routed, now took command of the army but, lacking the confidence of the regular officers, he was unable to rally the troops effectively.[50]

The collapse of military morale may also have been heightened by civilian panic. Most civilians were quickly aware of the disaster. Indeed, many seem to have watched the battle from the walls of the city or other vantage points. In the General Hospital, on the edge of the battlefield, the nuns witnessed the carnage first-hand. Soon the hospital was filled with the dead and dying, both French and British. One nun recorded:

> We witnessed the carnage from our windows. It was in such a scene that charity triumphed, and caused us to forget self-preservation and the danger we were exposed to, in the immediate presence of the enemy. We were in the midst of the dead and the dying, who were brought in to us by hundreds, many of them our close connexions; it was necessary to smother our griefs and exert ourselves to relieve them. Loaded with the inmates of three convents, and all the inhabitants of the neighbouring suburbs, which the approach of the enemy caused to fly in this direction, you may judge of our terror and confusion.[51]

Vaudreuil now summoned the officers of the army to a council of war, and sent a message to Montcalm on his deathbed asking for his advice. Montcalm simply advised him that he had three choices: make a new attack; surrender; or retreat to Jacques Cartier, between Quebec and Montreal. Vaudreuil argued passionately for the army to counter-attack, possibly waiting until the following morning. However, the officers, still shaken by the rout, and having little faith in Vaudreuil's leadership, argued that the army should now retreat to Jacques Cartier to protect their supply lines with Montreal.[52]

Sometime after midday, Bougainville arrived on the western edge of the battlefield. Seeing that the battle was lost, he waited for instructions from Vaudreuil. With the determined opposition of the army officers to any counter-attack, Vaudreuil realised that he had little choice but to retreat, abandoning much of the army's equipment and provisions in the Beauport camp. He sent instructions to Jean-Baptiste-Nicolas-Roch de Ramezay, the governor of Quebec City, on how to conduct the siege, explicitly ordering him not to wait until the 'last extremity' before surrendering, and even drafting the terms on which he could accept surrender. He also hurriedly recalled Lévis from Montreal, where he had been sent a few weeks earlier to co-ordinate that city's defence against any advance by Amherst, to take over command of the army on the St Lawrence.[53]

The battle on the Plains of Abraham had been one of the most important in North American history. Before the battle ,the British army had been frustrated and seemed on the verge of retreat. The French had begun to sense victory. In just one morning all had changed. The British victory on the Plains was clearly in part the result of good fortune. Divine providence, which had protected Canada previously, had finally deserted the colony. The decision to recall the Guyenne Regiment which had been stationed on the Plains, the confusion over the supply convoy expected from Montreal and the poor readiness of Vergor's men were all determined by luck rather than by any skill (or treachery). The successful navigation of the British fleet from St-Nicholas to L'Anse au Foulon probably owed as much to luck as to the skill of the naval officers. While skill certainly determined the judgement of tide and moonlight, it could not control the weather, nor could the British know for certain how easily they could approach the shore at L'Anse au Foulon.

Leadership also played a central role. Much of the debate over the relative merits of both Montcalm and Wolfe has stemmed from the bitter disputes they both endured with their subordinates. Both Wolfe and Montcalm clearly had their strengths. Wolfe was a charismatic leader of his men and during the battle his presence served to steady his men and preserve their good order. He was also a good tactician, if not strategist, who had redesigned the training and exercises of his troops. In particular, as early as 1755 Wolfe had formulated a new tactic for countering French column attacks in force. This was the tactic he used when the French army charged on 13 September. He had also adopted a new method of platoon-firing in battle which simplified the mass fire of the army and was used to such devastating effect on the Plains of Abraham. It might be true to say, as some of his detractors have, that he was a better regimental commander than army commander. However, he faced a difficult task and was further handicapped by ill health, which plagued him for much of the expedition. Even had he not taken Quebec, if his success or failure was judged by one of the original aims of the campaign, to divert Montcalm's troops until Amherst could drive into the heart of Canada from the south, he had succeeded.[54]

Montcalm, for his part, had a good grasp of strategy and of the best way of preserving his force. He had the confidence of his military officers, if not the civilian officers of Canada. On 13 September, however, Montcalm's fatal decision to attack was a major blunder which was central to the French defeat. Montcalm also seems to have made a tactical mistake in combining Canadians with regular units. Although this may have made sense in fighting irregular skirmishes, when it came to a regular battle it proved a major shortcoming. In addition, Montcalm had become preoccupied with defending the Beauport shore, to the detriment of any other quarter. Wolfe's obsession with secrecy, and his constant attempts throughout the campaign to mislead Montcalm, served to leave the French general completely unsure about Wolfe's attack. This was not necessarily a major positive trait of Wolfe; indeed, C.P. Stacey wrote rather cogently that 'Wolfe's planning had an illogical and unpredictable quality that made it a very difficult intelligence problem.'[55] But that 'illogical and unpredictable quality' was central in winning the battle on 13 September. Even as British troops were marching onto the Plains of Abraham, Montcalm still worried that this was merely a ruse for Wolfe's attack on the Beauport shore.

The qualities of the troops who fought in the battle were also central in securing the British victory. The British troops, highly trained and disciplined, had a great advantage in regular combat against the French and Canadian forces, who were better prepared and equipped for wilderness fighting. Although the morale of the British troops had dropped during the weeks of waiting, on the morning of 13 September as they waited for the French to attack it was as high as it had been at their first landing. As the French advanced towards them, the British troops held their nerve and their fire, waiting until their first volley would have the greatest impact. In contrast, French and Canadian morale had been wavering. Hope that the British would soon withdraw was tempered by the chronic lack of supplies and provisions. As they advanced towards the British line, the lack of discipline and poor morale proved central in the rout of the regular forces. All these separate influences – luck, skill, training, leadership – combined on 13 September to give the British a major victory. By that evening British forces were encamped outside the walls of Quebec City. The real siege had now begun, but the conquest of Canada was very far from over. The next task of the British army was to take the city itself, if necessary by storm. For the French, every attempt had to be made to relieve the town before it was stormed.

The city's defences were substantial enough to resist an attack, even on the weaker landward side where the British were now encamped. However, if the British artillery was brought ashore, and if some of the cannon from Pointe-Lévy were transported to the new batteries overlooking the city, it could only be a matter of time before the British would batter down the walls and enter the city. Most pressing was the lack of supplies. The decision during the bombardment of the city to evacuate supplies to more secure warehouses outside the city and the range of British artillery meant that there were no food stores within the city. In addition, Lévis reported that the haste with which the army abandoned their camp at Beauport was so great that each company was only allowed 'to take one tent and a cooking pot or two'. Some men lost their packs and the officers had to abandon their baggage. Worse still, they were forced 'to leave the artillery, the ammunition, and the supplies'.[56]

Ramezay had the thankless task of conducting the city's defence. His first task was to make an invoice of the supplies and provisions available in Quebec. He found to his horror that the city had only enough supplies for five or six days, even if the men were reduced to half rations. Even the garrison was grossly under-strength. Most of the troops now in Quebec were militia and sailors, and there were only about 200 regular troops. That number grew less as daily some of the militia deserted and returned to their homes.[57]

Townshend's first task was to secure the British army's camp on the Plains. He thus sent his men to cut down all the scrub around the camp, to secure the houses on the Ste-Foy road, and to throw up redoubts around the camp. This was all done by nightfall on the day of the battle. It was not until the next day that the troops began to bury their dead. To facilitate the landing of supplies and artillery, Townshend also ordered the construction of a new road up the cliff from L'Anse au Foulon to the Plains of Abraham to replace the narrow path. Only once these tasks had been completed did Townshend order his men to begin the construction of batteries and entrenchments to besiege the town. He also sent out men to secure the General Hospital, which lay to the north of the Plains of Abraham outside the city walls. For the nuns in the hospital, the arrival of the British troops created alarm. They reported that 'the silence and consternation which prevailed, was suddenly interrupted by loud and repeated knocks at our doors. Two young Nuns, who were carrying broth to the sick, unavoidably happened to be near when the door was opened. The palor and fright which overcame them, touched the officer, and he prevented the guard from entering; he demanded the appearance of our Superiors, and desired them to assure us of protection; he said that part of the English force would enter and take possession of the house.'[58]

On 17 September, Lévis arrived to take over command of the French army. He realised that the British positions outside Quebec were vulnerable. The British were sandwiched between his force at Jacques Cartier and the city of Quebec. They could not divide their force to attack French detachments from Jacques Cartier, nor did they have enough men to surround Quebec completely and prevent communication between the French army and the town. His men could harass the British from the woods at Cap Rouge, Ste-Foy and St-Michel, taking full advantage of their skill in fighting in the woods. This might even allow the garrison to sortie and supplies to be transported into the town. Plans for an attack, Lévis argued, would help to recover the army's morale. With Lévis in command, the army began its move back towards Quebec.[59]

Within Quebec, however, military and civilian morale had collapsed. On 15 September, Ramezay called a council of war to discuss the city's defence. The inhabitants begged him to surrender. They had seen the devastation wrought by the British on the settlements of the St Lawrence and worried that the town would be sacked and many of its residents massacred if it were taken by storm. Civilian pressure, as much as military necessity, forced Ramezay to open negotiations with Townshend. The following day, 16 September, he sent word to Vaudreuil that he had only six days' provisions remaining and warned him that he would have to surrender if he did not receive speedy relief.[60] Vaudreuil had already drafted a surrender document and, before his departure on 13 September, had specifically instructed Ramezay that he was not 'to wait for the enemy carrying the town by assault; therefore, as soon as he shall fail of provisions, he is to hoist the white flag and send the most capable and intelligent officer of his garrison to propose its capitulation'.[61]

Negotiations between the beleaguered garrison and the British began on 16 September. Ramezay's first request was to allow the women and children who were still in the town to be evacuated. Townshend agreed to this, and that evening a party of bedraggled civilians left the town across the St Charles River bridge. Ramezay now opened formal negotiations for the city's surrender. Negotiations continued for two days, but eventually Townshend agreed to relatively generous terms which granted the garrison the honours of war and promised that it would be immediately transported back to

France. Civilian property was to be respected and protected, as was the Roman Catholic Church. Nothing better could have been expected. Indeed, Townshend may have worried that the terms were too generous, for he wrote to Pitt that 'the terms you find we granted will I flatter myself be approved of by his Majesty considering the Enemy assembling in our Rear & what is far more formidable The very whet & Cold Season which threatened our Troops'.[62]

On the morning of 18 September, as Lévis was mustering his troops in an attempt to relieve the city, he heard that Ramezay had surrendered. He was angered, as relief was so close to hand – there were even suggestions that Ramezay had known this but had still gone ahead with the surrender. Vaudreuil wrote to Paris that he had 'expected a more protracted resistance, having adopted the surest measures to convey provisions into that town'.[63] However, as it was Vaudreuil himself who had drafted the surrender terms before departing with the troops on 13 September, his opposition seems rather perverse. The principal motives for surrender seem to have been civilian fear of a massacre rather than simply the lack of military supplies. Indeed, François Daine, who remained in Quebec and acted as the French mayor during the occupation, queried whether 'in such a position, can it be said with justice that the Commandant was in too great a hurry, and might have waited? No, without doubt, unless to expose his garrison and the people to be put to the sword, which would indubitably have been the case.'[64] Whatever the reasons, on the afternoon of 18 September British troops took possession of the city of Quebec.

As news of the surrender rippled through the French camp, the Canadian troops and militia began to desert in droves. It was soon clear that the campaign of 1759 was over. The French army would go into winter quarters and hope to renew the fight the following spring. After so many failed attempts, the capital of Canada had now fallen to the British. Whether the British army could hold Quebec, however, was a different matter. The campaign of 1759 might have finished, but the campaign for control of Quebec was far from over. Now the British army would have to prepare to face a new enemy: the bitter Canadian winter.

7

Survivors

In Britain, people had waited all summer for news of
Quebec's fate. The wives and sweethearts that soldiers
had left behind in Britain hankered for news. Townshend's
wife, Charlotte Compton, Baroness Ferrers and Compton,
was no different and fretted at the lack of definite news
from Quebec. She wondered if her husband were still alive.
A close family friend attempted to reassure her, writing to
her 'Give me Leave to observe... that I a little fear, least yr
Ladyships Spirits should Sink a little, because Good News is
long a Coming from Quebec... No News therefore is good
News.'[1] On 14 October, Wolfe's disheartening dispatch written
on 2 September arrived in London. Wolfe began his letter by
informing Pitt that 'I wish I could upon this occasion have
the honour of transmitting to you, a more favourable Account
of the Progress of His Majesty's Arms; But the Obstacles we
have met with in the operations of the Campaign are much
greater than we had reason to expect or could forsee.'[2] He
doubted he would capture Quebec. Wolfe's news spread gloom

amongst the government and the country. So much political
and financial capital had been invested in the campaign. The
government was not alone in worrying.

On 16 October the London gazettes were full of Wolfe's
gloomy predictions of failure. The mood in the capital was glum.
Then, towards evening, fresh news arrived. Quebec had fallen.
Throughout the city there was wild jubilation. The following
morning, according to the *Gentleman's Magazine*, 'His Royal
Highness the Prince of Wales and the Royal Family with most
of the Nobility in town, waited upon his majesty at Kensington,
to pay their compliments on the joyful news of taking Quebec.
The Park and Tower guns were fired, flags every where displayed
from steeples, and the greatest illuminations were made throughout the city and suburbs that were ever known.'[3] Throughout
Britain church bells were rung and grand illuminations held.
Jubilation at the great victory, however, was tinged with grief at
the death of Wolfe, whose tragic death at the moment of victory
had ensured his place in myth.

If there were mixed feelings in Britain about the victory,
for the British soldiers who remained in the city the conquest was a distinctly mixed blessing. The surrender of the
city of Quebec on 18 September marked a dramatic shift in
the campaign for control of Canada, but it did not mark the
end of the campaign. The British garrison would now have to
survive the bitter Canadian winter. If the French army rallied
in the spring, especially if it received aid from Europe, there
was every chance that it could drive the British from the city.
The campaign for Quebec and the conquest of Canada were
far from over. Indeed, one French diarist recorded that 'the
taking of this town and the destruction of the villages and
settlements on which it depended did not mean the loss of
Canada, since we were still master of the upper country and
the English could not be considered strong in such a weakly
defended town during the winter'.[4]

On 19 September, the French troops who had surrendered in Quebec began their departure for France, while most of the militia were allowed to return to their homes. Some of the troops, particularly the *troupes de la Marine*, left behind their wives and children, as under the terms of the surrender civilians were not allowed to leave the colony until its fate had been determined by a treaty in Europe. Consequently, many government officers were also allowed to stay behind to look after the French civilians who remained in the city. Most wealthy Canadian merchants, with Monckton's permission, abandoned the city for the relative comfort and safety of Montreal, while poorer families sought shelter in the surrounding towns and villages. Most had to leave behind valued possessions and food stocks, for they were prohibited from taking anything which might prove of use to their conquerors and their carts were searched as they left the city.[5]

As the British garrison entered Quebec, they found the city in a battered state. Major Patrick MacKellar recorded that he 'found the buildings in general in a most ruinous condition, infinitely worse than we could have imagined; for, besides those burnt, there was hardly a house in the town that was not hurt by either shot or shells, and scarce habitable without some repairing'.[6] Captain John Knox agreed that 'the havoc is not to be conceived. Such houses as are standing are perforated by our shot, more or less; and the low town is so great a ruin, that its streets are almost impassable.'[7] Monckton, who now commanded the British army, had only a few short weeks to prepare the garrison before the onset of the bitter Canadian winter. The French army remained a potent threat and was lurking at Jacques Cartier, only two days' brisk march away. The city's defences were not overly impressive. Murray described the city as 'at best a strong Cantonment and that it's safety must chiefly depend upon the Vigilance and bravery of those who guard it'.[8] A French counter-attack might succeed. Perhaps even more importantly, the garrison had to be prepared to overcome cold and short rations through the winter.

Monckton immediately put the entire garrison to work. The first task was to prevent injury from falling buildings and Monckton ordered the demolition of all structures in danger of collapse. Only then could the men begin the tasks of repairing the city's defences, patching up buildings for winter quarters, cutting wood, collecting food, and in addition carry out all the regular duties of soldiers, especially maintaining order among an uneasy Canadian population. All these tasks needed to be completed quickly, as the approach of winter would not only mean that the men would be unable to work outside, but also that the fleet would soon have to depart, taking with it the labour of the sailors. Not only would the departure of the fleet mean the loss of the sailors but also the hospital ship, the Louisbourg Grenadiers and many of the rangers. The loss of the rangers would be a particular burden to the garrison over the winter, when their skills in cold-weather combat would have been most valuable. In addition, the two superior brigadiers were also planning on leaving Quebec. Townshend, disheartened by the nature of the campaign and fearful about political gossip and rumours over his opposition to Wolfe, was desperate to leave as soon as he could. Monckton, still recovering from the wounds he had received on the Plains of Abraham, would spend the winter recuperating in New York. This would leave Murray in command of the garrison over the winter, a thankless and difficult task.[9]

By the end of September, there were sufficient habitable buildings available for Monckton to quarter his men in the city. He divided the city into districts, and on 27 September each regiment drew lots to determine where in the city they would take quarters. As British troops moved into the city, the Bishop de Pontbriand, Catholic Bishop of Quebec, wrote to Paris lamenting that 'the Episcopal palace is almost destroyed and supplies only one habitable apartment... The Recollet convent and Jesuit college are nearly in the same condition. The English however, have somewhat repaired them for quarters for the troops; they have taken possession of such houses in the town as are the least damaged, and even daily drive citizens from their houses, who, by means of money, having had some apartment fitted up; or confine them to such narrow compass, by the number of soldiers whom they billet on them, that almost all are forced to abandon that unfortunate town.'[10]

Once they had taken possession of their quarters, the men did their best to make them as warm and habitable as they could. John Montrésor reported that he was 'quartered in a house that has no roof, not a single Board', but he believed that he could 'make my quarters as good as any, in the idle hours, I get a couple of carpenters or rather aim to get, tomorrow to begin roofing'.[11] The demand for labour was so great that some civilians even returned to the city to labour. Carpenters, smiths, bricklayers and many others all laboured repairing the devastation. However, language problems were severe. A few officers had a smattering of French and some of Fraser's Highlanders had served in the French army following the battle of Culloden (their language skills would prove extremely valuable). Beyond this, British officers had few means of communicating with the Canadian civilians they now controlled, few of whom spoke any English. In an attempt to ease the situation Murray appointed François Cugnet, a Canadian who was fluent in English, as judge of Beauport and Charlesbourg. But one judge could do little by himself.[12]

Language problems do not seem to have prevented British troops from making other close liaisons with Canadian civilians. As early as 6 October, orders had to be issued banning marriages between troops and Canadians. Less than a month later, Murray had to repeat the orders. The speed with which British troops began to marry Canadian civilians, less than three weeks after the surrender of Quebec, suggests that some of these liaisons had begun long before the city's surrender. Around the fixed camps on the Île d'Orléans and at Pointe-Lévy, the men had plenty of opportunity to develop relationships with the Canadian women whose farms were close to the army camps or who ventured to the markets to sell their produce. The repeated investigations of Canadian civilians for selling liquor or encouraging desertion also suggest a significant amount of day-to-day interaction. Indeed, one resident was convicted by an army court of providing deserters with traditional Canadian winter clothing to escape army patrols. Many of the Irish and Highland troops may also have been Roman Catholics (who were not officially allowed to join the British army), for otherwise it is difficult to explain the influence some of the Canadian priests seem to have held over them. For instance, Murray discovered one priest who was 'instruct[ing] some of our Sick Soldiers in the Hospital'.[13]

While these developing relationships, and the demand for Canadian food and labour, may have helped to win the support of some Canadians for the new British regime, the effect of the liquor, which seems to have flowed surprisingly freely, served to threaten such benefits. As early as 16 September, the army was receiving 'complaints… of the great disorders that have been already Committed in the Neighbourhood of the Camp by the Soldiers which has obliged the Country People who were Coming in with fresh Provisions to return'. On 19 September, the day that the British army first marched into Quebec, orders were issued that 'Whereas Several Soldiers have been Robbing & Plundering, notwithstanding the General's strict Orders to the Contrary, whoever will discover the Persons Concerned in Robbing & Plundering shall receive 5 Guineas Reward.' By the beginning of October Monckton was even compelled to order his officers to 'take great care to keep their Guards Sober'.[14]

After such a long and hard campaign, facing a long and bitter winter, with few supplies and comforts, the British troops seem to have attempted to make the most of the few weeks before the onset of cold weather. Throughout October and November the extent of drunkenness grew. Murray attempted to control the sale of liquor by demanding licenses for all sutlers, but many of the Canadian inhabitants openly flouted his restrictions. He forbade the troops from leaving their quarters after dark unless on duty, but many still found ways to sneak out to the nearest liquor-seller. Eventually Murray was forced to ban the sale of all liquor within the city or its suburbs. This still did not prevent the widespread abuse of alcohol and Murray recorded that 'as drunkenness & Theft continued to reign Predominant vices in the Garrison, highly Prejudicial to the service, I... orderr'd for the future every man who was found drunk to receive Twenty lashes every morning till he acknowledged where he got it'.[15] It soon became clear that it was not only the Canadians who provided liquor to the troops. Indeed, the major source of liquor was probably the many sutlers who accompanied the army, particularly the wives, sweethearts and mistresses of the troops. Because Quebec was under martial law, and removed from the prying eyes and sensibilities of the British public, women could be exposed to the full vigour of military discipline. Indeed, in November Knox reported that 'two women have been whipped through the streets for selling rum contrary to orders'.[16] Such fierce and public corporal punishment on female camp followers was almost unheard of in Europe.

As the weather began to close in, maintaining order and discipline became an even greater problem for the isolated garrison. With little to relieve the tedium of garrison life, with no contact with the outside world, fearing French attack, dreading the coming bitter cold, it is not entirely surprising that soldiers sought some means of escape. Increasing numbers of men, drunk or hungover, missed duty. As Murray attempted to punish troops for their drunken antics, their response was to desert before they were caught. Throughout early November there was a worrying increase in desertion. On 14 November, Murray woefully recorded in his journal that 'a very unusual Desertion at this time prevail'd among the Troops, the Plunderg kind of war wch had been carried on this last Campaign, had so debauch'd the Soldier'.[17] Throughout the autumn and early winter, regular courts martial were convened to sentence drunks and, more importantly, deserters. Their sentences became increasingly severe. At one court martial in November, for instance, one soldier received the death penalty and two others 1,000 lashes each for desertion. At another in December, four men were tried for quitting their posts and, in a drunken binge, breaking open the king's stores to steal liquor. Two of them were sentenced to death, while the others received 800 lashes each.[18]

While many of the deserters were simply trying to avoid punishment for drunkenness, others seem to have been encouraged by their Canadian associates. In some cases these were merely the sellers of liquor attempting to continue their clandestine trade. Others were the girlfriends and mistresses of the men, who sought to continue their relationships despite the prohibitions on soldiers leaving their quarters after dark. Some, however, were clearly estranged Quebecers. In particular, some of the Jesuit priests and Ursuline nuns who tended to the sick seem to have actively encouraged desertion.[19]

The growing association between the ranks and Canadian civilians caused new problems for Murray. His natural inclination seems to have been to treat the Canadians with much tolerance. Indeed, he wrote to Amherst:

...the Canadians have been taught to look upon us as Barbarians, whose only view was their destruction; hence the obstinate resistance they have made, and the eagerness they shew'd to take up arms against us; They begin now to be astonish'd with our conduct, [and] will soon be convinced that there is no deceit in it, and hardly here after so easily be perswaded to take up arms against a nation they must admire, & who will always have it in their power to burn, and distroy. Sufficient examples they have had this summer of the horrors of War; they were not treated tenderly before we had the good fortune to take Quebec; they will remember that no doubt, and it may be supposed they will not forget any instances of Clemency, & generosity that may be shewn then, since they have been entirely in our power.[20]

Initially, Murray sought to provide as great a degree of normality as possible for the residents of Quebec: markets were established; priests continued to say Mass; property was protected; some officials of the French regime were allowed to continue their functions. Officers were even ordered to raise their hats to any Canadian civilians that they passed in the street, 'because it is a civility due to the people who have chosen to live under our laws'.[21] However, Murray's willingness to provide a degree of toleration for the Quebecers was soon tempered by his need to protect the garrison. Restrictions on the civilian population became increasingly strict as the winter progressed. Initially, the only limits placed on civilian activity related to their potential role as spies; they were banned, for instance, from walking on the city walls or near the batteries. Soon restrictions were placed on the removal of goods from the city. Any item which might assist the garrison had to remain and all carts were searched at the city gates to ensure that they carried no 'Provisions, Leather & Soap and Candles'. In November, a curfew was placed on all civilians, who also had to report all guests who resided in their homes. All unauthorised correspondence with friends and relations in Montreal was banned 'on pain of death'. By December, so strict had the restrictions become that some civilians were 'whipped through the streets, for appearing abroad at an unseasonable time of night, without a lanthorn'.[22]

The increasingly strict measures, not surprisingly, drew some opposition from the Canadian residents of Quebec. However, there seems to have been an understanding that while the rule of the British was strict, it was not arbitrary. Indeed, one of the nuns at the General Hospital later wrote that 'we could not, without injustice, complain of the manner in which they treated us'.[23] The reason for the increasingly draconian nature of these measures was the failure of the British garrison to control the region outside the city. Following the surrender of Quebec, Murray had published a manifesto to the inhabitants on the St Lawrence River, warning them not to take up arms against the British. Each parish priest was to read the manifesto to his assembled parishioners and post a copy on the church door. Of course only those in areas firmly under British control did so. The inhabitants were compelled to hand over their guns, only two men in each parish being allowed to retain their guns for hunting. Everyone was required to take an oath of loyalty to King George II and each parish was to send a hostage to Quebec to ensure the good behaviour of the residents.[24]

Such measures did not serve to end French attacks on the British troops. As one of the nuns in the General Hospital reported, the Canadians

> did not remain inactive, but were constantly on the alert, harassing the enemy. The English were not safe beyond the gates of Quebec... Prisoners were frequently made, which so irritated the Commander, that he sent out detachments to pillage and burn the habitations of the country people... The English did not fail to require the oath of allegiance to their King; but,

notwithstanding this forced obligation, which our people did not consider themselves bound to observe, they joined the flying camps of the French, whenever an opportunity offered.[25]

As opposition to the British regime continued outside Quebec, Murray, like Wolfe before him, was goaded into a series of punitive raids. However, Murray's raids and retribution were more limited than Wolfe's. In November he sent out a number of detachments to the west of Quebec to Lorette and Ste-Foy and towards the French post at Jacques Cartier. These detachments were to disarm the civilian population, and to destroy the homes and property of those who were still openly fighting with the French.[26]

Murray's actions reflected his realisation that Lévis was dependent upon civilians for both intelligence and supplies. As the winter passed, this dependence increased. Shortly after the surrender of Quebec, Lévis had dismissed the militia to reduce the burden on the army's already strained food supplies. He set his remaining men, mostly regulars, to work constructing a fort at Jacques Cartier, hoping that the post would prevent any advance from Quebec on Montreal. When that was completed he sent out small parties in an attempt to maintain civilian morale and support, and to round up what supplies and firewood they could find. On occasion these parties skirmished with the advanced guards of the British forces around Quebec. Finally, as mid-winter approached, he sent his men into winter quarters amongst the *habitants* between Trois Rivières and Montreal.[27]

For the British garrison in Quebec, skirmishes with the French in the autumn and early winter of 1759 were more a nuisance than a serious threat. The real threat came from the deepening cold and the shortage of supplies. Throughout October there were fierce storms and gales which battered the few remaining naval vessels in the basin. Then in mid-November the weather turned cold. By the end of November most of the smaller rivers and lakes had frozen over. For the men, the change to cold weather was initially enjoyable. On 13 November, Knox reported that 'the winter weather is now set in, though it is not yet severe, and is much more agreeable than the extreme wet season we have had for some time past'. The bright sunshine which lasted through the end of November was a welcome change from the grey skies and wind which had preceded it. The men soon began to amuse themselves with tobogganing and skating on the frozen ponds and rivers.[28]

Then the men encountered their first problem, not the cold but the ice. On 26 November, Knox reported that 'our streets and passages are so slippery, that it is with the greatest difficulty we can walk in them'.[29] The snow and ice made transporting wood and provisions difficult, as well as walking. Murray ordered his men to prepare 'creepers' (grips which fastened over the bottom of the men's boots), snow shoes, toboggans and sleighs. As the snow grew deeper, Murray ordered beacons to be built along the sides of the roads out to the blockhouses at Lorette and Ste-Foy. He also requisitioned sleighs from the inhabitants of the parishes surrounding Quebec. Then came the cold. On 13 December, Knox reported that 'the weather is now become inconceivably severe'.[30] Over the next two weeks more than 200 men suffered from frostbite. They resorted to whatever skins or furs they could find to keep themselves warm while on duty. Such was their range of attire that Knox reported 'our Guards on the grand parade, make a most grotesque appearance in their different dresses; and our inventions to guard us against the extreme rigour of the climate are various beyond imagination: the uniformity, as well as the nicety, of the clean, methodical soldier, is buried in the rough fur-wrought garb of the frozen Laplander; and we rather resemble a masquerade than a body of regular troops'.[31]

The problems of cold were compounded by the lack of fresh provisions. The basic diet with which the troops were provided was scarcely adequate in calories. However, any soldier who complained about the rations was threatened with 'trial for *sedition*, and… the punishment which such a notorious crime deserves'.[32] Even if the quantity of food was adequate, it was hardly appetising. Relying principally on flour, salted beef and salted pork, it was bland and dull. This was hardly assisted by the cooking directions, for the 'pork or beef [was] to be steeped, at least, twenty hours, changing the water three times, scraping and washing the salt off at each time that the water is removed, and then boil it with the pease, as usual; but the soldiers are desired, as they value their own health, never to eat their salt meat raw or broiled'.[33]

The shortage and drabness of rations encouraged a flourishing black market in provisions. The Canadians had some stores of dried fruit and vegetables, as well as small amounts of butter and cheese. They also knew how to make holes in the frozen rivers to fish and how to hunt for game in the snow-covered forests. This could provide some relief to the monotonous diet. However, the British troops had nothing with which to buy such produce. They had received no pay since the early summer, and there was no money with which to pay them. Some money had been collected from the officers (who received notes promising payment in the spring in return) and redistributed to the men in October, but this was scarcely sufficient. Murray had proposed issuing his own paper money, but his proposal was quickly voted down by his subordinates. As French paper money was forbidden in the British-controlled areas, and there was a desperate shortage of hard currency, there were few ways that troops could trade, except by bartering their salt pork and flour for fresh provisions. Such a trade was strictly banned, as it was feared that these supplies would end up in the hands of the French army. Consequently, a flourishing clandestine market developed.[34]

As in the liquor trade, the main participants in this black market were not the few French merchants who remained in Quebec, but rather the women who followed the army. The women served as an important link between the Quebec civilians and the garrison and were able to provide the men with many luxuries or necessities, or rather were able to provide the officers with many luxuries. Knox reported in December that 'at present we are tolerably well supplied with fresh provision, (I mean the Officers!) which, however, except the articles of beavers, hares, partridges, and other game, are very indifferent in their kinds'.[35] Indeed, Murray had specifically sought to develop this trade by distributing many of the French supplies which were found hidden in Quebec, particularly salt, to his officers. The officers could then barter their provisions to the men in return for services, such as repairing damaged buildings or cutting firewood, or even for some of the booty which had been acquired during the campaign. Not surprisingly, the clandestine trade grew quickly, forcing Murray to warn the women that if they were found selling any rations which they had bought from the garrison they would be 'liable to corporal punishment, and never more be allowed to follow the army'.[36]

For the French army, supplies were also desperately short. However, Lévis hoped that by quartering the regular troops among the *habitants* of the Montreal region he could relieve his supply problems over the winter. For the *habitants* on whom these troops were billeted, this burden was not totally unwelcome, as the troops provided a needed source of labour, especially as many of the Canadians' draft animals had already been pressed into army service, slaughtered for food or killed in British raids. It was the low level of ammunition that gave Lévis most concern. While it was possible to manufacture shot in Canada, all gunpowder had to be imported from Europe. With only paltry supplies arriving from France in both 1758 and 1759, levels of ammunition were desperately low. This state of affairs had grown worse with the abandonment of supplies in Quebec and at the Beauport camp in September. The shortage of ammunition and powder meant that Lévis could not mount a serious attack on Quebec during the winter, despite the fears of the British garrison. However, if he could assemble his forces in the spring, and march on the city in time for the arrival of a French supply fleet, he could retake the city. Such a plan, of course, depended upon France sending supplies to its beleaguered colony. To ensure that this took place, in November Vaudreuil and Lévis dispatched the Chevalier Le Mercier to France to argue for urgent aid to be sent to Canada. All would now depend on the decision of the ministry in Versailles.[37]

Realising that he would need an abundant supply of provisions if he was to launch a campaign to retake Quebec in the spring, in mid-February Lévis dispatched a party of *troupes de la Marine* to forage along the south shore and gather what they could. In particular, he was hopeful the region between Cap-St-Ignace and the Etchemin river could provide supplies. This region had not been heavily damaged by raids in the summer, as it had been occupied by British troops, but following the surrender of Quebec most of the troops had withdrawn across the river. It seemed that it might be possible to collect a substantial quantity of supplies from the *habitants* in this region. At the village of St-Michel, the French party received shelter and intelligence about British positions, as well as collecting a considerable quantity of provisions. However, the party was soon discovered by the British, and Murray sent out several detachments who drove the French back to Jacques Cartier.[38]

Murray was incensed by the actions of the villagers of St-Michel. He viewed their support for the French party as a clear violation of the oath of allegiance that they had taken in October. He recorded in his journal: 'as I was inform'd, the French Detachmt had conceal'd itself for two nights in the houses at Pointe-Lévy, within about six miles of our post; without any of the inhabitants giving the least notice, I thought it proper Punishment to burn these houses, at the same time that it put it out of the Enemys Power to make use of them a second time'.[39] He sent out a detachment of Fraser's Highlanders commanded by Captain Donald MacDonald, with orders to obliterate the village. According to Knox, the party 'consumed every house throughout that parish'.[40] The destruction of St-Michel seems to have been an effective warning, for the Canadians were reluctant to offer the same degree of protection and intelligence to future French raiding parties.

St-Michel was not the only village on the St Lawrence to feel the wrath of the British over the winter. In late September, Jeffery Amherst sent out a raiding party from Crown Point, led by the British ranger Major Robert Rogers, to attack the Abenakis mission on the south shore of the St Lawrence at St-Francis. The destruction of the village was to punish the Abenakis for their support of the French, and their supposed involvement in the massacre of Fort William Henry in 1757. On the morning of 4 October Rogers's party descended on the settlement. Catching many of the villagers asleep, they set fire to the village, burning women and children as they cowered in cellars and attics. Although many of the villagers escaped, and Rogers's claim to have killed 200 of them was almost certainly too high, the destruction of the mission village at the beginning of the winter was a blow to French and especially Abenaki morale. While encouraging the Abenakis to seek revenge, the attack on St-Francis may have served to convince many of France's traditional Native American allies that their warriors would serve a better purpose protecting their villages than fighting for a cause that already looked lost.[41]

The destruction of St-Michel and St-Francis did not prevent Canadians from supplying Lévis's army. However, it did make some *habitants* more circumspect about providing intelligence and supplies, while Lévis could not offer them protection from British retaliation. It was not only for Lévis that the chronic shortage of supplies within the French army caused problems. Numerous French deserters headed for the British camp, claiming that they were driven to such extremes by near-starvation. This created a quandary for Murray. He did not have the supplies to feed them, even if they could be of use to his army, but the 'laws of war' meant that he had to treat these men humanely. Initially, Murray sent the deserters to the Île d'Orléans and quartered them upon Canadian families at their own expense. Eventually, his own shortages of supplies forced him simply to give French deserters their liberty.[42]

If Murray faced a problem feeding French deserters, he faced an even bigger problem feeding and supporting the hundreds of camp followers who remained with his army. At the beginning of December, Murray warned that 'no French servants or boys, hired since the army took the field will be victualled'.[43] He ordered the commissaries to investigate the number of women accompanying each regiment. To his horror he discovered that there were 569 women still officially accompanying the troops, or about 7 per cent of his total force, far higher than the total Wolfe had originally permitted. He ordered the women to receive rations at two-thirds of the rate of the men. In return, they were ordered to work, tending to the growing numbers of sick, cooking in the canteens, or even assisting in filling sandbags and stacking wood. The plight of those who were unable to receive army rations was dire. The price of food and wood increased dramatically throughout the winter, but with little cash available for purchases many British civilians were left on the verge of starvation. Murray ordered all Canadians who could not afford to live in the city to leave.

Most wealthy residents had already done so. Left behind was a smattering of labourers, artisans and merchants, who all hoped that the demand for goods and services from the British garrison might provide them with sufficient support through the long winter.[44]

It was not, however, the lack of food, the dreariness of rations or even the cold that caused the biggest problem for the British over the winter, but rather the lack of fresh water, fresh fruit and vegetables. This caused widespread sickness. From early December onwards the hospitals in the city were filled with sick and dying men. At first the men were cared for in the Ursuline and General Hospitals, but these were soon filled. Murray thus opened his own hospitals, staffed by the women who accompanied the army. Through the bitter winter all the hospitals lacked adequate blankets and heating. In cold and cramped conditions, it is not surprising that many sick men never recovered, and those who did recovered very slowly.[45]

Dysentery was the first big killer. With the wells frozen, the men had only a few sources of water, and many drank melted snow. Attempts to 'disinfect' the water with rum proved futile and by February the ranks had been decimated by the scourge of dysentery. At the beginning of January John Knox reported that 'the men grow more unhealthy as the weather advances… it is, indeed, melancholy to see such havock among our brave fellows'. At the beginning of February he added that 'our soldiers grow more sickly, and many of them are daily carried off by the inveteracy of their disorders, notwithstanding all imaginable care is taken of them'. By the end of the month he confessed that there were 'immense numbers of sick and weak men'.[46]

Dysentery, however, was not the major health problem which faced the garrison. The lack of fresh supplies meant that by February increasing numbers of men were suffering from scurvy. There were various efforts made to combat scurvy.

Murray ordered supplies of vinegar for the men, and wine for the officers, but these had little effect. Other attempted remedies were ginger and tar water, but not surprisingly they had little positive impact on the men's health. However, by the end of March the army's doctors had discovered a remedy: Canadian spruce beer. Spruce beer, made from spruce bark and molasses and containing substantial quantities of ascorbic acid or vitamin C, had long been brewed by the region's Native American population and Canadians had quickly discovered its use as an antidote to scurvy. Spruce beer was soon being issued to all the men with scurvy in the army's hospitals. However, its distribution was too late to prevent many men from dying.[47]

As the first signs of spring began to show, the effects of the winter on the British garrison were all too apparent. At the beginning of the winter there had been 7,300 men in the garrison; by the beginning of March there were only 4,800 men fit for duty. Murray dejectedly commented that 'We are very low, the Scurvy makes terrible havock… Whoever winters here again must be better provided with beding and warm cloaths than we were. Our medicines are entirely expended.'[48] Knox commented that this was 'far from being surprising, when we consider the… indifferent cloathing, uncomfortable barracks, worse bedding, and their being intirely confined to a salt provision diet'.[49]

The weakness of the garrison made military operations very difficult. Throughout the winter Murray was convinced that Lévis would take advantage of the Canadians' superiority in cold-weather warfare to launch a surprise attack on the city. For this reason he established advanced posts at Lorette and Ste-Foy and then later at Pointe-Lévy on the south side of the St Lawrence. These would give him advance notice of any attack. Murray also began the construction of a network of blockhouses across the Plains of Abraham. Once the St Lawrence had frozen, the city was also dangerously exposed to attack across the river, for the lower town had few defences against a 'land attack' across the frozen ice. So worried was Murray about such an attack that he ordered his men to move all stores of food and ammunition from the lower town to the upper town. The winter attack that Murray feared never came. Vaudreuil and Lévis both knew that Canada lacked supplies and ammunition. To launch an expedition in mid-winter would strain the colony's resources past breaking point. Moving men and supplies was all but impossible. While Canadians were inured to the hardships of winter, this did not mean that they were immune to frostbite and exposure. Spring was the most opportune time to attack. Spring flood-waters would prevent the British from sailing down the Richelieu river. Lévis could concentrate all his forces against Quebec. If Quebec could be retaken before the end of May, the troops resupplied by a French relief squadron, they could return to Montreal to hold off any other forces that might be thrown against the colony. Canada could still be saved.[50]

Most Canadians, however, hoped not for the repulse of the British, which would merely continue the war, but rather for news of the conclusion of a peace in Europe that would restore Canada to France and end their suffering. Rumours of such a peace had been circulating for some time. Indeed, in September 1759, Governor Thomas Pownall of Massachusetts had written to Jeffery Amherst that rumours from Europe suggested France would soon come to terms and there was 'a fine opportunity for a Good Peace'.[51] Among Canadians such rumours had a distinct tinge of desperation, but with Canada isolated from Europe for six months during the winter it was easy for rumours to spread. By March there were even rumours that a British fleet had been sunk and the French had landed in Ireland. Many Canadians were openly proclaiming that the next fleet would 'bring us an account of a peace being concluded, Quebec will be restored, and Canada once more flourish under a French government'.[52] Governor Vaudreuil himself gave credence to such rumours, in an attempt to maintain morale as Lévis prepared the expedition against Quebec. Murray resorted to his own propaganda to counter Vaudreuil's. At the beginning of April he ordered a sergeant and four men of one of the ranging companies to cross the river and make a grand arrival in Quebec, purporting to be an express sent from Amherst with news of great British victories. Murray's simple ruse was very successful, and 'gave great Sprits to the Garrison, & visibly affected the French Inhabitants'.[53]

While rumours abounded in Quebec of battles in Europe that would bring a peace, the most decisive battle of the war, and the battle which would ultimately seal the fate of Quebec, had been fought off France's Atlantic coast. On 20 November 1759, Admiral Sir Edward Hawke had delivered a crushing blow to French naval power at the battle of Quiberon Bay. Trusting in the superior tactical ability of his captains, and the superior training of his crews, he attacked the French fleet in atrocious weather that later drove many of the French fleet ashore. He also dispensed with traditional rules of attack, allowing his captains to attack at will rather than attacking in the traditional line formation. As the French admiral, Hubert de Brienne, Comte de Conflans, attempted to form his fleet into the traditional defensive line, the gales, the shallows and then the irregular British attack broke his fleet apart. The result was a stunning victory. Of the French fleet of twenty-one ships of the line, only eight would ever reach safety in the port of Rochefort. Even more damaging, the French lost 2,500 sailors. Hawke for his part lost only two ships and 300 men. The French Atlantic Fleet would not be able to challenge the British again. The battle of Quiberon Bay was in many ways as decisive for Canada's future as the Battle on the Plains of Abraham on 13 September.[54]

As French officials read Vaudreuil's and Lévis's missives sent in the autumn, begging desperately for aid, they were amazed. Canada, Vaudreuil and Lévis had argued, needed 4,000 troops, supplies and ammunition to stave off the British for another year. If the sending of supplies and men to Canada had been too dangerous in early 1759, following the battle of Quiberon Bay such a scheme seemed downright foolhardy. Canada would not get 4,000 soldiers, but 400. Instead of a fleet of supply ships, the crown sent five merchantmen escorted by the merchant-frigate the *Machault*. Perhaps most damning, the ships were not ready to depart until 10 April. By the time they arrived at the Gulf of St Lawrence, the British fleet was already waiting. In desperation, they put ashore in the Baie des Chaleurs, but the few supplies they brought would never reach the beleaguered French army.[55]

While French officials may have been doubtful about the chances of retaining Canada, Murray was equally concerned about his ability to hold Quebec. To delay the expected French attack, on 19 March he dispatched Captain Donald MacDonald and a party of Fraser's Highlanders, with orders to attack one of the French advanced posts at Calvaire. Descending on the post at dawn, MacDonald's party was brutal in its pursuit of the French defenders and took over sixty prisoners. Such attacks on the French posts, however, could do little more than delay the inevitable attack. To improve the city's defences, Murray had begun construction of a network of blockhouses over the winter, but they were far from complete. The city walls were unfinished and had suffered some damage in the British bombardment. They would not protect the city for long from a determined assault and Murray had had little time to repair them. He thus took the advice of Major Patrick MacKellar, his chief engineer, who recommended that at first notice of a French advance he should entrench his men on the Plains of Abraham and await their arrival there.[56]

While Murray was considering how best to defend Quebec, Vaudreuil and Lévis were considering how best to raise an army. In early April Vaudreuil had sent orders to all the *curés* in Canada, urging them to use all their influence among their parishioners to convince them to support the campaign. He begged them 'to make them [their parishioners] know that it is for the sake of their religion, for their honour, and in their real interest to join the army'.[57] He urged all Canadians to fight. They had seen 'the dire straits to which the misfortunes of war have reduced the Canadians of the government of Quebec'. They must be aware of the 'humiliation [Murray] has forced upon them, and of the hard and cruel way he has treated most Canadians'. He begged them to 'undertake everything, risk everything, to preserve your religion and the safety of your homeland'.[58] He also issued a proclamation promising an amnesty to all deserters who returned to the army, even those who had enlisted with the British. By 20 April Lévis had assembled an army of over 7,000 men, including 3,000 militia, at Montreal and was ready to march on Quebec. Initially, it was difficult to navigate through the ice floes of the partially frozen river, but three days later the ice sheet across the St Lawrence completely broke up, opening the river for navigation for the first time. On 21 and 22 April, scouts from Murray's advanced posts at Lorrette and Ste-Foy warned him of increased activity among the French. Murray sensed that an attack was imminent. He immediately ordered all the Canadian residents of Quebec to leave the city. The British troops watched them depart with some pity. Knox wrote that 'the wretched citizens have evacuated the town: it is impossible to avoid sympathising with them in their distress. The men prudently restrained their sentiments on this occasion, but the women were not so discreet; they charged us with a breach of the capitulation.'[59]

Desperately aware of the weakness of his garrison, Murray attempted to put McKellar's plan into action and prepared to

entrench his men on the Plains of Abraham. However, below
the surface the ground was still frozen hard and the men could
not dig more than nine inches deep. Clearly the plan of preparing entrenchments would not work. Weather also caused the
French to change their plans. Lévis had initially planned to
transport his men by water and land at Sillery. However, drifting
ice in the river meant that he decided to land at St-Augustin
and march overland. His plan was to surprise the advanced
posts at Lorette and Ste-Foy, but unfortunately one of his men
fell overboard when landing, and drifted downstream on the
ice floes. He was spotted by the garrison in Quebec, and pulled
to safety. It was not long before he divulged the presence of
the French army and their plans to attack. The next morning,
27 April, Murray withdrew his men from Lorrette and Ste-Foy
just before Lévis's force moved in.[60]

On the night of 27-28 April, Lévis's men moved up to L'Anse
au Foulon. Murray was in a quandary. He had just under 3,900
men fit for duty; Lévis had nearly twice that number. The
plan he had developed through the winter was to fortify the
Plains of Abraham, but now those plans had been defeated
by the weather. Lévis was already moving his men onto the
Plains. Murray later wrote that 'as the Place is not Fortified,
and Commanded every where towards the Land, my Garrison
which was now melted down to Three Thousand Fighting
Men, by the most Inveterate Scurvy, were daily mouldering
away, and it was now impossible for me to Fortify the Heights
of Abraham, tho' Fascines and every Requisite Material had
been provided long ago, I could not hesitate a moment about
giving the Enemy Battle; As every One knows the Place is not
tenable against an Army in possession of the Heights.' He had
to prevent the French from establishing their position on the
Plains of Abraham overlooking the city.[61]

At 7 a.m. on 28 April, Murray's army moved onto the Plains
of Abraham, accompanied by twenty-two artillery pieces.

Murray formed his men on the rising ground, the Buttes-à-Neveu, where Montcalm had formed his army in September. At the same time Lévis's men were beginning to arrive on the Plains. Lévis had intended to rest his men, land more supplies, and prepare for a siege, but now it was clear that Murray was preparing for battle. Lévis posted two brigades on his right in two blockhouses built by Murray at the top of the road leading to the Plains from L'Anse au Foulon. The left, composed of five grenadier companies, was some distance away, occupying a windmill on the Ste-Foy road. The main body of Lévis's men was still on the march and the centre of his line was very weakly defended.[62]

Murray soon had his men in order of battle. On his right, commanded by Colonel Burton, were the 15th Regiment or Amherst's, Anstruther's 58th, the Second Battalion of the 60th Royal Americans and Webb's 48th. On the left, Colonel Fraser commanded Kennedy's 43rd, Lascelles's 47th, the 78th Regiment or Fraser's Highlanders and Braggs's 28th. Murray ordered Otway's 35th and the Third Battalion Royal Americans to remain as a reserve, while covering his flanks with light infantry and rangers. The light infantry and the rangers on the two flanks were the first to engage the French, who soon retreated in some haste and abandoned the windmill on the Ste-Foy road. Murray recorded in his journal that he 'now reconnoitred the Enemy, and perceived [*sic*] their Van busy throwing up Redoubts while their Main body was yet on their March. I thought this was the Lucky Minute, mov'd the whole in great Order to attack them before they could have time to form.'[63]

Hoping to engage the French before they were in battle order and while they were in some confusion, Murray ordered his men to throw away their entrenching tools and to advance down from their advantageous position on the Plains in much the same manner as Montcalm's men had done. However, the light infantry on the right were soon checked by the French, and dispersed irregularly across the entire right wing of Murray's army, delaying the advance of the British right for some time. At this point the French left counter-attacked. Forming a column attack, as Montcalm had attempted in September, this time the French manoeuvre was successful. Advancing quickly across the field with bayonets drawn, defying the heavy fire from the British artillery, the French columns tore into the British ranks. The British right collapsed and was quickly driven back from the windmill in some confusion. A second French column attack now attacked the British left with almost as devastating an effect.[64]

Murray now committed his reserves: the third battalion of the Royal Americans to the left, Otway's to the right. It was too late. According to Knox, 'our troops fought almost knee-deep in dissolving wreaths of snow and water, whence it was utterly impracticable to draw off our artillery'.[65] Without the advantage of their artillery support, the British army was desperately outnumbered. Within minutes the British left gave way, and according to Murray 'the disorder spread from the left to the Right & the whole Retreat'd, under the Musquetry of our Blockhouses, abandoning their Cannon to the Enemy'.[66]

The battle of Ste-Foy, as the battle of 28 April is usually known, had been as devastating as the battle of the Plains of Abraham; indeed, the casualties were higher. Murray listed a total of 1,104 casualties, including 259 men killed, while Lévis recorded 833, with 193 men killed. Murray had little choice but to withdraw his battered army back into Quebec. The second siege of Quebec had begun with Murray's army, already decimated by disease, now besieged by a much larger French force. Within the walls, the morale of some of the troops all but collapsed. Knox reported that 'immense irregularities are hourly committed by the soldiery, in break[ing] open store and dwelling houses to get at liquor: this is seemingly the result of panic and despair, heightened by drunkenness; one man was hanged this evening *in terrorem,* without any trial, which it is hoped will effectually prevent farther disorders'.[67] Murray was even forced to order the destruction of all private liquor supplies to prevent them falling into the hands of his men.[68]

Lévis was less hopeful about the chances of a French victory. He still had to construct siege trenches and batter down the city walls before his army could attempt to take the city. However, the French besiegers lacked heavy artillery and were desperately short of powder – so short that Lévis limited firing to only twenty rounds per gun per day. Indeed, the British garrison inside the fort outgunned their besiegers and did more damage to the French batteries than the French did to them. If, however, a French fleet were to arrive with only some of the supplies and reinforcements that had been requested, there was every chance that the city of Quebec would again be French. In London, news of Murray's defeat caused more than a little consternation. Government bonds dropped sharply in value, and signs of war-weariness surfaced. Horace Walpole summed up the feelings of many when he wrote, 'Who the deuce was thinking of Quebec? America was like a book one has read and done with, but here we are on a sudden reading our book backwards.'[69] If Quebec were lost, it was quite apparent that the British government might not have the determination to continue the conflict and might come to terms with France. For one last time Canadians waited for providence to rescue them from catastrophe, or rather they waited for supplies to arrive from France. If a French fleet could get into the St Lawrence before the British, Murray could not hold out for long.

Murray was all too aware of the importance of French supplies. On 1 May he dispatched the ship *Racehorse* to Halifax, begging Amherst to rush aid to the city. As the French edged their siege works closer and closer to the city, the British batteries poured their fire into the besiegers, greatly retarding their progress. On 3 May Vaudreuil wrote to Versailles with some optimism. He informed the ministry that 'the victory which Chevalier de Levis has just gained is a very good omen, provided always that the obstinate defence of the English do not give time to their reinforcements to arrive'.[70] On 9 May, the first warship arrived in the St Lawrence. It was not French but the British *Lowestoft*. To the men in the besieged garrison, its arrival was a wonderful boost. Knox reported that 'both Officers and soldiers mounted the parapets in the face of the enemy, and huzzaed, with their hats in the air, for almost an hour; the garrison, the enemy's camp, the bay, and circumjacent country for several miles, resounded with our shouts and the thunder of our artillery; for the Gunners were so elated, that they did nothing but fire and load for a considerable time: in short, the general satisfaction is not to be conceived'.[71]

Lévis had not abandoned all hope. The *Lowestoft* was but one warship. Surely the French supply fleet would not be far behind? On 11 May, the French batteries finally opened fire on Quebec, targeting their fire on the Glacière bastion, which Lévis knew from personal experience to be the weakest part of the city's defences. On 15 May, however, two more British ships arrived and messengers from the Côte du Sud brought Lévis news that there were more British warships in the St Lawrence. There was no sign of a French fleet. Indeed, the tiny fleet which had been dispatched from France so late in the season would not arrive off the Canadian coast for several weeks. Realising that all hope of taking Quebec was now gone, on the morning of 16 May Lévis ordered his men to abandon the siege. They left behind their guns and many of their supplies.[72]

The French army was distraught. Many felt that it was not their failure which had now cost them Quebec. As one French diarist confided:

'Twas never expected, when leaving Montreal, that we could take Quebec with the mere resources the country was able to furnish, as that town was provided with an immense artillery and guarded by a numerous garrison, composed of good troops. under an active and experienced chief. The plan was to confine that garrison within the walls of the town sufficiently early, to deprive it of the power of constructing external works before the fronts which have been attacked, and to wait under cover of the first approaches until the arrival of the reinforcements demanded from France should enable us to continue the siege. One single French flag would have been sufficient to produce that effect.[73]

Most Canadians felt that they had been abandoned by France. For many, the campaign to save Canada was now over. The arrival of the British fleet in the St Lawrence in mid-May lacks the drama and pathos of the battle of the Plains of Abraham on 13 September. In many ways, it was an anti-climax to a year's campaigning. Nevertheless, as much as Wolfe's great victory this sealed the fate of Canada. Murray's men had struggled for nearly six months against the bitter winter weather, almost as much as they had struggled against the French during the summer. They had suffered more from sickness and the weather than they had from battle. Civilians had suffered even more, enduring near-starvation and martial law. The campaign was clearly far from over. However, by mid-May the bedraggled French army was retreating back to Montreal. The British were preparing to pour men and supplies into one final push against Canada. It was clear to everyone that the French army would not be able to resist for much longer.

Conclusion:

Conquest

The arrival of the British fleet finally secured the British hold over Quebec. It extinguished the last hope of the Canadians that the British Army could be driven from Canada. The only possibility that the colony could be saved for France lay in the conclusion of a peace treaty in Europe before the colony was finally overrun. The only hope was to delay the inevitable capitulation for as long as possible. Lévis withdrew his main forces from Quebec to Montreal, leaving Dumas in command of a detachment of 1,500 men near Jacques Cartier. Dumas's task was simply to delay any advance by Murray, but this was not expected for some time, as Lévis guessed correctly that Murray's men would be exhausted after the rigors of the winter and the siege, and would be unable to commence offensive operations against Montreal immediately.[1]

The greatest threat seemingly came not from Quebec, but from the large army which Amherst was already massing at Oswego on Lake Ontario to attack Montreal from the west.

Amherst had almost 11,000 men in his army, including 5,600 regulars. A third army was being assembled at Crown Point on Lake Champlain; commanded by General William Haviland, it contained 3,400 men. He would attack Montreal from the south. Canada was being overwhelmed on all sides. Both Haviland and Amherst, however, faced substantial obstacles before they could arrive in Montreal. On an island in the St Lawrence the French had hastily constructed Fort Lévis. If Amherst intended to ascend the river and transport his supplies by boat, he would need first to take the fort. On the Richelieu river, Bougainville was preparing to defend another island fortress at Île-aux-Noix. Both these forts would have to be captured before the British could reach Montreal.[2]

The military crisis was not all the Canadians had to endure. For some time Canadians had worried about the security of their paper money and of the loans that they had made to the government. Now the first dispatches received from Paris revealed that the French Crown had defaulted on the payment of Canadian bills of exchange. The loans which Canadians had made to the government would not be repaid on schedule. The government would only start paying the debts accumulated since 1757 three months after the end of the war, and would only pay a total of 6 million livres per year. As by the beginning of 1760 there were 120 million livres outstanding; most Canadians felt that they had little chance of ever recovering their debts. Lévis wrote in anger to Paris that 'all the farmers [were] in despair; they have sacrificed everything for the preservation of Canada; they now find themselves ruined beyond recovery'.[3]

With no money to buy provisions and no supplies from France, it was little wonder that much of the French army now dispersed. Indeed, Lévis and Vaudreuil were forced to disperse their men in an attempt to prevent them from starving. Lévis bemoaned the situation: 'We are utterly unable to keep the field; provisions, warlike stores, everything is lacking. 'Tis a wonder that we yet exist.'[4] Scattered in farms and farmsteads across the St Lawrence, many of the militia and the *troupes de la Marine* simply abandoned the army. Even France's staunchest Native American allies were now reluctant to take to the field as the French Empire crumbled away.[5]

Murray's force was the first of the British armies to set out for Montreal. Only two months after the relief of Quebec, Murray's men were prepared. Departing Quebec on 14 July, the expedition initially made swift progress up the St Lawrence. On 15 July, the expedition passed the French post at Jacques Cartier, which Murray was concerned might retard their progress. However, the river was so wide that without boats or floating batteries the French were unable to oppose Murray's advance but merely shadowed the expedition along the northern shore. Contrary winds then slowed the expedition's progress, but by 4 August Murray had reached Trois Rivières. From this point onwards the greatest delay to the army would not be French resistance but the hundreds of *habitants* who swarmed around the army to sell their produce, or who came to lay down their arms and swear an oath of allegiance. The resistance which Murray did meet was disorganised and sporadic, but often consisted of ambushes and traps. In an attempt to quell this activity, Murray issued a series of threatening proclamations, echoing Wolfe's the previous summer. He enjoined Canadians to remain in their homes as the British army advanced, and warned that if they continued their resistance 'I shall treat severely Canadians taken with arms in their hands and I shall burn all villages that I find abandoned.'[6] Murray had a chance to put his warnings into effect at Sorel. When a party of his men were lured into an ambush near the village, Murray unleashed his full retribution. He explained in a letter to William Pitt that he had 'found the inhabitants of the parish of Sorrel had deserted their habitations and were in arms; I was therefore under the cruel necessity of burning the greatest part of these poor unhappy people's houses; I pray God this example may suffice, for my nature revolts when this becomes a necessary part of my duty'.[7] Perhaps the destruction of Sorel did serve as a warning to the Canadians, for there were no more surprise attacks on his troops. More likely, however, as the three armies neared Montreal Canadian *habitants* were all too aware of what their future held.

The task of assembling the other British armies took longer than it did for them to advance to Montreal. Haviland did not leave Crown Point until 11 August, the same date that Amherst's men departed from Oswego. However, while Amherst and Haviland faced greater geographical obstacles than Murray, they were not slowed by the continual need to deal with Canadian civilians. Haviland reached Île-aux-Noix on 19 August and besieged the post for eight days before Bougainville evacuated his men and headed for Montreal. Amherst's force reached Fort Lévis on the same day, but in his usual methodical fashion it took Amherst's men five days to open the siege trenches. On 25 August, the French surrendered the fort, leaving the route to Montreal open for Amherst. Instead of continuing down the Richelieu river and into the St Lawrence, Haviland took a more direct overland route towards Montreal from the south. Meanwhile Amherst carefully guided his boats through the rapids of the upper St Lawrence, loosing more men in their navigation than he had in the attack on Fort Lévis. By 5 September, Amherst's men were within sight of the Island of Montreal.[8]

The meeting of the armies could not have been better choreographed, arriving almost simultaneously at Montreal from three different directions, although luck seems to have played as great a role as planning. Within a few days Lévis's army had all but disintegrated without a shot being fired. On

3 September, Knox reported that 'The regulars now desert to us in great numbers, and the Canadian militia are surrendering by hundreds.' The following day he continued to be amazed at the 'Crowds of Canadians... surrendering to us every minute, and the regulars, worn out with hunger and despair, desert[ing] to us in great numbers'.[9] On 6 September, Amherst's troops landed at Lachine, a few miles to the west of Montreal. That evening Vaudreuil summoned a council of war in Montreal. The council agreed that further resistance would be futile. Unlike Quebec, the city had few natural defences. Lévis's men were now outnumbered by the combined British armies by perhaps ten to one. The council drew up terms for the surrender of the colony, seeking the best terms they could. Amherst accepted the proposed terms, with one notable exception: he would not allow the garrison to have the honours of war. The French had committed too many atrocities to be allowed this final honour. This refusal forced Lévis to request that he be allowed to take his army out of the town to Île-Ste-Helene, 'in order to sustain there, in our own name, the honour of the king's arms, resolved to expose ourselves to every extremity rather than submit to conditions which appear to use so contrary thereto'. Vaudreuil refused. On 8 September 1760 he signed the Articles of Capitulation. The British had conquered Canada.[10]

The articles were in many ways quite generous to the Canadians. In particular they guaranteed that 'the free exercise of the Catholic, Apostolic, and Roman Religion, shall subsist intire... without being molested in any manner'. They also guaranteed that 'the Chapter, Priests, Curates, and Missionaries, shall continue, with an intire liberty, their exercise and functions of cures, in the parishes of the towns and countries'. For the eighteenth century, this was a remarkably liberal document that may well have prevented Quebec from becoming another Ireland.[11]

Despite the seeming finality of the capitulation, many Canadians still did not see the Articles as marking the conclusion of the French Empire. Indeed, many Canadians, and many of the British troops in Canada, presumed that at the final treaty negotiations Canada would be returned to the French in exchange for gains the French had made in Europe. Such hopes continued to surface even in government circles as late as 1762. Consequently, even in the aftermath of the British military conquest it was not at all clear who would control Canada in the long term.

Many Canadians accepted the presence of the British remarkably quickly. In part, this may be because there was a rapid return to normal life. Militia captains continued to exercise troops; judicial tribunals established by the British continued to conduct justice according to French law; Roman Catholic priests continued to celebrate Mass. Members of the elite who could not tolerate British rule simply left for France, while many who remained often found the increased economic opportunity as members of the British Empire more than compensated for the loss of their French identity. Hundreds of young Canadian women married British soldiers. In particular, many of Fraser's Highlanders, who were disbanded in 1763, permanently settled in Canada around Rivière du Loup, where their descendants became francophone.[12]

British rule may also have been easier to accept because for many Canadians there was a sense of betrayal by France. France had not come to Canada's aid and had left the colony to fend for itself. The failure of France to provide either military or economic support in 1758 and 1759 had deeply shocked many Canadians. As François Bigot's machinations became more widely known, and as he was put on trial in France for the corruption of his administration, the sacrifices of ordinary Canadians for the French cause seemed even more meaningless. Ironically, Wolfe's war of devastation in the summer of 1759 may also have served to underscore the lack of protection offered to most *habitants* by the French presence. With a French army sitting motionless in Quebec, while the British plundered the St Lawrence seemingly at will, many Canadians must have questioned the cost of their loyalty.

French 'betrayal' surfaced once more at the Treaty of Paris in 1763. To the horror of many Canadians, France did the unthinkable and formally surrendered sovereignty to the British. Canada was now a British colony. In 1783 at another Treaty of Paris, this time ending the Revolutionary War, with Britain defeated, France could well have demanded the return of her former colony in Canada, in much the same way as Spain received her former colony in Florida. When France failed to press for the return of Canada, once more, Canadians felt abandoned.

The British 'conquest' of Canada was thus clearly not one single event. Conquest was not achieved on 13 September 1759 on the Plains of Abraham, but was an extended process. The military conquest of Canada, which began in late 1758 as preparations commenced for the expeditions of 1759, concluded with the capitulation in September 1760. The political and social 'conquest' was an ongoing process. This conquest involved far more than just soldiers and armies. Indeed, even the military conquest of Canada involved far more than just armies manoeuvring for victory and included the activities of civilians and camp followers. The war itself had an impact on the lives not only of those who fought it, but on the lives of ordinary Canadian civilians. The military conquest devastated Canadian society; indeed, Canadian historian Guy Frégault has concluded that 'the framework of the Canadian community, destroyed in the crisis, was never properly rebuilt'.[13] In part this was because British merchants and settlers were able to move into Quebec after the conquest to take advantage of the dire plight of the *habitants* to buy up land and property at bargain prices. The war had left Canada devastated, particularly the region from Quebec City eastwards. The Bishop de Pontbriand, Bishop of Quebec, reported the destruction of the colony. He claimed that the

> Côte de Beaupré and the Island of Orleans have been wholly destroyed before the end of the siege; the barns, farmers' houses and priests' residences, have been burned, and the cattle that remained, carried off; those removed above Quebec have almost all been taken for the subsistence of our army; so that the poor farmer who returned to his land with his wife and children, will be obliged to hut himself, Indian fashion; his crops, which could not be saved, except on halves, will be exposed, as well as the cattle, to the inclemency of the weather.... The farmer is without clothing, furniture, plough and without any implements to cultivate the soil and to cut wood... On the other, or South, side of the river about 36 leagues of settled country have been almost equally devastated; it contained 19 parishes, the greater number of which have been destroyed.[14]

The impact of the conquest was also far-reaching. This was total war, on a scale not previously witnessed in North America. The whole of Canadian society was mobilised to resist the invading force. As some contemporaries noted, the removal of France as a continental power in North America also removed a threat to Britain's North American colonies and gave them further confidence to seek independence from the protection of Great Britain. The British government's enormous spending on the war left the government with £137 million of debt by the end of the war. To recoup some of that debt the government attempted to find new means of raising taxes, and in the process of doing so sparked revolution in the British North American colonies. Thus the war which gained an empire, in many ways, was also responsible for losing much of that empire.

For Canadians, the experience of the British conquest of Canada was a psychologically devastating affair. This was not the carefully regulated war which occurred – or at least was supposed to occur – in Europe. Vattel in his *Law of Nations* argued that 'since women and children are subjects of the state, and members of the nation, they are to be ranked in the class of enemies. But it does not thence follow that we are justifiable in treating them like men who bear arms, or are capable of bearing them....'[15] In the struggle in Canada, however, the line between combatant and non-combatant was extremely blurred. Indeed, Vattel had also argued that civilians only merited protection 'provided the inhabitants submit to him who is master of the country, pay the contributions imposed, and refrain from all hostilities'.[16] Wolfe and Murray could both argue, with some justification, that the *habitants* of Canada did not lay down their arms and 'refrain from all hostilities' but continued to wage war against the British. For that reason they merited the destruction of their property and villages. Such actions also affected the troops who committed them. While some British troops may have delighted in the plundering and destruction of civilian property, others did not. For many Highlanders, such a campaign may have brought reminders of the devastation of the Highlands in the wake of the 1745 Jacobite Rebellion. Perhaps such feelings may in part account for the propensity of the Highland troops who settled in Canada to intermarry with the Francophone population.

The British campaign for Quebec – the conquest of Canada – was consequently a total war, both in its conduct and in its outcome. It was a conquest fought over an extended period of time, not just during the high summer of 1759. While in many ways it resembled campaigns in Europe in its reliance upon regular troops, the experiences of the soldiers who fought and of the civilians who witnessed the conflict were very different from wars elsewhere, particularly in Europe.

Notes

Introduction

1   Francis Parkman, *Montcalm and Wolfe*, 2 vols (London: 1884).
2   'Letters and Papers Relating to the Siege of Quebec in the
     Possession of the Marquess Townshend' in *The Siege of Quebec and
     the Battle of the Plains of Abraham*, ed. Arthur Doughty (Quebec: 1901)
     5:195.

Chapter 1: Two Empires

1   *Memoirs of the Siege of Quebec, Capital of All Canada and of the Retreat
     of Monsieur de Bourlamaque to the Isle Aux Noix in Lake Champlain
     from the Journal of a French Officer* (London: 1761) 15.
2   Richard Middleton, *The Bells of Victory: The Pitt-Newcastle Ministry
     and the Conduct of the Seven Years' War, 1757–1762* (Cambridge: 1985);
     Guy Frégault, *Canada: The War of the Conquest*, trans. Margaret M.
     Cameron (Toronto: 1969) 233-239.
3   Matthew C. Ward, *Breaking the Backcountry: The Seven Years' War in
     Virginia and Pennsylvania, 1754–1765* (Pittsburgh: 2003) 34-36.
4   Duke of Newcastle to Sir Benjamin Keene, 28 April 1755, Additional
     Mss. 32,854:299-302, British Library.

5   J.R. Jones, *Britain and the World, 1649–1815* (London: 1980) 209-210;
     W.A. Speck, *Stability and Strife: England 1714–1760* (London: 1977)
     262-263; Lawrence Henry Gipson, *The Great War for the Empire: The
     Years of Defeat*, 15 vols, vol. 6, *The British Empire before the American
     Revolution* (New York: 1946) 398-417.

6   Alan Rogers, *Empire and Liberty: American Resistance to British
     Authority, 1755–1763* (Berkeley: 1974).

7   Fred Anderson, *Crucible of War: The Seven Years' War and the Fate of
     Empire in British North America, 1754–1766* (New York: 2000) 183-
     184,208.

8   Ian K. Steele, *Betrayals: Fort William Henry and the 'Massacre'* (New
     York: 1990).

9   Arthur G. Doughty, *The Siege of Quebec and the Battle on the Plains of
     Abraham*, 6 vols (Quebec: 1901) 1:207-211.

10   Anderson, *Crucible of War* 250-252; Ian K. Steele, *Guerillas and
     Grenadiers: The Struggle for Canada, 1689–1760* (Toronto: 1969) 116-
     117.

11   Arthur G. Doughty, ed., *An Historical Journal of the Campaigns in
     North America: For the Years 1757, 1758, 1759, and 1760 by Captain John
     Knox*, 3 vols (Toronto: 1914–1916) 241-243; Frégault, *War of the
     Conquest*, 217-220.

12   Stuart Reid, *Wolfe: The Career of General James Wolfe from Culloden to
     Quebec* (Rockville Centre, New York: 2000) 145-154.

13   Dale Miquelon, 'Canada's Place in the French Imperial Economy:
     An Eighteenth Century Overview', *French Historical Studies* 15 (1988)
     432-443; Allan Greer, *The People of New France* (Toronto: 1997).

14   Lord Loudoun to Henry Fox, 3 October 1756, CO 5/47 217-218,
     The National Archives: Public Record Office, Kew, England.

15   Gov. Pownall, 'Idea of the Service in North America for the year
     1759', 5 December 1758, WO 34/25 165, The National Archives:
     Public Record Office, Kew, England.

16   R. Cole Harris, ed., *Historical Atlas of Canada: From the Beginning to
     1800*, 3 vols, vol. 1 (Toronto: 1987).

17   Gov. Pownall, 'Idea of the Service in North America for the year
     1759', 5 December 1758, WO 34/25 165.

18   Eliga H. Gould, *The Persistence of Empire: British Political Culture in the
     Age of the American Revolution* (Chapel Hill: 2000) 72-96.

19   Linda Colley, *Britons: Forging the Nation, 1707–1837* (London: 1996)
     59-97.

20   Frank O'Gorman, *The Long Eighteenth Century: British Political and
     Social History 1688–1832* (London: 1997) 182-185; Patrick K. O'Brien,
     'Inseparable Connections: Trade, Economy, Fiscal State, and the
     Expansion of Empire, 1688–1815', *The Oxford History of the British*

Empire: The Eighteenth Century, ed. P.J. Marshall (Oxford: 1998), 65–70.

21   Speck, *Stability and Strife*, 267.

22   Richard Harding, 'Sailors and Gentlemen of Parade: Some Professional and Technical Problems Concerning the Conduct of Combined Operations in the Eighteenth Century', *Historical Journal*, vol.32 (1989) 33-355.

23   Middleton, *Bells of Victory*, 108-109; N.A.M. Rodger, 'Sea Power and Empire, 1688–1793' in *The Oxford History of the British Empire: The Eighteenth Century*, ed. P.J. Marshall (Oxford: 1998) 169-183; Gerald Graham, *Empire of the North Atlantic: The Maritime Struggle for North America*, 2nd edn (Toronto: 1958) 109,146,153.

24   Howard H. Peckham, *The Colonial Wars, 1689–1762* (Chicago: 1962) 165; Frégault, *War of the Conquest*, 112-113,137.

25   Edmund B. O'Callaghan and Berthold Fernow, eds, *Documents Relative to the Colonial History of the State of New York; Procured in Holland, England and France*, 15 vols (Albany: 1853–1887) 413.

26   Frégault, *War of the Conquest*, 234-236.

27   Bruce Lenman, *Britain's Colonial Wars 1688–1783* (London: 2001) 20-21; Steele, *Guerillas and Grenadiers*, 28-30.

28   Steele, *Guerillas and Grenadiers*, 38-40; Lenman, *Britain's Colonial Wars*, 37-38.

29   Steele, *Guerillas and Grenadiers*, 50-51.

30   *Narrative of the Doings During the Siege of Quebec, and the Conquest of Canada; by a Nun of the General Hospital of Quebec, Transmitted to a Religious Community of the Same Order in France* (Quebec: 1855[?]).

31   Doughty, ed., *Knox's Journal*, 22-23n.

32   Henri Raymond Casgrain, ed., *Journal Du Marquis De Montcalm Durant Ses Campagnes en Canada de 1756 à 1759* (Quebec: 1895) 492,510-511.

33   Middleton, *Bells of Victory*, 97-101.

Chapter 2: Two Armies

1   Quoted in Richard Middleton, *The Bells of Victory: The Pitt-Newcastle Ministry and the Conduct of the Seven Years' War, 1757–1762* (Cambridge: 1985) 101.

2   Stuart Reid, *Wolfe: The Career of General James Wolfe from Culloden to Quebec* (Rockville Centre, New York: 2000) 141.

3   Middleton, *Bells of Victory*, 18,103-104; Reid, *Wolfe*, 165.

4   Secret Instructions of George II to Gen. Wolfe, 5 February 1759, Robert Monckton Papers, Northcliffe Collection, 19:2, Library and Archives Canada, Ottawa.

5   Embarkation Return of His Majesty's Forces, 6 June 1759, CO 6/51 67, The National Archives: Public Record Office, Kew, England.

6   Army for Lake George, 19 June 1759, CO 7/55 236; Wolfe to Amherst, 1 May 1759, WO 34/46B 297-298, The National Archives: Public Record Office, Kew, England.

7   Wolfe to Maj. Walter Wolfe, 19 May 1759, Beckles Wilson, *The Life and Letters of James Wolfe* (London: 1909) 427; Wolfe to Monckton, 8 July 1759, Monckton Papers, vol. 5; Fred Anderson, *A People's Army: Massachusetts Soldiers and Society in the Seven Years' War* (Chapel Hill: 1984).

8   Hew Strachan, *European Armies and the Conduct of War* (London: 1983) 17.

9   17 and 30 July 1759, *Diary of Proceedings up the River St Lawrence*, Townshend Papers, vol. 9, Northcliffe Collection, Library and Archives Canada, Ottawa; Middleton, *Bells of Victory*, 25,63-64; Sylvia R. Frey, *The British Soldier in America: A Social History of Military Life in the Revolutionary Period* (Austin: 1981) 3-21.

10   Orders Given for the Preparation of… the Expedition…, 14 March 1759, CO 5/54 272; Arthur G. Doughty, ed., *An Historical Journal of the Campaigns in North America: For the Years 1757, 1758, 1759, and 1760 by Captain John Knox*, 3 vols (Toronto: 1914–1916) 1:348-353; Strachan, *European Armies and the Conduct of War*, 28-31.

11   Frey, *British Soldier in America*, 60-61.

12   Paul E. Kopperman, 'The British High Command and Soldiers' Wives in America, 1755–1783', *Journal of the Society for Army Historical Research* LX (1982) 26-29; Doughty, ed., *Knox's Journal*, 1:355, 2:338; Major General Wolfe's Orders, General Wolfe's Order Book, 1748–1759, Series 3, Separate Items Northcliffe Collection, vol. 23, Library and Archives Canada, Ottawa.

13   Amherst to Mr Napier, 29 March 1759, CO 5/54 280; Alan J. Guy, *Oeconomy and Discipline: Officership and Administration in the British Army 1714–63* (Manchester: 1985); Kopperman, 'British High Command and Soldiers' Wives in America', 14-34.

14   Kopperman, 'British High Command and Soldiers' Wives in America', 22-26.

15   C.P. Stacey, *Quebec, 1759: The Siege and the Battle* (Toronto: 1959) 7-8; Embarkation Return, 6 June 1759, CO 5/51 67; Amherst to Joshua Loring, 1 February 1759, CO 5/54 166; Amherst to Gov. Pownall, 19 March 1759, CO 5 54/224.

16   Instructions of George II to General Wolfe, 5 February 1759, Monckton Papers, vol. 2.

17   Townshend to Pitt, 20 September 1759, CO 5/51 92.

18   Stephen Brumwell, *Redcoats: The British Soldier and War in the*

Americas, 1755–1763 (Cambridge: 2002) 60.

19   Aegidius Fauteux, ed., 'Journal du Siège de Québec du 10 Mai au 18 Septembre 1759', *Rapport de l'Archiviste de la Province de Québec*, vol.1 (1920-1921): 166,169,185,196; Embarkation Return, 6 June 1759, CO 5/51 67; Wolfe to Amherst, 1 May 1759, CO 5/55 190-191.

20   Brumwell, *Redcoats*, 110.

21   Desmond Morton, *A Military History of Canada: From Champlain to the Gulf War*, 3rd edn (Toronto: 1999) 20-21; Lee Kennett, *The French Armies in the Seven Years' War: A Study in Military Organization and Administration* (Durham NC: 1967) 56-59.

22   Morton, *Military History of Canada*, 20; Peter N. Moogk, 'Reluctant Exiles: Emigrants from France in Canada before 1760', *William and Mary Quarterly*, 46 (1989) 500-502; Edmund B. O'Callaghan and Berthold Fernow, eds, *Documents Relative to the Colonial History of the State of New York; Procured in Holland, England and France*, 15 vols (Albany: 1853–1887) 1017 [hereafter *DRCHNY*].

23   Stacey, *Quebec*, 15.

24   George F.G. Stanley, *Canada's Soldiers 1604–1954: The Military History of an Unmilitary People* (Toronto: 1954) 21-23.

25   *DRCHNY* 10:1017; Henri Raymond Casgrain, ed., *Journal du Marquis de Montcalm durant ses Campagnes en Canada de 1756 à 1759* (Quebec: 1895) 551.

26   Casgrain, ed., *Journal de Montcalm*, 606; J.C. Panet, 'Journal du Siège de Québec en 1759', *Quebec Literary and Historical Society Documents*, Series 4, 10; Henri Titu, ed., 'M. Jean-Felix Récher, Curé de Québec, et Son Journal, 1757–1760', *Bulletin des Recherches Historiques*, vol.9 (1903) 339.

27   *DRCHNY* 947.

28   *Journal of the Siege of Quebec*, Monckton Papers, vol. 13, 74.

29   Daniel K. Richter, *The Ordeal of the Long-House: The Peoples of the Iroquois League in the Era of European Colonization* (Chapel Hill: 1992).

30   *DRCHNY* 10:754.

31   *Ibid.*, 10:966.

32   Martin L. Nicolai, 'A Different Kind of Courage: The French Military and the Canadian Irregular Soldier During the Seven Years' War', *Canadian Historical Review*, 70 (1989) 65; *DRCHNY* 10:1017-1018.

33   Kennett, *French Armies in the Seven Years' War*, 23-26.

34   *DRCHNY* 10:904.

35   *Ibid.*, 906-907; Guy Frégault, *Canada: The War of the Conquest*, trans. Margaret M. Cameron (Toronto: 1969) 242-244.

36   *DRCHNY* 960-961; Casgrain, ed., *Journal de Montcalm*, 492, 513-

516,534.

37   Frégault, *War of the Conquest*, 242-243; *DRCHNY* 10:1017.

38   Casgrain, ed., *Journal de Montcalm*, 526,552.

39   Panet, 'Journal du Siège de Québec en 1759', 4-5; Casgrain, ed., *Journal de Montcalm*, 553.

40   *DRCHNY* 1016-1017; Fauteux, 'Journal du Siège', 151.

41   *DRCHNY* 1017,1050.

42   20-30 May, *Journal of the Siege*, Monckton Papers, vol. 13.

43   Montcalm, *Mémoir sur la défense de Québec, Lettres et Pièces Militaires, Instructions, Ordres, Mémoirs, Plans de Campagne et de Défense, 1758–1760*, ed. Henri Raymond Casgrain, vol. 4, Collection des Manuscrits de Maréchal De Lévis (Quebec: 1891) 4:168-170; Fauteux, 'Journal du Siège', 148,154.

44   Gaston Deschênes, *L'Année des Anglais: La Côte-du-Sud à l'Heure de la Conquête* (Sillery, Quebec: 1988) 33-38.

45   29 August 1758, Captain Thomas Bell Journal, Manuscript Quebec Journals, Separate Items No. 24, Northcliffe Collection, Library and Archives Canada, Ottawa; 30 October 1758, Journal of Operations 1757–1765, Frederick Mackenzie Collection, Library and Archives Canada, Ottawa; Fred Anderson, *Crucible of War: The Seven Years' War and the Fate of Empire in British North America, 1754–1766* (New York: 2000) 112-114.

46   M.S. Anderson, *War and Society in Europe of the Old Regime* (London: 1988) 191-192.

47   Emmerich de Vattel, *The Law of Nations: Or the Principles of the Law of Nature Applied to the Conduct and Affairs of Nations and Sovereigns*, trans. Joseph Chitty (Philadelphia: 1863) 351.

Chapter 3: Beginnngs

1   Admiral Holmes to William Pitt, 2 March 1759, CO 5/51 23-24, The National Archives: Public Record Office, Kew, England; Instructions of George II to General Wolfe, Robert Monckton Papers, Northcliffe Collection vol. 2, Library and Archives Canada, Ottawa.

2   Hutchinson to Amherst, 12 May 1759, WO 34/25 248, The National Archives: Public Record Office, Kew, England.

3   Wolfe to Monckton, 17 May 1759, Monckton Papers vol. 81; Saunders to Pitt, 1 May 1759, CO 5/51 29-30.

4   'Journal of Major Moncrief', *The Siege of Quebec and the Battle of the Plains of Abraham*, ed. Arthur Doughty (Quebec: 1901) 34; Henri Raymond Casgrain, ed., *Journal du Marquis de Montcalm durant ses Campagnes en Canada de 1756 à 1759* (Quebec: 1895) 506-507;

Guy Frégault, *Canada: The War of the Conquest*, trans. Margaret M. Cameron (Toronto: 1969) 240.

5   Edmund B. O'Callaghan and Berthold Fernow, eds, *Documents Relative to the Colonial History of the State of New York; Procured in Holland, England and France*, 15 vols (Albany: 1853–1887) 10:925-930 [hereafter *DRCHNY*]; *Journal of the Siege of Quebec*, Monckton Papers, vol. 13; *Précis de Plan d'Operations Générales*, Henri Raymond Casgrain, ed., *Collection des Manuscrits de Maréchal de Lévis*, vol. 4, *Lettres et Pièces Militaires, Instructions, Ordres, Mémoirs, Plans de Campagne et de Défense, 1758–1760* (Quebec: 1891) 157.

6   Oliver Warner, *With Wolfe to Quebec: The Path to Glory* (London: 1972) 82; *DRCHNY* 10:952-956.

7   Frégault, *War of the Conquest*, 233-238.

8   *DRCHNY* 10:943-944.

9   *Memoirs of the Siege of Quebec, Capital of All Canada and of the Retreat of Monsieur De Bourlamaque to the Isle Aux Noix in Lake Champlain from the Journal of a French Officer,* (London: 1761) 15.

10   Aegidius Fauteux, ed., 'Journal du Siège de Québec du 10 Mai au 18 Septembre 1759' *Rapport de l'Archiviste de la Province de Québec* 1 (1920–1921) 145; Casgrain, ed., *Journal De Montcalm*, 524.

11   May 1759, *Journal of the Siege*, Monckton Papers, vol. 13.

12   15-20 June 1759, *Ibid.*

13   *Journal of Wolfe's Campaign of 1759* [hereafter *McCord Museum Journal*], M 277, McCord Museum of Canadian History, Montreal.

14   Arthur G. Doughty, ed., *An Historical Journal of the Campaigns in North America: For the Years 1757, 1758, 1759, and 1760 by Captain John Knox*, 3 vols. (Toronto: 1914–1916) 1:355.

15   *Ibid.*, 1:308,323.

16   29 May 1759, *[McCord Museum] Journal*.

17   *A Journal of the Expedition up the River St. Lawrence (by a Sgt Major in Hopson's Grenadiers)* [hereafter *Hopson's Journal*], Siege of Quebec Collection, vol. 4, file 5, f.3, Library and Archives Canada, Ottawa; Doughty, ed., *Knox's Journal* 1: 362, 372-373.

18   20-30 May, *Journal of the Siege*, Monckton Papers, vol. 13; Casgrain, ed., *Journal de Montcalm* 546; Fauteux, 'Journal du Siège', 153; *Memoirs of the Siege of Quebec, Capital of All Canada and of the Retreat of Monsieur De Bourlamaque to the Isle Aux Noix in Lake Champlain from the Journal of a French Officer*, 18.

19   Casgrain, ed., *Journal de Montcalm*, 556-559; Arthur G. Doughty, *The Siege of Quebec and the Battle on the Plains of Abraham*, 6 vols (Quebec: 1901) 2:78-79.

20   Casgrain, ed., *Journal de Montcalm*, 554.

21   Stuart Reid, *Wolfe: The Career of General James Wolfe from Culloden to*

Quebec (Rockville Centre, New York: 2000) 164.

22   Beckles Wilson, *The Life and Letters of James Wolfe* (London: 1909) 428.

23   Captain Thomas Bell Journal, Manuscript Quebec Journals Separate Items No. 24, Northcliffe Collection, Library and Archives Canada, Ottawa; Doughty, *Siege of Quebec*, 2:66; Wolfe's Journal, James Wolfe Collection, vol. 5, Library and Archives Canada, Ottawa.

24   25-27 June, *Journal of the Siege*, Monckton Papers, vol. 13.

25   John Johnson Journal, Siege of Quebec 1759 Collection, vol. 3, ff. 12-13, Library and Archives Canada, Ottawa.

26   J.C. Panet, 'Journal du Siège de Québec en 1759', *Quebec Literary and Historical Society Documents*, Series 4:5; 'Journal Abrégé de la Campagne de 1759 en Canada', *The Siege of Quebec and the Battle of the Plains of Abraham*, ed. Arthur Doughty (Quebec: 1901) 5:284.

27   *Journal of the Siege*, Monckton Papers, vol. 13, 25.

28   Doughty, ed., *Knox's Journal*, 1:381-382.

29   Casgrain, ed., *Journal de Montcalm*, 561.

30   *Journal of the Siege*, Monckton Papers, vol. 13, 27-29.

31   Henri Titu, ed., 'M. Jean-Felix Récher, Curé de Québec, et Son Journal, 1757–1760,' *Bulletin des Recherches Historiques* 9 (1903) 330; Fauteux, 'Journal du Siège', 170.

32   29 June 1759, Journal of Operations, 1757–1765, Frederick Mackenzie Collection, Library and Archives Canada, Ottawa; Wolfe to Pitt, 2 September 1759, CO 5/51 73; 29 June, Bell's Journal; *DRCHNY* 1019.

33   Wolfe's Journal.

34   *Ibid.*; James Murray, *Journal of the Expedition against Quebec*, Series 4, James Murray Collection, Library and Archives Canada, Ottawa.

35   Casgrain, ed., *Journal de Montcalm*, 571-583.

36   *Journal of the Siege*, Monckton Papers, vol. 13, 30-31.

37   Casgrain, ed., *Journal de Montcalm*, 562-565.

38   *DRCHNY* 10:996.

39   Wolfe's Journal.

40   Titu, 'Journal de Récher', 332; C.P. Stacey, *Quebec, 1759: The Siege and the Battle* (Toronto: 1959) 57; Johnson Journal, 16-17.

41   Doughty, *Siege of Quebec*, 2:87-89; Capt. John Montrésor, 'Journal of the Siege of Quebec', *The Siege of Quebec and the Battle of the Plains of Abraham*, ed. Arthur Doughty (Quebec: 1901) 4:312; 'Journal of the Siege of Quebec, by Brigadier General Townshend' in *The Siege of Quebec and the Battle on the Plains of Abraham*, ed. Arthur Doughty (Quebec: 1901) 4:261.

42   Casgrain, ed., *Journal de Montcalm*, 570.

43   *Ibid.*, 571.

44   Titu, 'Journal de Récher', 339.

45   *Journal of the Siege*, Monckton Papers, vol. 13, 44; *DRCHNY* 10:1023.

46   *Journal of the Siege*, Monckton Papers, vol. 13, 44.

47   *Ibid.*, 45.

48   Casgrain, ed., *Journal de Montcalm*, 573.

49   Wolfe's Journal; Wolfe to Monckton, 16 July 1759, Monckton Papers, Northcliffe Collection vol. 5, Library and Archives Canada, Ottawa; *Journal of the Particular Transactions During the Siege of Quebec by an Officer of Fraser's Regiment* (Quebec: 1901) 9.

50   Wolfe to Monckton, 20 July 1759, Monckton Papers, vol. 81.

51   Wilson, *Life and Letters of Wolfe*, 384-385; *DRCHNY* 10:1025; Doughty, ed., *Knox's Journal*, 589; Fauteux, 'Journal du Siège', 174.

52   Casgrain, ed., *Journal de Montcalm*, 580.

53   Emmerich de Vattel, *The Law of Nations: Or the Principles of the Law of Nature Applied to the Conduct and Affairs of Nations and Sovereigns*, trans. Joseph Chitty (Philadelphia: 1863) 352; *DRCHNY* 10:1025.

54   Doughty, ed., *Knox's Journal*, 1:441.

55   M.S. Anderson, *War and Society in Europe of the Old Regime* (London: 1988) 193; Precautions taken for the safety of proposed negotiations between Le Mercier & Wolfe, 24 July 1759, Admiral Saunders to General Townshend, 25 July 1759, Monckton Papers, vol. 21; Alexander Schomberg Journal, Siege of Quebec 1759 Collection, vol. 2, 20, Library and Archives Canada, Ottawa; Fauteux, 'Journal du Siège', 177; Panet, 'Journal du Siège de Québec en 1759', 17; Titu, 'Journal de Récher', 353; *Journal of the Siege*, Monckton Papers, vol. 13, 53-54.

56   *DRCHNY* 10:1046-1047.

57   *Journal of an Officer of Frasers' Regt.*, 4; Panet, 'Journal du Siège de Québec en 1759', 9; Titu, 'Journal de Récher', 353.

58   *DRCHNY* 10:999-1001, 1025; Titu, 'Journal de Récher', 345; Panet, 'Journal du Siège de Québec en 1759', 17.

Chapter 4: Frustration

1   'Journal Abrégé de la Campagne de 1759 en Canada', in *The Siege of Quebec and the Battle of the Plains of Abraham*, ed. Arthur Doughty (Quebec: 1901) 6:288-289.

2   23 July 1759, Wolfe's Journal, James Wolfe Collection, vol. 5, Library and Archives Canada, Ottawa.

3   'Journal of Major Moncrief' in *The Siege of Quebec and the Battle of the Plains of Abraham*, ed. Arthur Doughty (Quebec: 1901) 5:39.

4   Wolfe to Monckton, 20 July 1759, Monckton Papers, Northcliffe

Collection, vol. 81, Library and Archives Canada, Ottawa; Maurice de Saxe, 'My Reveries Upon the Art of War', in *Roots of Strategy: A Collection of Military Classics*, ed. Maj. Thomas R. Philips (London: 1943) 146.

5   Edmund B. O'Callaghan and Berthold Fernow, eds, *Documents Relative to the Colonial History of the State of New York; Procured in Holland, England and France*, 15 vols (Albany: 1853–1887) 10:1025 [hereafter *DRCHNY*].

6   Arthur G. Doughty, ed., *An Historical Journal of the Campaigns in North America: For the Years 1757, 1758, 1759, and 1760 by Captain John Knox*, 3 vols (Toronto: 1914-1916) 1:428.

7   *Journal of the Siege of Quebec* [hereafter *Journal of the Siege*], vol. 13, 51.

8   Beckles Wilson, *The Life and Letters of James Wolfe* (London: 1909) 448.

9   7 July 1759, Wolfe's Journal.

10   *DRCHNY* 1024.

11   Amherst to Pitt, 27 July 1759, CO 5/56 1, The National Archives: Public Record Office, Kew, England; Fred Anderson, *Crucible of War: The Seven Years' War and the Fate of Empire in British North America, 1754–1766* (New York: 2000) 340-343.

12   Quoted in Guy Frégault, *Canada: The War of the Conquest*, trans. Margaret M. Cameron (Toronto: 1969) 260; Amherst to Thomas Gage, 14 August 1759, WO 34/46A 175-176, The National Archives: Public Record Office, Kew, England.

13   Wolfe to Amherst, 29 December 1758, WO 34/46B 286-289.

14   *Journal of the Siege*, Monckton Papers, vol. 13, 51,52.

15   29 July 1759, Wolfe's Journal; René Chartrand, *Québec: The Heights of Abraham 1759; the Armies of Wolfe and Montcalm* (Oxford: 1999) 70-71; C.P. Stacey, *Quebec, 1759: The Siege and the Battle* (Toronto: 1959) 74-75.

16   30 July 1759, Wolfe's Journal.

17   Arthur G. Doughty, *The Siege of Quebec and the Battle on the Plains of Abraham*, 6 vols (Quebec: 1901) 2:130.

18   30 July 1759, Wolfe's Journal.

19   Lévis to Bellestre, 2 August 1759, *Lettres de Monsieur le Marquis de Lévis Concernant la Guerre du Canada, 1756–1762*, Fonds Chevalier de Lévis 11:275, Library and Archives Canada, Ottawa; James Murray, *Journal of the Expedition against Quebec*, Series 4, James Murray Collection 14-16, Library and Archives Canada, Ottawa; Wolfe to Saunders, 30 August 1759, Wilson, *Life and Letters of Wolfe*, 460-463.

20   31 July 1759, Wolfe's Journal .

21   Wolfe to Pitt, 2 September 1759, CO 5/51 77.

22   Wolfe to Saunders, 30 August 1759, Wilson, *Life and Letters of*

Wolfe, 461; 'Journal of the Siege of Quebec, by Brigadier General Townshend', in *The Siege of Quebec and the Battle on the Plains of Abraham*, ed. Arthur Doughty (Quebec: 1901) 4:264.

23   Alexander Schomberg Journal, Siege of Quebec 1759 Collection vol. 2, 33-35, Library and Archives Canada, Ottawa.

24   Montcalm to Lévis, 31 July 1759, Henri Raymond Casgrain, ed., *Lettres du Marquis de Montcalm au Chevalier de Lévis* (Quebec: 1894) 211.

25   Henri Raymond Casgrain, ed., *Journal des Campagnes du Chevalier de Lévis en Canada de 1756 à 1760* (Montreal: 1889) 185-186.

26   *DRCHNY* 10:1029; Casgrain, ed., *Journal de Lévis*, 186.

27   Doughty, ed., *Knox's Journal*, 2:452-454.

28   *Extract from a Letter from an officer in Maj Genl. Wolfe's Army*, 10 August 1759, Seven Years' War Collection, Library and Archives Canada, Ottawa.

29   *A Journal of the Expedition up the River St Lawrence (by a Sgt Major in Hopson's Grenadiers)* [hereafter *Hopson's Journal*], Siege of Quebec Collection, vol. 4, File 5, 10, Library and Archives Canada, Ottawa.

30   *Ibid.*

31   31 July 1759, 'Journal of Operations, 1757–1765', Frederick Mackenzie Collection, Library and Archives Canada, Ottawa.

32   *Journal of the Siege*, Monckton Papers, vol. 13, 63, Northcliffe Collection, Library and Archives Canada, Ottawa.

33   *DRCHNY* 10:1029.

34   *Murray's Journal*, 18-19.

35   John Johnson Journal, Siege of Quebec 1759 Collection, vol. 3, 22, Library and Archives Canada, Ottawa.

36   *Narrative of the Doings During the Siege of Quebec, and the Conquest of Canada; by a Nun of the General Hospital of Quebec, Transmitted to a Religious Community of the Same Order in France*, (Quebec: 1855[?]) 7.

37   Doughty, *Siege of Quebec*, 2:159-163.

38   31 July 1759, *Wolfe's Journal*.

39   Henri Raymond Casgrain, ed., *Journal du Marquis de Montcalm durant ses Campagnes en Canada de 1756 à 1759* (Quebec: 1895) 585; Oliver Warner, *With Wolfe to Quebec: The Path to Glory* (London: 1972) 127-128.

40   1 August 1759, General Wolfe's Order Book, 1748–1759, Series 3: Separate Items Northcliffe Collection, vol. 23, Library and Archives Canada, Ottawa.

41   Wolfe to Monckton, 15 August 1759, Monckton Papers, vol. 5.

42   Wolfe to Monckton, 16 August 1759, *Ibid.*

43   Johnson Journal, 34; Wolfe's Order Book.

44   Doughty, ed., *Knox's Journal*, 2:18, 41.

45   *Ibid.*, 2:40; Stuart Reid, *Wolfe: The Career of General James Wolfe from*

Culloden to Quebec (Rockville Centre, New York: 2000) 93.

46   Doughty, ed., *Knox's Journal*, 2:19.

47   16 September 1759, General Monckton's Orderly Book, Robert Monckton Papers, vol. 6, Library and Archives Canada, Ottawa.

48   *Journal of the Particular Transactions During the Siege of Quebec by an Officer of Frasers' Regiment*, (Quebec: 1901) 29.

49   26 June 1759, Brigadier General Townshend's General Orders, Townshend Papers, vol. 8, Library and Archives Canada, Ottawa; Sylvia R. Frey, *The British Soldier in America: A Social History of Military Life in the Revolutionary Period* (Austin: 1981) 22-23, 40-42.

50   29 July 1759, Wolfe's Order Book.

51   23 July 1759, *Ibid.*; Capt. John Montrésor, 'Journal of the Siege of Quebec', in *The Siege of Quebec and the Battle of the Plains of Abraham*, ed. Arthur Doughty (Quebec: 1901) 4:329.

52   7 August 1759, General Monckton's Orderly Book.

53   23 July 1759, Wolfe's Order Book.

54   22 July 1759, *Ibid.*; Paul E. Kopperman, 'The British High Command and Soldiers' Wives in America, 1755–1783', *Journal of the Society for Army Historical Research* LX (1982) 19.

55   Doughty, ed., *Knox's Journal*, 2:7.

56   Doughty, ed., *Knox's Journal*, 1:407; 20 August 1759, General Monckton's Orderly Book.

57   2 July, 6 July, 29 July 1759, 7 August, Wolfe's Order Book; Stephen Brumwell, *Redcoats: The British Soldier and War in the Americas, 1755–1763* (Cambridge: 2002) 105.

58   7 August 1759, General Monckton's Orderly Book; Frey, *British Soldier in America*, 64-65.

59   Henri Titu, ed., 'M. Jean-Felix Récher, Curé de Québec, et son Journal, 1757–1760', *Bulletin des Recherches Historiques* 9 (1903) 345; Frégault, *War of the Conquest*, 239-240.

60   *DRCHNY* 10:1044.

61   Aegidius Fauteux, ed., 'Journal du Siège de Québec du 10 Mai au 18 Septembre 1759', *Rapport de l'Archiviste de la Province de Québec* 1 (1920–1921) 178; 'Relation Du Siege De Québec', *Rapport de l'Archiviste de la Province de Québec* 18 (1937–38) 19.

62   Doughty, *Siege of Quebec*, 163-164; *Narrative of the Siege of Quebec by a Nun of the General Hospital*, 1-6.

63   Titu, 'Journal De Récher', 343.

Chapter 5: The Distasteful War

1   *A Journal of the Expedition up the River St. Lawrence (by a Sgt Major in Hopson's Grenadiers)* [hereafter *Hopson's Journal*], Siege of Quebec

Collection, vol. 4 File 5, 18, Library and Archives Canada, Ottawa.

2   Wolfe to his mother, 31 August 1759, James Wolfe Collection, vol. 1,
    Library and Archives Canada, Ottawa.

3   Wolfe to his mother, 17 October 1757, *Ibid.*, vol. 3.

4   Quoted in Stuart Reid, *Wolfe: The Career of General James Wolfe from
    Culloden to Quebec* (Rockville Centre, New York: 2000) 59.

5   Arthur G. Doughty, ed., *An Historical Journal of the Campaigns in
    North America: For the Years 1757, 1758, 1759, and 1760 by Captain John
    Knox*, 3 vols (Toronto: 1914–1916) 2:40,42,55.

6   John Johnson Journal, Siege of Quebec 1759 Collection, vol. 3, 29-
    30, Library and Archives Canada, Ottawa.

7   Aegidius Fauteux, ed., 'Journal du Siège de Québec du 10 Mai au
    18 Septembre 1759', *Rapport de l'Archiviste de la Province de Québec* 1
    (1920–1921) 164,185.

8   *Journal of the Siege of Quebec* [hereafter *Journal of the Siege*],
    Monckton Papers, vol. 13, 68, Northcliffe Collection, Library and
    Archives Canada, Ottawa; Montcalm to Lévis, 2 August 1759, Henri
    Raymond Casgrain, ed., *Lettres du Marquis de Montcalm au Chevalier
    de Lévis* (Quebec: 1894) 212-213.

9   Doughty, ed., *Knox's Journal*, 2:310; Sylvia R. Frey, *The British Soldier
    in America: A Social History of Military Life in the Revolutionary Period*
    (Austin: 1981) 90; Stephen Brumwell, *Redcoats: The British Soldier and
    War in the Americas, 1755–1763* (Cambridge: 2002) 106.

10 Brumwell, *Redcoats*, 112-120.

11 Frey, *British Soldier in America*, 72-73,80-81.

12 Vaudreuil to Lévis, 18 August 1759, Henri Raymond Casgrain,
    Lettres du Marquis de Vaudreuil au Chevalier de Lévis (Quebec: 1895)
    86.

13 'Journal Abrégé de la Campagne de 1759 en Canada', in *The Siege
    of Quebec and the Battle of the Plains of Abraham*, ed. Arthur Doughty
    (Quebec: 1901) 293; Henri Raymond Casgrain, ed., *Journal du
    Marquis de Montcalm Durant ses Campagnes en Canada de 1756 à 1759*
    (Quebec: 1895) 587.

14 *Journal of the Siege*, Monckton Papers, vol. 13, 40-41; 'Journal Abrégé
    de la Campagne de 1759', 5:292-293.

15 Edmund B. O'Callaghan and Berthold Fernow, eds, *Documents
    Relative to the Colonial History of the State of New York; Procured in
    Holland, England and France*, 15 vols (Albany: 1853–1887) 10:947
    [hereafter *DRCHNY*].

16 *Journal of the Siege*, Monckton Papers, vol. 13, 68.

17 Vaudreuil to Lévis, 18 August 1759, Casgrain, *Lettres de Vaudreuil à
    Lévis*, 86.

18 *Journal of the Siege*, Monckton Papers, vol. 13, 54; 15 July, Captain

Thomas Bell Journal, Manuscript Quebec Journals Separate Items No. 24, Northcliffe Collection, Library and Archives Canada, Ottawa.

19 Henri Titu, ed., 'M. Jean-Felix Récher, Curé de Québec, et Son Journal, 1757–1760', *Bulletin des Recherches Historiques,* vol. 9 (1903): 342-344,353; Capt. John Montrésor, 'Journal of the Siege of Quebec', in *The Siege of Quebec and the Battle of the Plains of Abraham,* ed. Arthur Doughty (Quebec: 1901) 316.

20 'Relation du Siege de Québec', *Rapport de l'Archiviste de la Province de Québec,* vol. 18 (1937–38) 15; *Journal of the Siege,* Monckton Papers, vol. 13, 65.

21 *Journal of the Siege,* Monckton Papers, vol. 13, 66-67.

22 James Murray, *Journal of the Expedition against Quebec,* Series 4, James Murray Collection, 14, Library and Archives Canada, Ottawa; *Journal of the Particular Transactions During the Siege of Quebec by an Officer of Frasers' Regiment,* (Quebec: 1901) 12; 11 August, Journal of Operations, 1757–1765, Frederick Mackenzie Collection, Library and Archives Canada, Ottawa; Charles Saunders to William Pitt, 5 September 1759, CO 5/51 40, The National Archives: Public Record Office, Kew, England.

23 *Journal of the Siege,* Monckton Papers, vol. 13, 57.

24 *DRCHNY* 10:1047-1048.

25 2 August, Wolfe's Journal, James Wolfe Collection, vol. 5, Library and Archives Canada, Ottawa.

26 Johnson Journal, 33.

27 Gorham to Wolfe, 19 August 1759, Robert Monckton Papers, Northcliffe Collection, vol. 21, Library and Archives Canada, Ottawa.

28 Gaston Deschênes, *L'Année des Anglais: La Côte-du-Sud à l'Heure de la Conquête* (Sillery, Québec: 1988).

29 Report of a Tour to the South Shore of the River St Lawrence, Monckton Papers, vol. 21; Gorham to Amherst, 30 September 1759, WO 34/4 1, The National Archives: Public Record Office, Kew, England.

30 J.C. Panet, 'Journal du Siège de Québec en 1759', *Quebec Literary and Historical Society Documents,* Series 4, 27; Titu, 'Journal de Récher', 369-370,386; *Murray's Journal,* 19-20; *Journal of an Officer of Frasers' Regt.,* 22, 29-30; James Murray to Admiral Holmes, 11 August 1759, James Murray to Gen. Wolfe, 25 August 1759, James Murray Collection, Series 1, in *Library and Archives Canada* (Ottawa); Henri Raymond Casgrain, ed., *Journal des Campagnes du Chevalier de Lévis en Canada de 1756 à 1760* (Montreal: 1889) 193.

31 *DRCHNY* 10:1059.

32 Emmerich de Vattel, *The Law of Nations: Or the Principles of the Law of Nature Applied to the Conduct and Affairs of Nations and Sovereigns*, trans. Joseph Chitty (Philadelphia: 1863) 352.

33 *Ibid.*, 369.

34 *Journal of the Siege*, Monckton Papers, vol. 13, 90; Fauteux, 'Journal Du Siège', 194; *Journal of Wolfe's Campaign of 1759* [hereafter *McCord Museum Journal*], M 277, McCord Museum of Canadian History, Montreal.

35 Vattel, *Law of Nations*, 367.

36 Beckles Wilson, *The Life and Letters of James Wolfe* (London: 1909) 473.

37 *DRCHNY* 10:1026.

38 Wolfe to Monckton, 25 July 1759, Monckton Papers, vol. 22.

39 Johnson Journal, 10.

40 *Narrative of the Doings During the Siege of Quebec, and the Conquest of Canada; by a Nun of the General Hospital of Quebec, Transmitted to a Religious Community of the Same Order in France* (Quebec: 1855[?]) 7; Johnson Journal, 22.

41 Vaudreuil to Lévis, 5 July 1759, Casgrain, *Lettres de Vaudreuil à Lévis*, 64; Fred Anderson, *Crucible of War: The Seven Years' War and the Fate of Empire in British North America, 1754–1766* (New York: 2000) 238-239.

42 Daniel K. Richter, *The Ordeal of the Long-House: The Peoples of the Iroquois League in the Era of European Colonization* (Chapel Hill: 1992); Ian K. Steele, *Betrayals: Fort William Henry and the 'Massacre'* (New York: 1990).

43 Wilson, *Life and Letters of Wolfe*, 474; *DRCHNY* 10:954-955.

44 Casgrain, ed., *Journal de Montcalm*, 589.

45 Panet, 'Journal du Siège de Québec en 1759', 11; Casgrain, ed., *Journal de Montcalm*, 589.

46 Doughty, ed., *Knox's Journal*, 2:56; Deschênes, *L'Année des Anglais* .

47 2 July 1759, *[McCord Museum] Journal*; *DRCHNY* 10:1032; James Axtell and William C. Sturtevant, 'The Unkindest Cut, or Who Invented Scalping?', *William and Mary Quarterly*, Series 3, 37 (1980) 451-472; Daniel K. Richter, 'War and Culture: The Iroquois Experience', *William and Mary Quarterly*, Series 3, 40 (1983) 528-529.

48 Johnson Journal, 10-11.

49 *DRCHNY* 10:1047.

50 Doughty, ed., *Knox's Journal*, 2:36.

51 *Journal of the Siege*, Monckton Papers, vol. 13, 78.

52 10 July 1759, *[McCord Museum] Journal*.

53 General Wolfe's Order Book, 1748–1759, Series 3, Separate Items

Northcliffe Collection, vol. 23, 172, Library and Archives Canada, Ottawa.

54 Wolfe to Monckton, 16 August 1759, Monckton Papers, vol. 22; 29 August 1759, *Journal of an Officer of Frasers' Regt.*, 29.

55 *[McCord Museum] Journal*; *DRCHNY* 10:1034.

56 Casgrain, ed., *Journal De Montcalm*, 602.

57 Doughty, ed., *Knox's Journal*, 1:443.

58 5 March 1759, Journal of Operations; *Journal of an Officer of Frasers' Regt.*, 29; 30 June 1759, Bell's Journal.

59 29 August 1758, Bell's Journal.

60 7 July 1759, *Ibid*.

61 Journal of Operations, 30 October 1758, 12 February 1759, 5 March 1759; Amherst and Boscawen Letter, 10 August 1758, CO 5/53 52; Amherst to Brigadier-General Lawrence, 9 March 1759, WO 34/46B 99; Murray to Amherst, 24 December 1759, James Murray Collection, Series 1, 1:16-19.

62 Townshend to Lady Ferrers, 6 September 1759, Arthur G. Doughty, *The Siege of Quebec and the Battle on the Plains of Abraham*, 6 vols (Quebec: 1901) 5:195.

63 Townshend to Amherst, 7 October 1759, WO 34/46B 217-218.

64 Gaston Deschênes, *L'Année Des Anglais: La Côte-du-Sud à l'Heure de la Conquête* (Sillery, Quebec: 1988).

65 Doughty, ed., *Knox's Journal*, 1:431.

66 Montcalm to Lévis, 25 July 1759, Casgrain, *Lettres de Vaudreuil à Lévis*, 197.

67 *Journal of the Siege*, Monckton Papers, vol. 13, 48, 52.

68 Townshend to Amherst, 7 October 1759, WO 34/46B 217-218; Doughty, ed., *Knox's Journal*, 2:90n.

Chapter 6: The Plains of Abraham

1 Lévis to Montcalm, 6 September 1759, Lévis Collection, 11:282, Library and Archives Canada, Ottawa.

2 Wolfe to Pitt, 2 September 1759, CO 5/51 84, The National Archives: Public Record Office, Kew, England.

3 Saunders to Pitt, 5 September 1759, CO 5/51 40.

4 *Journal of the Siege of Quebec*, Monckton Papers, vol. 13, 86, Northcliffe Collection, Library and Archives Canada, Ottawa.

5 Wolfe to Monckton, 22 August 1759, Robert Monckton Papers, Northcliffe Collection, vol. 81, Library and Archives Canada, Ottawa.

6 Wolfe's Instructions to Brigadiers, [August] 1759, George Townshend Papers, Northcliffe Collection, vol. 1, Library and Archives Canada, Ottawa; Christopher Hibbert, *Wolfe at Quebec* (London: 1959) 107;

Barré to Monckton, 24 August 1759, Arthur G. Doughty, *The Siege of Quebec and the Battle on the Plains of Abraham*, 6 vols (Quebec: 1901) 6:69.

7   Reply of the Brigadier-Generals to Wolfe, 29 August 1759, Monckton Papers, vol. 48; 28-31 August 1759, *Diary of Proceedings up the River St Lawrence*, Townshend Papers, vol. 9, Northcliffe Collection, Library and Archives Canada, Ottawa.

8   Beckles Wilson, *The Life and Letters of James Wolfe* (London: 1909) 463-464; Stuart Reid, *Quebec 1759: The Battle That Won Canada* (Oxford: 2003) 51.

9   Arthur G. Doughty, ed., *An Historical Journal of the Campaigns in North America: For the Years 1757, 1758, 1759, and 1760 by Captain John Knox*, 3 vols (Toronto: 1914–1916) 57-59,70-71; Edmund B. O'Callaghan and Berthold Fernow, eds, *Documents Relative to the Colonial History of the State of New York; Procured in Holland, England and France*, 15 vols (Albany: 1853–1887) 1035-1036 [hereafter *DRCHNY*].

10 4 September 1759, General Monckton's Orderly Book, Robert Monckton Papers, vol. 6, Library and Archives Canada, Ottawa; Hibbert, *Wolfe at Quebec*, 120-121.

11 J.C. Panet, 'Journal Du Siège De Québec en 1759', *Quebec Literary and Historical Society Documents*, Series 4, 31; Vaudreuil to Lévis, 7 September 1759, Henri Raymond Casgrain, *Lettres du Marquis de Vaudreuil au Chevalier de Lévis* (Quebec: 1895) 100-101; Henri Raymond Casgrain, ed., *Journal du Marquis de Montcalm durant ses Campagnes en Canada de 1756 à 1759* (Quebec: 1895) 603-604.

12 'Journal of Major Moncrief', in *The Siege of Quebec and the Battle of the Plains of Abraham*, ed. Arthur Doughty (Quebec: 1901) 47; Doughty, ed., *Knox's Journal*, 80-83.

13 8 September 1759, *Diary of Proceedings up the River St Lawrence*; 'Journal of Major Moncrief', 48.

14 Murray to Townshend, 5 October 1759, Townshend Papers, vol. 12; C.P. Stacey, *Quebec, 1759: The Siege and the Battle* (Toronto: 1959) 108-109.

15 Doughty, *Siege of Quebec*, 4:296.

16 Monckton, Townshend and Murray to Wolfe, 12 September 1759, Townshend Papers, vol. 12.

17 *Journal of the Particular Transactions During the Siege of Quebec by an Officer of Frasers' Regiment* (Quebec: 1901) 32.

18 Doughty, ed., *Knox's Journal*, 2:82-83.

19 *Journal of an Officer of Frasers' Regt.*, 33.

20 Saunders to Pitt, 21 September 1759, CO 5/51 45; Donald W. Olson *et al.*, 'Perfect Tide, Ideal Moon: An Unappreciated Aspect of Wolfe's Generalship at Québec, 1759', *William and Mary Quarterly*, Series 3,

59 (2002) 957-975.

21   Hibbert, *Wolfe at Quebec*, 122-124; Stacey, *Quebec*, 106-107.

22   Quoted in Guy Frégault, *Canada: The War of the Conquest*, trans. Margaret M. Cameron (Toronto: 1969) 253; Vaudreuil to Lévis, 9 September 1759, Casgrain, *Lettres de Vaudreuil à Lévis*, 104.

23   René Chartrand, *Québec: The Heights of Abraham 1759; the Armies of Wolfe and Montcalm* (Oxford: 1999) 81.

24   'Journal of Major Moncrief', 50; Stuart Reid, *Wolfe: The Career of General James Wolfe from Culloden to Quebec* (Rockville Centre, New York: 2000) 187.

25   'Journal of Major Moncrief', 50; Stacey, *Quebec*, 130-131; *Journal of an Officer of Frasers' Regt.*, 35-37; Reid, *Wolfe*, 188.

26   James Murray, *Journal of the Expedition against Quebec*, Series 4, James Murray Collection 29-31, Library and Archives Canada, Ottawa.

27   Quoted in Frégault, *War of the Conquest*, 254; Henri Raymond Casgrain, ed., *Journal des Campagnes du Chevalier de Lévis en Canada de 1756 à 1760* (Montreal: 1889) 207-208.

28   'Journal of Major Moncrief', 52.

29   *Ibid.*, 51-52.

30   *DRCHNY* 10:1038.

31   Robin Reilly, *The Rest to Fortune: The Life of Major-General James Wolfe* (London: 1960) 308-309.

32   *DRCHNY* 10:1052; Vaudreuil to Bougainville, Doughty, *Siege of Quebec,* 4:204.

33   *DRCHNY* 10:1017-1018,1039; Chartrand, *Quebec, 1759,* 86-87; Stacey, *Quebec*, 144-145.

34   Townshend to Pitt, CO 5/51 91; 'Journal Abrégé de la Campagne de 1759 en Canada', in *The Siege of Quebec and the Battle of the Plains of Abraham*, ed. Arthur Doughty (Quebec: 1901), 296-297; Reid, *Quebec 1759*, 73.

35   *DRCHNY* 10:1039.

36   Doughty, ed., *Knox's Journal*, 2:99.

37   'Journal of the Siege of Quebec, by Brigadier General Townshend', in *The Siege of Quebec and the Battle on the Plains of Abraham*, ed. Arthur Doughty (Quebec: 1901), 269.

38   Reid, *Quebec 1759*, 74.

39   *Journal of an Officer of Frasers' Regt.*, 37.

40   *Ibid.*

41   Townshend to Pitt, 20 September 1759, CO 5/51 91.

42   'Journal of Major Moncrief', 53.

43   *DRCHNY* 10:1039.

44   Doughty, ed., *Knox's Journal*, 2:102.

45   Reilly, *The Rest to Fortune: The Life of Major-General James Wolfe*, 310-311.

46 W.A.J. Archbold, 'A Letter Describing the Death of General Wolfe', *English Historical Review,* vol. 12 (1897) 768.

47 'Journal of Major Moncrief', 54; Townshend to Pitt, 20 September 1759, CO 5/51 91.

48 'Return of the Killed and Wounded at the Battle of Quebec', 13 September 1759, CO 5/51/97.

49 *DRCHNY* 10:1040.

50 Stacey, *Quebec,* 152-153.

51 *Narrative of the Doings During the Siege of Quebec, and the Conquest of Canada; by a Nun of the General Hospital of Quebec, Transmitted to a Religious Community of the Same Order in France,* (Quebec: 1855[?]) 9.

52 *DRCHNY* 10:1040, 1053.

53 'Journal Abrégé de la Campagne de 1759', 299.

54 Reid, *Quebec 1759,* 74-75; Stephen Brumwell, *Redcoats: The British Soldier and War in the Americas, 1755–1763* (Cambridge: 2002) 251.

55 Stacey, *Quebec,* 168.

56 Casgrain, ed., *Journal de Lévis,* 211.

57 'Journal Abrégé de la Campagne de 1759', 299.

58 *Narrative of the Siege of Quebec by a Nun of the General Hospital,* 10; Doughty, ed., *Knox's Journal,* 2:106; *Murray's Journal,* 37-38.

59 Casgrain, ed., *Journal de Lévis,* 212-213.

60 *DRCHNY* 10:1041; *Narrative of the Siege of Quebec by a Nun of the General Hospital,* 11; 'Journal Abrégé de la Campagne de 1759', 299-300.

61 *DRCHNY* 10:1004.

62 Townshend to Pitt, 20 September 1759, CO 5/51 92; Articles of Capitulation, CO 5/51 47; Doughty, ed., *Knox's Journal,* 2:119.

63 *DRCHNY* 10:1011.

64 *Ibid.,* 10:1015.

Chapter 7: Survivors

1 Arthur G. Doughty, *The Siege of Quebec and the Battle on the Plains of Abraham,* 6 vols (Quebec: 1901) 5:206.

2 Wolfe to Pitt, 2 September 1759, CO 5/51 72, The National Archives: Public Record Office, Kew, England.

3 *Gentleman's Magazine,* 1759, 495.

4 'Relation du Siege de Québec', *Rapport de l'Archiviste de la Province de Québec,* vol. 18 (1937–38) 20.

5 'Journal Abrégé de la Campagne de 1759 en Canada', in *The Siege of Quebec and the Battle of the Plains of Abraham,* ed. Arthur Doughty (Quebec: 1901) 301; Edmund B. O'Callaghan and Berthold Fernow,

eds, *Documents Relative to the Colonial History of the State of New York; Procured in Holland, England and France*, 15 vols (Albany: 1853–1887) 10:1015 [hereafter *DRCHNY*]; *Narrative of the Doings During the Siege of Quebec, and the Conquest of Canada; by a Nun of the General Hospital of Quebec, Transmitted to a Religious Community of the Same Order in France* (Quebec: 1855[?]) 11.

6   'Journal of Major Moncrief', in *The Siege of Quebec and the Battle of the Plains of Abraham*, ed. Arthur Doughty (Quebec: 1901), 55.

7   Arthur G. Doughty, ed., *An Historical Journal of the Campaigns in North America: For the Years 1757, 1758, 1759, and 1760 by Captain John Knox*, 3 vols (Toronto: 1914–1916) 2:135.

8   James Murray Letter, 11 October 1759, WO 34/4 8, The National Archives: Public Record Office, Kew, England.

9   14 October 1759, General Monckton's Orderly Book, Robert Monckton Papers, vol. 6, Library and Archives Canada, Ottawa; Saunders to Pitt, 6 October 1759, CO 5/51 49–50; Saunders to Capt. Spry, 11 October 1759, CO 5/51 53.

10   *DRCHNY* 10:1057; James Murray, *Journal of the Expedition against Quebec*, Series 4, James Murray Collection, f.50, Library and Archives Canada, Ottawa; Monckton to MacKellar, 30 September 1759, Robert Monckton Papers, Northcliffe Collection, vol. 32, Library and Archives Canada, Ottawa.

11   John Montrésor to his Father, 18 October 1759, Doughty, *Siege of Quebec*, 4:331.

12   J.R. Harper, *78th Fighting Frasers in Canada: A Short History of the Old 78th Regiment or Fraser's Highlanders, 1757–1763* (Laval: 1966) 11; Doughty, *Siege of Quebec*, 2:302.

13   *Murray's Journal*, 59; 6 October 1759, General Monckton's Orderly Book; Doughty, *Siege of Quebec*, 2:257.

14   General Monckton's Orderly Book.

15   *Murray's Journal*, 57,73.

16   Doughty, ed., *Knox's Journal*, 2:280.

17   *Murray's Journal*, 57.

18   Doughty, ed., *Knox's Journal*, 2:278, 307.

19   *Murray's Journal*, 59; Doughty, ed., *Knox's Journal* 2:277.

20   Murray to Amherst, 1 November 1759, WO 34/4 13.

21   Doughty, ed., *Knox's Journal*, 2:260.

22   *Ibid.*, 2:259,263,306; *Murray's Journal*, 52,57,71; 26 September 1759, Brigadier General Townshend's General Orders, Townshend Papers, vol. 8, Library and Archives Canada, Ottawa.

23   *Journal of the Particular Transactions During the Siege of Quebec by an Officer of Frasers' Regiment* (Quebec: 1901) 11.

24   Murray to Major Hussey, 20 November 1759, James Murray

Collection, Series 1, 1:15-16, Library and Archives Canada, Ottawa; *Murray's Journal*, 56.

25   *Narrative of the Siege of Quebec by a Nun of the General Hospital*, 13.

26   Instructions to Colonel Hunt Walsh, 15 November 1759, James Murray Collection, Series 1, 1:8-9.

27   Henri Raymond Casgrain, ed., *Journal des Campagnes du Chevalier de Lévis en Canada de 1756 à 1760* (Montreal: 1889) 221-227.

28   Doughty, ed., *Knox's Journal*, 2: 238.

29   *Ibid.*, 2:289.

30   *Ibid.*, 2:273,288,306; *Murray's Journal*, 65,67.

31   Doughty, ed., *Knox's Journal*, 2:309; *Murray's Journal*, 66-67.

32   Doughty, ed., *Knox's Journal*, 2:278.

33   *Ibid.*, 2:355.

34   Charles Saunders to William Pitt, 24 November 1759, CO 5/51 57; James Murray Letter, 11 October 1759, WO 34/4 8; Declaration of Murray, 23 November 1759, James Murray Collection, Series 1, 1:13; Doughty, ed., *Knox's Journal*, 2:326.

35   Doughty, ed., *Knox's Journal*, 2:306.

36   *Ibid.*, 2:258; *Murray's Journal*, 53.

37   Desmond Morton, *A Military History of Canada: From Champlain to the Gulf War*, 3rd edn (Toronto: 1999) 20; Guy Frégault, *Canada: The War of the Conquest*, trans. Margaret M. Cameron (Toronto: 1969) 269-275; Lawrence Henry Gipson, *The Great War for the Empire: The Victorious Years, 1758–1760*, 15 vols, vol. 7, *The British Empire before the American Revolution* (New York: 1949) 433-435.

38   *DRCHNY* 10:1079.

39   *Murray's Journal*, 80.

40   Doughty, ed., *Knox's Journal,* 2:349.

41   Gordon M. Day, 'Oral Tradition as Complement', *Ethnohistory*, vol. 19 (1972): 99-108.

42   Doughty, ed., *Knox's Journal*, 2:313; *Murray's Journal*, 70.

43   Doughty, ed., *Knox's Journal*, 2:293.

44   *Ibid.*, 2:323,338,348,403; *Murray's Journal*, 69-71.

45   Doughty, *Siege of Quebec* 2:365; *Narrative of the Siege of Quebec by a Nun of the General Hospital*, 12.

46   Doughty, ed., *Knox's Journal*, 2:318,337,352; *Murray's Journal*, 81.

47   *Murray's Journal*, 81; Doughty, ed., *Knox's Journal*, 2:357, 374.

48   Murray to Amherst, 19 May 1760, WO 34/4 19-20.

49   Doughty, ed., *Knox's Journal*, 2:292.

50   *Ibid.* 2:334; Frégault, *War of the Conquest*, 270.

51   Pownall to Amherst, 23 September 1759, WO 34/25 298.

52   Doughty, ed., *Knox's Journal*, 360.

53   *Murray's Journal*, 87.

54 Michael A. Palmer, "'The Soul's Right Hand": Command and Control in the Age of Fighting Sail, 1652–1827', *The Journal of Military History*, 61 (1997) 688-690; Fred Anderson, *Crucible of War: The Seven Years' War and the Fate of Empire in British North America, 1754–1766* (New York: 2000) 382-383.

55 Gilles Proulx, *Fighting at Restigouche: The Men and Vessels of 1760, in Chaleur Bay* (Hull, Quebec: 1998) 10-11; Frégault, *War of the Conquest*, 273.

56 *Murray's Journal*, 70,84.

57 Lettre circulaire écrite à MM. les curés..., 16 April 1760, Henri Raymond Casgrain, ed., *Collection des Manuscrits de Maréchal de Lévis*, vol. 4, *Lettres et Pièces Militaires, Instructions, Ordres, Mémoirs, Plans de Campagne et de Défense, 1758–1760* (Quebec: 1891) 222.

58 Lettre circulaire écrite aux capitaines des milices, 16 April 1760, *Ibid.*, 219-221

59 Doughty, ed., *Knox's Journal*, 2:379, 382; *DRCHNY* 10:1074-1075, 1080; *Murray's Journal*, 91.

60 *Murray's Journal*, 92-94; *DRCHNY* 10:1080.

61 Murray to Amherst, 30 April 1760, CO 5/58 192; *DRCHNY* 10:1082.

62 Doughty, ed., *Knox's Journal*, 2:390-391;Stuart Reid, *Quebec 1759: The Battle That Won Canada* (Oxford: 2003) 85-86.

63 *Murray's Journal*, 95-96.

64 Murray to Amherst, 30 April 1760, CO 5/58 192-193; Doughty, ed., *Knox's Journal*, 2:393-394; *DRCHNY* 10:1083.

65 Doughty, ed., *Knox's Journal*, 2:394.

66 *Murray's Journal*, 97.

67 Doughty, *Siege of Quebec*, 2:401; C.P. Stacey, *Quebec, 1759: The Siege and the Battle* (Toronto: 1959) 164.

68 *Murray's Journal*, 98-99.

69 Quoted in Frégault, *War of the Conquest*, 278; Stacey, *Quebec*, 165.

70 *DRCHNY* 10:1077; *Murray's Journal*, 99-100.

71 Doughty, ed., *Knox's Journal*, 2:415.

72 *Murray's Journal*, 108-109; *DRCHNY* 10:1088.

73 *DRCHNY* 10:1089.

Conclusion: Conquest

1 George F.G. Stanley, *New France: The Last Phase, 1749–1760* (Toronto: 1968) 250-251.

2 Guy Frégault, *Canada: The War of the Conquest*, trans. Margaret M. Cameron (Toronto: 1969) 282-283; Fred Anderson, *Crucible of War: The Seven Years' War and the Fate of Empire in British North America,*

1754–1766 (New York: 2000) 400-401.

3   Edmund B. O'Callaghan and Berthold Fernow, eds, *DRCHNY* 10:1099, 1101.

4   *Ibid.*, 10:1101.

5   Lawrence Henry Gipson, *The Great War for the Empire: The Victorious Years, 1758–1760*, 15 vols, vol. 7, *The British Empire before the American Revolution* (New York: 1949) 448-451.

6   Quoted in Frégault, *War of the Conquest*, 285; Arthur G. Doughty, ed., *An Historical Journal of the Campaigns in North America: For the Years 1757, 1758, 1759, and 1760 by Captain John Knox*, 3 vols (Toronto: 1914–1916) 467-500.

7   Doughty, ed., *Knox's Journal*, 2:504.

8   *Ibid.*, 2:528-543; Amherst to Pitt, 8 September 1760, CO 5/58 442-444, The National Archives: Public Record Office, Kew, England.

9   *Ibid.*, 2:512, 515.

10 Quoted in Stanley, *New France: The Last Phase, 258*; Amherst to Pitt, 8 September 1760, CO 5/58 442-444.

11 Doughty, ed., *Knox's Journal*, 2:579.

12 Michel Brunet, *French Canada and the Early Decades of British Rule, 1760–1791*, trans. Naomi E.S. Griffiths (Ottawa: 1963) 4-6; J.R. Harper, *78th Fighting Frasers in Canada: A Short History of the Old 78th Regiment or Fraser's Highlanders, 1757–1763* (Laval: 1966) 74-77.

13 Frégault, *War of the Conquest*, 344.

14 *DRCHNY* 10:1058-1059.

15 Emmerich de Vattel, *The Law of Nations: Or the Principles of the Law of Nature Applied to the Conduct and Affairs of Nations and Sovereigns*, trans. Joseph Chitty (Philadelphia: 1863) 321.

16 *Ibid.*, 352.

Maps

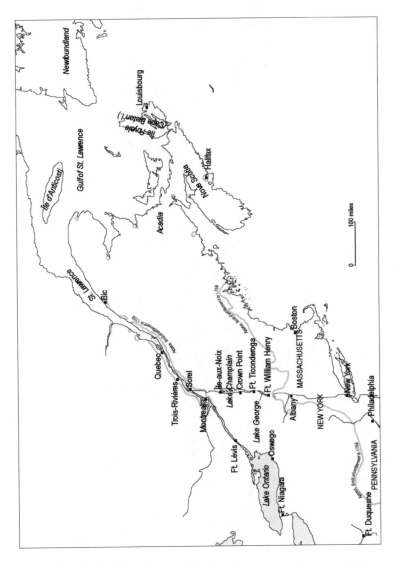

Figure 1 North-eastern North America in the Seven Years' War.

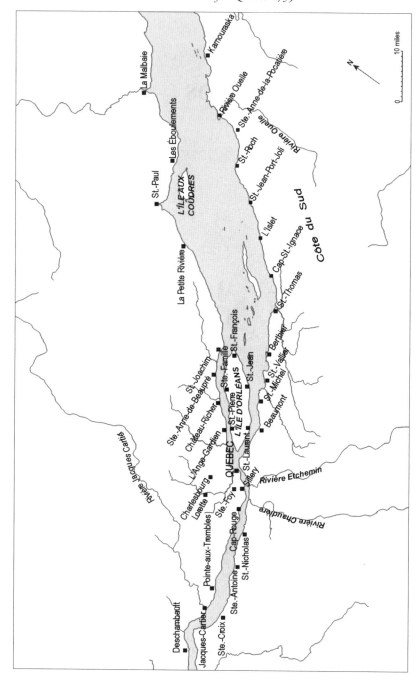

Figure 2 The lower St Lawrence River in 1759.

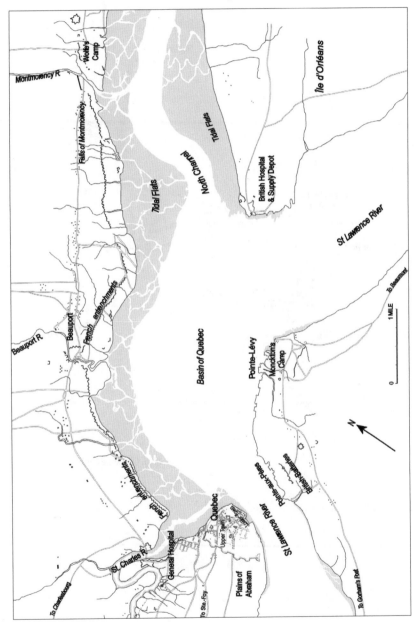

Figure 3 The Basin of Quebec in 1759.

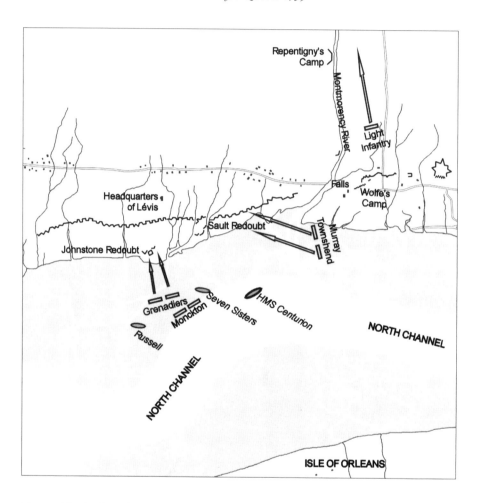

Figure 4 The battle at the Falls of Montmorency.

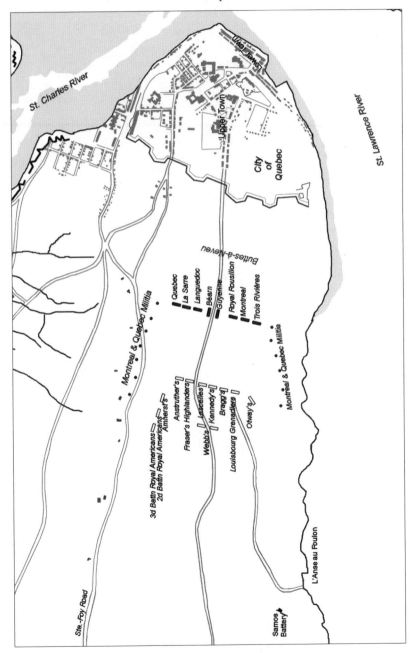

Figure 5 The battle on the Plains of Abraham.

Further Reading

There are many works published on aspects of the Quebec campaign and the Seven Years' War for those who wish to read further.

General Surveys

One of the most accessible studies of Britain's global struggle with France is Bruce Lenman, *Britain's Colonial Wars 1688–1783* (London: Longman, 2001). Focused purely on North America, Ian K. Steele, *Warpaths: Invasions of North America* (Oxford: Oxford University Press, 1994) provides a sound survey of the colonial struggle. J.R. Jones, *Britain and the World, 1649–1815* (London: Fontana, 1980) provides much of the context for British history during this period, while Richard Middleton, *The Bells of Victory: The Pitt-Newcastle Ministry and the Conduct of the Seven Years' War, 1757–1762* (Cambridge: Cambridge University Press, 1985) provides a good academic study of Pitt's administration and the conduct of the war. P.J. Marshall, *The Oxford History of the British Empire: The Eighteenth Century* (Oxford: Oxford University Press, 1998) contains several excellent essays dealing with different aspects of Britain's rise to power. W.J. Eccles, *The Canadian Frontier, 1534–1760,* 2nd edn (Albuquerque: University of New Mexico Press, 1984) and George F.G. Stanley, *New France: The Last Phase, 1749–1760* (Toronto: McClelland and Stewart, 1968) provide a good discussion of Canadian affairs while Allan

Greer, *The People of New France* (Toronto: University of Toronto Press, 1997) provides a brief and very readable discussion of life in New France before the conquest.

Warfare

There are several good discussions of the changing nature of warfare in the eighteenth century. In particular, G. Parker, *The Military Revolution: Military Innovation and the Rise of the West, 1500–1800* (Cambridge: Cambridge University Press, 1988) and Jeremy Black, *European Warfare, 1660–1815* (Frome: The University College London Press, 1994) provide good overviews of changing military strategy, tactics and technology. For the Royal Navy, Jeremy Black and Philip Woodfine, eds, *The British Navy and the Use of Naval Power in the Eighteenth Century* (Leicester: Leicester University Press, 1988) and Richard Harding, 'Sailors and Gentlemen of Parade: Some Professional and Technical Problems Concerning the Conduct of Combined Operations in the Eighteenth Century', *Historical Journal,* vol. 32, no. 1 (1989) provide a similar discussion. For a discussion of the French navy and the Quebec campaign see Gilles Proulx, *Fighting at Restigouche: The Men and Vessels of 1760 in Chaleur Bay* (Hull, Quebec: Parks Canada, 1998). For discussion of military society and the life of soliders in the eighteenth-century military see Sylvia R. Frey, *The British Soldier in America: A Social History of Military Life in the Revolutionary Period* (Austin: University of Texas, 1981) and the excellent book by Stephen Brumwell, *Redcoats: The British Soldier and War in the Americas, 1755–1763* (Cambridge: Cambridge University Press, 2002). For a more detailed discussion of the role of women in the British army see Paul E. Kopperman, 'The British High Command and Soldiers' Wives in America, 1755–1783', *Journal of the Society for Army Historical Research* LX (1982). For an overview of the French army see André Corvisier, *Armies and Societies in Europe, 1494–1789,* trans. Abigail T. Siddal (Bloomington: Indiana University Press, 1979). For a particularly Canadian context see the excellent article by Martin L. Nicolai, 'A Different Kind of Courage: The French Military and the Canadian Irregular Soldier During the Seven Years' War', *Canadian Historical Review,* vol. 70 (1989). For the changing relationship between eighteenth-century armies and society see M.S. Anderson, *War and Society in Europe of the Old Regime* (London: Fontana, 1988) and Hew Strachan, *European Armies and the Conduct of War* (London: Allen & Unwin, 1983). For the peculiar American 'context' of warfare see John E. Ferling, *A Wilderness of Miseries: War and Warriors in Early America* (Westport: Greenwood Press, 1980), Douglas Edward Leach, *Arms for Empire: A Military History of the British Colonies in North America, 1607–1763* (New York: MacMillan, 1973) and Don Higginbotham, 'The Early American Way of War', *William and Mary Quarterly* 3rd ser. 44 (1987).

Irregular Warfare

For a specific study of the role of warfare in Native American society see Daniel K. Richter, *The Ordeal of the Long-House: The Peoples of the Iroquois League in the Era of European Colonization* (Chapel Hill: University of North Carolina Press, 1992). A broader discussion can be found in Colin Calloway, *New Worlds for All: Indians, Europeans and the Remaking of Early America* (Baltimore: Johns Hopkins University Press, 1997). For a more specific discussion of the debate over scalping see James Axtell and William C. Sturtevant, 'The Unkindest Cut, or Who Invented Scalping?', *William and Mary Quarterly* 37 (1980). Peter Way, 'The Cutting Edge of Culture: British Soldiers Encounter Native Americans in the French and Indian War', in *Empire and Others: British Encounters with Indigenous Peoples 1600–1850*, ed. Martin Daunton and Rick Halpern (London: UCL Press, 1999) provides a good discussion of how British troops responded to irregular warfare, as does Daniel J. Beattie, 'The Adaptation of the British Army to Wilderness Warfare', in *Adapting to Conditions: War and Society in the Eighteenth Century*, ed. Maarten Ultee (University: University of Alabama Press, 1986).

Seven Years' War

For the best general survey of the war see Fred Anderson, *Crucible of War: The Seven Years' War and the Fate of Empire in British North America, 1754–1766* (New York: Alfred A. Knopf, 2000). For the best study of Canada during the war see Guy Frégault, *Canada: The War of the Conquest*, trans. Margaret M. Cameron (Toronto: Oxford University Press, 1969). Lawrence Henry Gipson's fifteen-volume *The British Empire before the American Revolution* (New York: Alfred A Knopf, 1936–1970), in particular volume 6, 'The Years of Defeat', and volume 7, 'The Victorious Years', provides an excellent discussion of Britain's quest for empire during the Seven Years' War. For a strong Native American context, but also a sometimes rather contentious outlook, see Francis Jennings, *Empire of Fortune: Crowns, Colonies and Empires in the Seven Years' War* (New York: W.W. Norton, 1988).

Quebec Campaign

One of the best, although now rather dated, studies of the campaign is C.P. Stacey, *Quebec, 1759: The Siege and the Battle* (Toronto: Macmillan, 1959). There are many other useful studies including Christopher Hibbert, *Wolfe at Quebec* (London: Longmans, 1959) and Oliver Warner, *With Wolfe to Quebec: The Path to Glory* (London: Collins, 1972). Francis Parkman, *Montcalm and Wolfe*, 2 vols (London: MacMillan, 1884) is one of the most reprinted works on the topic. While a classic work of literature, Parkman's skills as a historian are rather more lacking, and this work should be approached with great care. The first three volumes of Arthur G. Doughty, *The Siege of Quebec and the Battle on the Plains of Abraham*, 6 vols (Quebec: Dussault & Proulx, 1901) also provide a very detailed narrative account of the expedition. Gaston Deschênes, *L'Année des Anglais: La Côte-du-Sud à l'Heure de la Conquête* (Sillery, Quebec: Septentrion, 1988) provides a good case study of the impact of the campaign on the French population of the Côte du Sud, while Gérard Filteau, *Par la Bouche de mes Canons: La Ville de Québec Face à l'Ennemi* (Sillery, Quebec: Septentrion, 1990) provides a sound discussion of the impact of the 1759 siege, and other sieges, on the civilians of Quebec City. For the global context of the campaign see the very readable Frank McLynn, *1759: The Year Britain Became Master of the World* (London: Jonathan Cape, 2004).

There have been several biographies written of the main participants in the campaign. For a recent biography of Wolfe, which also includes a good discussion of the British army, see Stuart Reid, *Wolfe: The Career of General James Wolfe from Culloden to Quebec* (Rockville Centre, New York: Sarpendon, 2000). For a more dated, but still valuable study see Robin Reilly, *The Rest to Fortune: The Life of Major-General James Wolfe* (London: Cassell, 1960) or Richard Garrett, *General Wolfe* (London: Barker, 1975).

Two brief but very accessible and useful studies are René Chartrand, *Québec: The Heights of Abraham 1759; the Armies of Wolfe and Montcalm* (Oxford: Osprey, 1999) which contains a useful discussion of the individual units involved in the campaign, and Stuart Reid, *Quebec 1759: The Battle That Won Canada* (Oxford: Osprey, 2003) which provides a good strategic overview of the campaign, although much of the work echoes comments in his biography of Wolfe.

British Sources

The most important collection of British documents can be found in the collections of the Library and Archives Canada, in particular the Townshend and Monckton Papers in the Northcliffe Collection, and the James Murray Papers. The Wolfe Collection in the Library and Archives Canada also contains much useful material, including copies of material held elsewhere. The National Archives, the former Public Record Office, in Kew, England also contains two important collections, including the Colonial Office, Class 5 Files which contain most of the correspondence between military commanders and the government in London, and the War Office, Class 34 Files – the Jeffery Amherst Papers.

Many British documents have also been published. Perhaps the best published collections are in Doughty, *Siege of Quebec* in the appendix held in volumes 4-6. Doughty also edited *An Historical Journal of the Campaigns in North America: For the Years 1757, 1758, 1759, and 1760 by Captain John Knox*, 3 vols (Toronto: Champlain Society, 1914–1916), one of the most detailed accounts of the expedition. The appendix in volume 3 of the journal also contains several important documents. Beckles Wilson, *The Life and Letters of James Wolfe* (London: William Heinemann, 1909) is a very dated history of Wolfe's life and the expedition, but it contains complete copies of many of Wolfe's letters.

French Sources

If anything, more French sources have been published than British sources. The papers of the major military officers were published in the late nineteenth century in a series edited by H.R. Casgrain, in particular *Lettres du Marquis de Vaudreuil au Chevalier de Lévis* (Quebec: L.J. Demers et Frère, 1895), *Journal des Campagnes du Chevalier de Lévis En Canada de 1756 à 1760* (Montreal: C.O. Beauchemin et Fils, 1889), *Journal du Marquis de Montcalm durant ses Campagnes en Canada de 1756 à 1759* (Quebec: L.J. Demers et Frère, 1895), *Lettres du Chevalier de Lévis Concernant la Guerre du Canada (1756-1760)* (Montreal: C.O. Beauchemin et Fils, 1889), and *Lettres du Marquis de Montcalm au Chevalier de Lévis* (Quebec: L.J. Demers et Frère, 1894). Other published collections include Jean-Claude Hébert, ed., *Le Siège de Québec en 1759 par Trois Témoins* (Montreal: Ministère des Affaires Culturelles, 1972), which contains three useful accounts from other sources, including the details of a French journal from the Townshend Papers. Other useful published French sources are J.C. Panet, 'Journal du Siège de Québec en 1759', *Quebec Literary and Historical Society Documents*, Series 4, and Henri Titu, 'M. Jean-Felix Récher, Curé de Québec, et Son Journal, 1757–1760', *Bulletin des Recherches Historiques* 9 (1903).

Some French documents dealing with this period have also been translated into English. The most important collection is in Edmund B. O'Callaghan and Berthold Fernow, eds, *Documents Relative to the Colonial History of the State of New York; Procured in Holland, England and France*, 15 vols (Albany: Parsons Weed, 1853-1887) of which volume 10 contains documents relating to the campaign.

List of Illustrations

Unless otherwise stated, all illustrations are from the author's collection.

MAPS

Index

TEMPUS REVEALING HISTORY

Quacks Fakers and Charlatans in Medicine
ROY PORTER
'A delightful book'
The Daily Telegraph
£12.99
0 7524 2590 0

The Tudors
RICHARD REX
'Up-to-date, readable and reliable. The best introduction to England's most important dynasty'
David Starkey
£9.99
0 7524 3333 4

The Kings & Queens of England
MARK ORMROD
'Of the numerous books on the kings and queens of England, this is the best'
Alison Weir
£9.99
0 7524 2598 6

The Covent Garden Ladies
Pimp General Jack & the Extraordinary Story of Harris's List
HALLIE RUBENHOLD
'Has all the atmosphere and edge of a good novel… magnificent'
Frances Wilson
£20
0 7524 2850 0

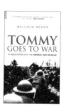

Okinawa 1945
GEORGE FEIFER
'A great book… Feifer's account of the three sides and their experiences far surpasses most books about war'
Stephen Ambrose
£17.99
0 7524 3324 5

Sex Crimes From Renaissance to Enlightenment
W.M. NAPHY
'Wonderfully scandalous'
Diarmaid MacCulloch
£10.99
0 7524 2977 9

Ace of Spies The True Story of Sidney Reilly
ANDREW COOK
'The most definitive biography of the spying ace yet written… both a compelling narrative and a myth-shattering *tour de force*'
Simon Sebag Montefiore
£12.99
0 7524 2959 0

Tommy Goes To War
MALCOLM BROWN
'A remarkably vivid and frank account of the British soldier in the trenches'
Max Arthur
£12.99
0 7524 2980 4

If you are interested in purchasing other books published by Tempus, or in case you have difficulty finding any Tempus books in your local bookshop, you can also place orders directly through our website

www.tempus-publishing.com